If These **WALLS** *Could* **TALK:**

San Jose Sharks

Dan Rusanowsky with Ross McKeon

TRIUMPH
B O O K S

Copyright © 2018 by Dan Rusanowsky and Ross McKeon

No part of this publication may be reproduced, stored in a retrieval system, or transmitted in any form by any means, electronic, mechanical, photocopying, or otherwise, without the prior written permission of the publisher, Triumph Books LLC, 814 North Franklin Street, Chicago, Illinois 60610.

Library of Congress Cataloging-in-Publication Data available upon request.

This book is available in quantity at special discounts for your group or organization. For further information, contact:

Triumph Books LLC
814 North Franklin Street
Chicago, Illinois 60610
(312) 337-0747
www.triumphbooks.com

Printed in U.S.A.

ISBN: 978-1-62937-525-0

Design by Amy Carter

Page production by Florence Aliesch

All photos are courtesy of the author unless otherwise noted.

Dedicated to the members of the Humboldt Broncos who perished, to the survivors of the tragic bus crash, and to the perseverance of the junior hockey team.

And also to all those who loyally support the San Jose Sharks/NHL in person, on the radio, on television, and in print, and to our wives and families, who support our efforts in covering the greatest game in the world.

—Dan Rusanowsky and Ross McKeon

CONTENTS

FOREWORD

Hockey players don't talk about themselves by nature. It's just our culture. By and large, players deflect attention because we play as much for who dresses next to us, the logo on the jersey, and for our fans as much as for ourselves.

Players are passionate—it's ingrained at an early age—and our fans share that same emotion. We feel their support, especially in San Jose, and understand they want to know everything about their favorite players.

For that, I pull back the curtain on my journey to the NHL—and my time spent here exclusively with the Sharks—as this is the kind of tale you'll read in these chapters.

Today, with 12 seasons in the NHL, what I know about San Jose is all I know about playing in the league. Back in 2003 when I got drafted, I didn't really know much about the Sharks.

I was a seventh-round pick while playing at Waterloo (Iowa) in the United States Hockey League. I was on Central Scouting's list toward the end—and that was on the American side of it. I didn't know what that translated to, whether I'd get drafted or not.

The day of the draft, I wasn't sitting around waiting. It really wasn't on my mind. I think my future wife, Sarah—who I met in Waterloo—said that I'd been drafted. Then I remember there was a voicemail. I wish I knew what I was doing—maybe golfing or fishing—and I know I was at my parents' house.

Pat Funk was my guy. He was the Sharks' scout for the area—the USHL and colleges in the Midwest. He was big on me. I think he wanted San Jose to take me earlier. It just so happened I went in the seventh round. The Sharks picked Milan Michalek, Steve Bernier, and Matt Carle in the first two rounds. It was a real good draft. Burnzie went in the first round to Minnesota.

It's weird. I was young, and my recollections are more just going through each day. But then I got my bag from the Sharks with a jersey and stuff, and that was pretty cool.

Earlier that season, which was my first in junior, those first 20-30 games were pretty slow moving for me. I kind of found something halfway through the season and started scoring a few more goals. The brain caught up to what was happening around me, my confidence took off, and I felt like I was scoring every night. I really enjoyed playing there.

I started talking to Wisconsin a little bit that first year. They weren't prepared to offer a full scholarship, and they asked me to return to Waterloo for a second year to earn playing time in all situations—power play, penalty kill, etc.—and work my way into a leadership role. I did that then committed pretty early to Wisconsin. The highlight of my two years with the Badgers was winning the NCAA Division I championship in 2005–06, and then turning pro.

The Sharks did a really good job in terms of development. I played three preseason games in 2006 and felt like I had some success. I scored a couple goals and even had an assist or two in the last game. I got sent down, and the talk was that I didn't create enough. As a young player, you don't realize how every game is so important at this level—preseason or not—when you're trying to make a team, and how you have to take somebody's job.

I went to the American League with Worcester and played for Roy Sommer. It felt new, and I was still very excited to play pro hockey. I went to the rink with the mindset I had to work with a goal to get better. I enjoyed my time there. I had mentors, great character guys like Mathieu Darche and Scott Ferguson. We had a pretty good veteran group who helped to share the things that go on in the locker room and keep you in tune with everything.

It was nice being around those guys in the professional life because you really are on your own. I got a lot of ice time and had success kind of right away. Once Milan Michalek went down with an injury in November, I got the call and played right away with Patty Marleau and Steve Bernier.

Ron Wilson was the coach. And I guess between us there was that sense of trust, which I'm grateful for, whether it was earned or not. I came in and played right around 15 minutes that first night. It's nice looking back, receiving those minutes and getting a real shot. It's important. It wasn't like coming in and playing six minutes, sitting on the bench and just watching.

I made some plays that night, scored a goal, and we beat the L.A. Kings, so I had the start I wanted. You don't want to wait three, four, five games still looking for a goal or some shots. I felt like I brought something to the team.

I joined when Joe Thornton, Patty Marleau, Kyle McLaren, and Scott Hannan had already been faces of the Sharks for a while. They carried a lot of the load, a lot of the pressures. I felt like I could fill in and help the team. It goes a long way as a younger kid to join a good team, win early, get confidence, and know what it feels like to win with the expectations. And I've been surrounded by great people ever since I got here.

Players love San Jose because as relaxed as it is and as much fun as we've had over the years, guys expect to win. We've never let games slide. Guys push to win and give ourselves the best opportunity. Players are allowed and encouraged to be themselves.

I received support in starting Kompany39, a digital platform to educate and entertain hockey fans with an under-the-hood glimpse into the lives, stories, and mental training of the game's most elite players.

In terms of the team's captaincy, I never really thought I'd get it. I have so much respect for the guys who had it before. It's kind of a tough topic for me to talk about because the guys who have had it—the guys who deserved to wear it—made my life so much easier in ways not everybody could see.

Getting by all that, it's those same guys who led the way and made it extremely easy for me. The transition was very fluid because they still carried so much weight and so much competitive level in their games. And they're just such good people.

Players in a position of leadership have a sense of pride in their game. You want to be the guy on the ice at the end to tie it, preserve a win, or score the overtime goal. You want to be in those moments. Being one of the leaders, I've always wanted to be in those types of moments right from the start. And I want to help out, just because, when it's all on the line, it's such a great time to play—whether it's in the regular season or the playoffs—and it's special to have the crowd behind you.

When it does work out in your favor it's a great release. Those are some of my most cherished memories—scoring a late game-tying goal or in overtime when the crowd hits that climax. There's not much more to say other than it's a feeling you never forget.

Sharks fans love their team, they really enjoy the game, and they flock to the Shark Tank. They love the atmosphere, and each one of them is a part of it.

For me, scoring my first goal in my first game, that's where my relationship with our rabid Sharks fans started. I've always been a player who has worked for what I've got, and I think there's a lot of that in San Jose. People who put in the hard work can relate to hockey players.

Driving to the rink, especially in the playoffs, I get a feeling to lay it all on the line for our fans. They make this game great, but having them behind us is special. You want to win for them as much as for your teammates.

It has been very easy to raise a family while living in San Jose. The hardest part is the distance from grandparents and close family. For us to be out here, with the type of weather we have, there's beautiful land all around us. The biggest thing is it's a big city, but it's got that small-city feeling.

For us going to the rink multiple times a day, I can drive through residential streets and I don't have to get stuck in traffic. There's so many times it only takes 10 minutes to get home. You can spend a little extra time with the family, or just relax and get away from the game a little bit.

We enjoy our time here. We enjoy Tahoe, Napa, Carmel, and the Peninsula. It seems endless at times. Coming from Wisconsin, this is a pretty cool spot to end up and spend a good chunk of time.

In closing, Sharks fans have a lot of respect for their team, and the guys who have put on the jersey. They have a good feel for what their character is by watching how they play. A lot of the personalities fans see on the ice, that's how the players are in the locker room. Maybe even a little looser at times, and having even more fun.

We really love coming to this rink, being together and sharing stories that a lot of fans will feel that they're a part of because they are. Enjoy.

—Joe Pavelski

INTRODUCTION

C alling the play-by-play in the National Hockey League is not only the stuff that dreams are made of, it's an exquisite privilege always to be savored and appreciated. I've had the distinct honor of having that privilege since the inception of the San Jose Sharks franchise in 1991, and along the way, there have been many thrilling rides for a team that has a loyal and dedicated fan base, a wonderful facility to play in, a great city to represent, and a fabulous history of its own.

For me, the history began in October 1971, when my uncle took me to my first NHL game at Madison Square Garden in New York. It was an early season matchup between the New York Rangers and Pittsburgh Penguins, and as luck would have it, traffic was delaying our arrival, so we turned on the radio to catch the pregame show.

The faceoff had been dropped and action was going on in the first period by the time we descended into the parking garage, the signal disintegrating into static because of the concrete building. We quickly got to our seats—yellows, in case any of you old MSG fans are wondering—and the score was still 0–0 with plenty of time left in the opening frame. We witnessed a 1–1 tie game, with Vic Hadfield scoring for New York and Jean Pronovost replying for Pittsburgh. It was mesmerizing.

That fateful encounter with the radio filled my imagination, and I began spending lots of nights at home tuning in to the action. My work in theater as a youngster gave me a love for the performing arts, and I was captivated by the word pictures that were coming alive for me through the radio. I felt as if I were there. I had found my calling.

On October 4, 1991, my lifelong dream came true, as a radio-only broadcast of the very first game in San Jose Sharks history was sent back to the Bay Area from Vancouver, B.C. A native Californian, Craig Coxe, scored the very first goal in franchise history, but Vancouver would get the win, 4–3, on a goal by Trevor Linden. It was now my voice that was providing the word pictures to the imaginations of a new generation of hockey fans in Silicon Valley.

I'm forever reminded of how far things have come since that first season, and recall an early example just a few days after moving to the Bay Area. Still without cable service and watching ABC-TV's *World News Tonight* program on over-the-air television, I heard anchor Peter Jennings head to a commercial break asking this question: "What is the largest city in Silicon Valley?"

Of course, I expected to hear the words "San Jose" when play resumed after the commercial break. But the esteemed anchor's answer was something very different: "San Francisco." It was at that moment that I realized that a team and a city were in for a memorable journey together.

Forty-five years after my first taste of the NHL, and nearly 25 years after my first NHL broadcast, the puck dropped on the Sharks' first foray into the rarefied air of the Stanley Cup Final, but unlike that game in 1971, I wasn't listening to someone else call the action. I was fulfilling a lifelong dream of painting those pictures to a whole slew of people, not only to those listening on the radio in Northern California, but to the entire world, using a Silicon Valley–developed technology called the Internet. Amazingly, the opponent was the same one that was on the ice in 1971—the Pittsburgh Penguins.

Beginning with George Gund III and continuing with Kevin Compton and now Hasso Plattner, the Sharks have been blessed to have supportive, visionary ownership. Doug Wilson and Pete

DeBoer are the two latest examples of outstanding management and coaches who have guided the team's amazing fan base through some wild adventures. Through it all, I've been very fortunate to have had the privilege of bringing that action to you.

The team has some great stories to share, both on and off the ice, and we thought that you'd enjoy hearing a few of our current favorites. Thanks for being there with us!

—Dan Rusanowsky

Chapter 1

The Players

Patrick Marleau

Joined by general manager Dean Lombardi and chief scout Ray Payne, Tim Burke shook the hand of NHL Commissioner Gary Bettman, strode decisively to the podium, and confidently announced, "San Jose is proud to select...from the Seattle Thunderbirds...Patrick Marleau."

A roar went up in Pittsburgh's old Igloo, which hosted the 1997 NHL Entry Draft on a warm early summer day. Down below, a few rows from the arena floor, the 17-year-old Marleau hugged his mother and shook his father's hand as the commentator told a national viewing audience, "Patrick Marleau will know the way to San Jose as he's taken second overall by the Sharks."

In spite of all the hype and expectations typically heaped upon that high a draft pick, no one—and I mean *no one*—could have anticipated the things Marleau would accomplish over two decades in San Jose.

The question was often asked, particularly early in his career, who really is Patrick Marleau? Fans and the media saw him as a quiet individual searching for consistency on the ice, and one who would typically deflect attention—a common trait among hockey players.

To at least start to understand Marleau, it's best to trace his roots. Marleau grew up with two older siblings—a sister, Denise, and a brother, Richard—on a 1,600-acre wheat, grain, and cattle farm in Aneroid, Saskatchewan. Three hours from the nearest airport in Regina, and more than 40 miles away from the closest recognizable city of Swift Current, Aneroid is described as a special service area in the rural municipality of Auvergne No. 76 in the southwestern portion of the province.

Population has hovered right around 50 people for the last several decades, down significantly since Aneroid's heyday when it boasted 450 residents during the 1940s and '50s. How did the town get its name, the one a commentator completely butchered before putting the mic in front of the shy Marleau during a televised predraft interview? One version suggests the first survey party lost its aneroid barometer on the present town site, and voila!

Marleau was born miles away in Swift Current and attended school and played midget hockey there, but he will always tell you he is from Aneroid.

Not long after Marleau was chosen by the Sharks, a large and distinctive sign was erected at the town's entrance that said "Home of Patrick Marleau." It replaced a similar sign that celebrated the village's 75th birthday, which had been more than a decade earlier.

On the family farm itself, not far from the modest home and two adjacent barns, is the old fence that took the brunt of Marleau's daily barrage of practice slap shots. A goal stands nearby, but the tattered net was left hanging from the crossbar, in no shape to hold any more of Marleau's rockets.

Work all day on the farm, carve out time for hockey. That was the life Marleau knew. And loved.

Is it really any surprise then that he'd arrive at his first pro training camp months after getting drafted and barely utter a peep? Even his dad had doubts. "Physically maybe he's ready to be up there, but mentally it would be quite a change," Denis told a reporter at the time. "But I've been watching him all these years thinking he was taking things a little too fast, and he's always made me eat my words."

Marleau's arrival coincided with new head coach Darryl Sutter's hiring. The Sharks were coming off consecutive last-place finishes, and Lombardi's first coaching hire, Al Sims, was a disaster the year before. Lombardi was given a second chance to right his wrong and was able to lure the demanding Sutter off his family farm in Viking, Alberta, to Silicon Valley.

Sutter had a large task at hand. He and management wanted to win, and they wanted to win now. But it wouldn't be easy. Lombardi paid established veterans well in the era before salary caps in an effort to change the culture and mentor a group of young talent that he hoped would form a successful core.

Grizzled vets such as Tony Granato, Bernie Nicholls, Todd Gill, Kelly Hrudey, Stephane Matteau, Bill Houlder, Johnny MacLean, Murray Craven, Marty McSorley, and Joe Murphy were trusted with the responsibility to nurture a young group while getting one more opportunity.

Sutter didn't have a lot of patience for rookie mistakes. It wasn't going to be an easy road for Marleau, who after making the Opening Night roster represented the youngest player in the league at only 18 years and 16 days old.

Marleau's first career goal came late in the Sharks' eighth game of the season. Trailing 5–2, San Jose defenseman Bill Houlder jumped on a turnover along the left boards, tossed a puck to the slot where Marleau beat a Coyotes defender and wristed a bullet over Phoenix goalie Nikolai Khabibulin with 25.9 seconds remaining.

Linemates Viktor Kozlov and Owen Nolan were first on the scene with the post-goal hockey hug as a smattering of boos and applause came from the fans at old America West Arena. It was the first of 13 goals scored during Marleau's 74-game rookie season, the fewest he'd earn in a season—lockout shortened or otherwise—before finishing with 508 during his two decades with the Sharks.

Patty may have been quiet, but he sure liked scoring goals. And while he certainly didn't overstep his bounds as a rookie, Marleau liked to be around the guys, enjoyed the locker room banter, showed his fun side from time to time, and displayed an eagerness for fitness. If you were to compare the future captain to military leaders, Marleau wasn't the George S. Patton type. He was more like Omar Bradley.

And when it came to getting attention? Well, that was another thing, especially early on.

I recall the time when a buddy of former Shark Igor Larionov wanted to start a fan club for Marleau in much the same manner he did for Pavel Bure with the Canucks. Nick Shevchenko was trusted because he was a friend of Igor's, and any friend of Igor's must be legit. He was a big hockey fan working along with his brother, Walter, for Air Canada. We'd see them all the time at the airport, in fact. Shevchenko called Patty's parents to get an okay, even though Marleau was still a little reluctant. But Patty warmed up to the idea and eventually made a number of appearances to sign autographs and mingle with those in his fan club.

Still, you could see this wasn't Patty's thing, and he probably wasn't going to change. Blame Aneroid? How about, "Applaud Aneroid."

The early part of Marleau's outstanding career was marked by slow yet steady ascent into NHL stardom. Twenty-one goals in Year 2, 17 the next, 25 more after that, and 21 in 2001–02 to give Marleau 97 lamplighters in his first 396 games. And let us not forget a perfect 5-for-5 in playoff appearances at the start of his career.

Missing the postseason in 2002–03 created a lot of change. Sutter was fired two months into his disappointing sixth campaign.

A housecleaning that included the ousting of Lombardi in favor of longtime NHL All-Star defenseman-turned-hockey-executive Doug Wilson shed a different light on Marleau, especially after captain Owen Nolan was dealt before the 2003–04 campaign.

The Sharks employed a rotating captaincy to start the year under new head man Ron Wilson. But the buck stopped at Marleau after passing through three older vets, who all agreed it was the highly skilled 24-year-old's time.

Marleau matched a career-high 28 goals set the year before in leading San Jose all the way to the conference final against Calgary that first season in which he displayed the C before the Sharks fell short of a first Stanley Cup Final appearance.

Then, after the entire 2004–05 NHL season was lost to labor strife, a funny thing happened a couple months into the 2005–06 campaign. The Sharks were off to a sputtering start, and headed for a 10th straight loss, and GM Doug Wilson shook up the hockey world by trading for Joe Thornton. Yes, the very same Jumbo Joe who was the only player selected ahead of Marleau in 1997.

It was a reunion for the ages.

Think about it. Marleau had been following Thornton around for almost his entire career, whether it was during their youth hockey days in Canada, junior international or all-star play, the draft, and even the early part of their NHL careers since they were forever linked as the back-to-back picks at the top of a draft. Now Marleau and former Boston Bruin defenseman Kyle McLaren were on their way to the Buffalo airport on December 1, 2005, to pick up their newest teammate.

Jumbo Joe would pass many a puck to a Sharks teammate who would find the back of the net. But he never found a better one to pass to, or enjoyed assisting more, than Patrick Denis Marleau.

At the time of the trade Marleau was starting to come out of his shell. While his team worked to right the ship, Marleau was sailing to his first of seven 30-plus goal seasons. And now Thornton shows up in his backyard, but instead of shrinking back into a supportive role, Marleau stepped up to give the team a dynamic one-two punch at center ice for many seasons to come before he eventually moved to a wing.

Off the ice, Marleau evolved from that shy teenager into a responsible family man, who reminded people who know the family of his father, Denis. Patty married a local girl, Christina, and the couple had four boys during the second half of his career in San Jose.

The paternal influence was evident at one charity endeavor that in typical Marleau fashion flies under the radar. He chose to have an asphalt parking lot at a San Jose–area school paved for use as a street hockey venue. The school wasn't in the best of neighborhoods, and Patty knew the recreational addition could benefit a number of children.

Marleau enjoyed visiting the site for pictures and autographs. He didn't just show up through. He interacted with each child and showed a genuine interest in each one, crouching down to have private conversations. The kids really looked up to him and almost melted in front of him as he got them to drop their guard. Patty was at complete ease with this kind of celebrity.

There was no escaping the celebrity he earned toward the end of his long-standing tenure in San Jose. In the lead-up to Marleau's last season with the Sharks, they made it to the Stanley Cup Final (only to lose in six games to Pittsburgh). During what would prove to be his 19th and final Sharks season, he reached the magical 500-

goal plateau while extending a consecutive-games-played streak to 624 by the end of the 2016–17 campaign.

I'll never forget the night the Sharks eliminated the St. Louis Blues to win the West in 2016. Patrick Marleau and Joe Thornton were brought to the postgame interview room, and the look on their faces, beaming with pride, was a sight to behold.

The following and final season in San Jose wasn't easy for Patty. He was asked to change lines, centering a third unit and taking on a more defensive role, before the team had scoring needs and he was moved back to a top-six role on the wing. It's a hard thing for a veteran to do sometimes—accepting a role for the betterment of the team. Instead of resisting, he wrapped his arms around it.

Marleau still managed to score 27 goals in the regular season and led the team in goal scoring during a first-round playoff loss to Edmonton. Patty was one of the best, if not *the* best Shark in that series, never mind that he was 37 years old.

Was I surprised Marleau would depart via free agency? A bit. Was I disappointed? Somewhat, but I was also happy because he could go where he wanted to go, to Toronto. Like many, I wanted to see Marleau finish his illustrious career as a Shark and remember him like they do Stan Mikita in Chicago or Steve Yzerman in Detroit—NHL stars who spent their entire career with one team.

Getting a chance to play in his native Canada with Toronto reminds me of a story one-time broadcast partner Jamie Baker shared. After stops in three other NHL cities, Baker landed in Toronto by the time he was 30. Jamie talks about the first time he put on the Maple Leaf sweater. He left his locker room stall and slipped into the bathroom to see in the mirror how he looked. That's what playing in Canada, especially for the Maple Leafs, means.

And I get a kick out of this: Marleau wears his usual No. 12 in Toronto. Who wore No. 12 when the Leafs won the Cup in 1967? None other than my good friend Pete Stemkowski, the Sharks' radio and television color guy in two stints between 1992 and 2004.

I truly believe Patty Marleau will reach the Hall of Fame. Five hundred goals, 1,000 points, and a game-winning goal against all 29 opponents—before getting a crack against San Jose and expansion Vegas—along with the amazing durability to rarely miss a hockey game is enough for me.

Owen Nolan

A bull in a china shop. That's how Dean Lombardi described Owen Nolan on October 27, 2005, after the Sharks general manager shipped young defenseman Sandis Ozolinsh to the Colorado Avalanche in exchange for the 23-year-old, former No. 1 draft pick. Having shown flashes of what was to come, Nolan was still evolving into the rough and tumble power forward that defied expectations others had of him throughout his early development.

He was a player the Sharks didn't have, yet a player they *had* to have.

Like so many NHLers, Owen had a fascinating background. He was born in Belfast, Northern Ireland, for starters. Only five other players in league history were born in Ireland or Northern Ireland. Fellow Belfast native Jim McFadden was a center and appeared in 412 NHL games for Detroit and Chicago from 1947–54. The other four—Sid Finney, Bobby Kirk, Sammy McManus, and Jack Riley—combined for 228 games in the NHL. Nolan would finish his career with 1,200 on the nose.

Nolan was seven months old when his family relocated to the St. Catharines, Ontario, suburb of Thorold, located not far from Niagara Falls and the US border. Nolan grew up playing baseball and soccer, and did not start skating until the advanced age of 9. But once he got involved in ice hockey, Nolan made big strides.

Nolan played minor hockey for hometown Thorold in the Ontario Minor Hockey Association, and after a stint of A hockey for the Thorold Bantam A's he was chosen in the second round in 1988 to play for Cornwall in the Ontario Hockey League. Nolan's skills were on full display with the Royals as he scored 34 goals and piled up 213 minutes at age 16 before producing an eye-popping 51 goals, 111 points, and 240 PIM in just 58 games a year later with Cornwall.

That was enough to convince the Quebec Nordiques to make Nolan the No. 1 overall pick in a 1990 draft that included Petr Nedved, Keith Primeau, Mike Ricci, Jaromir Jagr, and Derian Hatcher in the top 10 of the first round alone.

Bothered by injury, and able to produce only three goals and 13 points in 59 games of his rookie year, Nolan blossomed in his second season, 1991–92. Just 19, Nolan led the Nordiques with 42 goals. We're talking about a Quebec roster that included Joe Sakic and Mats Sundin. Nolan's 73 points were third-most on the team, and he compiled a runner-up-leading 183 penalty minutes in 75 games.

By 1995, and after the franchise relocated to Denver, the newly named Avalanche were on the precipice of a breakthrough. They were loaded with talent, especially up front. What they needed—a scoring threat from the blue line—is exactly what the Sharks had in Sandis Ozolinsh. And the Avs had a dynamic identity-establishing skater San Jose needed.

I'm sure it wasn't easy for Nolan to watch his original franchise march straight to the Stanley Cup Final and hoist the coveted chalice by year's end. It was a harsh education in the business of hockey, and a true-life lesson in the saying you have to give to get.

The Sharks were in transition when Nolan arrived. Actually, it looked more to him like a total reconstruction project as opposed to a rebuild. What Dean was trying to do—as he always tries to do—was build a team you hate to play against. He was just starting to put the pieces together after management had philosophical differences about how to build the franchise.

Owen epitomized the identity Lombardi was trying to establish.

The Sharks were seven games into a season-opening 11-game winless streak when Nolan debuted against Dallas on October 28. The other names on that night's lineup sheet included vets Jamie Baker, Dave Brown, Ulf Dahlen, Craig Janney, Jim Kyte, Kevin Miller, Jeff Odgers, Ray Sheppard, and Jayson More along with a number of San Jose's recent draftees: Jeff Friesen, Ray Whitney, Vlastimil Kroupa, Andrei Nazarov, Shean Donovan, Marcus Ragnarsson, Mike Rathje, and Michal Sykora. Arturs Irbe and Wade Flaherty were the goalies.

In that first home game Nolan played, there was a puck dumped into the right wing corner, and Owen absolutely throttled somebody. And the crowd went crazy. The team needed that. It didn't have that element at all before.

That's why Sandis was traded for him. And Ozie was that one guy the team drafted who turned into the No. 1 defenseman everyone wants. But Ozolinsh had his pluses and minuses. And he definitely helped a very talented Colorado team that was much further along in its development win that Stanley Cup.

Owen had what the Sharks really needed. He had that mean and grumpy disposition on the ice. To use a Brian Burke phrase, Owen had the truculence that you need on a championship team.

Dallas scored a tie-breaking goal early in the third and won 4–3 in Nolan's debut. Owen contributed his first Sharks point with a second assist on Sheppard's power-play goal to tie the game 2–2 early in the second period. In addition to three shots on goal, Nolan drew three minor penalties—charging, holding, and roughing. Two of the three certainly fit his style of play.

Three more games went by—two losses and a tie—before Nolan scored his second goal as a Shark and added three assists for a four-point night during a 7–3 win over visiting St. Louis. San Jose finally broke into the win column after an 0–7–4 start almost exactly one month into the season. Nolan knew then and there this would require patience on his part.

As we were all getting to see Owen's style of play on a nightly basis, and getting to know Nolan as a person, I remember a funny exchange between Lombardi and my always-opinionated good-buddy, analyst Pete Stemkowski. Dean was trying to convince Stemmer that Owen's style of play was similar to Gordie Howe.

"Gordie Howe?!" Stemmer shouted.

Dean wasn't saying he expected Nolan to embark on a 30-year career or that he'd score 800 goals. He was trying to suggest that Owen could play tough and physical, he had the potential to post big goal totals, and he could lead a team.

Stemmer might not have bought it, but I knew what Lombardi meant. Eventually, Stemmer did, too.

Nolan had to endure another tough season in 1996–97 when, despite his 31 goals and 63 points, the Sharks finished last again and fired one-year coach Al Sims before things started to turn.

Darryl Sutter was convinced to leave the family farm in Viking, Alberta, and jump back behind an NHL bench.

Lombardi added a group of character veterans that included Murray Craven, Bernie Nicholls, Tony Granato, Bryan Marchment, Mike Ricci, Stephane Matteau, Ron Sutter, Marty McSorley, John MacLean, Mike Vernon, and Kelly Hrudey. Nolan felt much more insulated with support moving forward.

Owen just wanted to do his job. He wasn't a big rah-rah guy in the room. He wasn't the loudest voice or the life of the party. He just wanted to be the best he could be on the ice. And showing that on a nightly basis would be the best way to show the guys the way.

Sutter saw that in Nolan, too. And that's why he took the leap of faith in 1998 and named the man nicknamed "Buster" the fifth captain in franchise history.

Nolan was tough on the young guys—just ask Patrick Marleau—as Owen was a throwback. I think he wanted to be captain at that time. I know he appreciated it. What was seen as surliness was really intensity. Owen really cared about this game, and he wanted to bring this team to the next level.

With Sutter, Nolan & Co. united, the team went on a run of five straight postseason appearances. It was in the third year of that streak that Nolan—now 27 years old—took over. He was coming off a career-best 44 goals and 84 points during the regular season. An opening-round series against the Presidents' Trophy–winning Blues came down to a seventh and deciding game in St. Louis.

Nolan was ready. His dump-in shot from center ice in the midst of a line change during the final 10 seconds of the opening period fooled and bounced past Blues goalie Roman Turek for a 2–0 Sharks lead on the way to a 3–1 win.

That flair for the dramatic reminded me of when he capped an All-Star Game hat trick in 1997 by pointing to the net and calling his shot against Dominik Hasek for goal No. 3 that brought the home crowd out of their seats in San Jose. While his All-Star goal was a great memory for local fans, his playoff strike was certainly more significant.

Those are two of the quintessential moments in the early history of this franchise, and they underscored that Nolan was going to give you all he had. I know Owen had his moments with teammates and the print media, who needed to talk to him every day because he wore the C. He wasn't always in the mood to talk, especially if things weren't going well for the team. It didn't matter if they were going well for him. He was all about the team.

He was old-time hockey, and always got a ton of respect from all corners of the dressing room and the organization. Owen was tough. I like to say he arrived in every corner of the rink in ill humor. Just ask Kyle McLaren. Before joining the Sharks, and as an 18-year-old high draft pick playing with the Boston Bruins, McLaren messed around with Owen once and ended up with a broken nose.

After stops in Toronto, Phoenix, Calgary, and Minnesota, and after Nolan finally called it a career after 18 seasons in the NHL, Owen made a commitment to San Jose. He had married a local woman and started his family here. There were a couple before him—Doug Wilson, Mike Rathje, and David Maley, to name a few—but Nolan was really the first to settle in, establish a business, and make San Jose his home.

When he had children and started a family, that changed him, too. Owen tries to be the best father he can be. He does all the stuff that is so healthy, and that's a tribute to him.

On a personal level, I would describe Owen as someone who was slow to get to know you, but he was loyal to the people he knew.

Owen was critical to the team, and without him they couldn't have turned the corner like they did. There were others like him who followed—Scott Thornton, Ron Sutter, and Bryan Marchment were all big parts of the turnaround. But without Buster, the Sharks wouldn't have gotten there.

He was the face of the franchise when he was here. And he loved being a Shark.

Igor Larionov and Sergei Makarov

It doesn't happen often, but sometimes when broadcasting a game, I feel an almost out-of-body experience. I recall way back in the Cow Palace days, I'd pinch myself because I thought I was dreaming when I heard myself say, "Gretzky to Kurri to Gretzky."

Offensively gifted linemates Wayne Gretzky and Jari Kurri, who first made magic during their prime years with the perennial champion or contending Edmonton Oilers, were reunited in Los Angeles where the Kings were instant geographical rivals of the expansion Sharks.

I compare that feeling of disbelief with the one I got for much of the first two seasons when the Sharks played in San Jose. That's when Russian superstars Igor Larionov and Sergei Makarov patrolled the ice like a pair of beautifully choreographed assassins the opposition just didn't know how to handle.

The difference between "Gretzky to Kurri" and "Larionov to Makarov" was saying it six times a year with San Jose playing Los

A reunion of the KLM line that won gold at the 1984 and '88 Olympics at Moscow's Red Square in 2006. From left, Vladimir Krutov, Vyacheslav Fetisov, Igor Larionov, Alexei Kasatonov, and Sergei Makarov. *(AP Photo/Ivan Sekretarev, File)*

Angeles compared to getting to say it *every night* when calling the Sharks!

Igor Larionov and Sergei Makarov were hockey royalty from the former Soviet Bloc. Larionov and Makarov were two-fifths of the famed "Russian Five" and "Green Unit"—so called for the green uniforms they wore during practice. This was the same Makarov who was a member of the USSR team the United States beat at the 1980 Winter Games at Lake Placid, New York, in that miracle moment for American hockey. Larionov was the Russian Gretzky.

And here they were in San Jose. Wearing teal. Together as members of the San Jose Sharks.

San Jose's front office had a plan to reunite the two stars, and they executed it with a subtle transaction, and another one that was one of the biggest in franchise history. The Sharks claimed Larionov during a waiver draft from Vancouver in October of 1992. It was basically a paper transaction because, after three seasons with the Canucks, Larionov was skating with HC Lugano in the Swiss League in 1992–93.

Makarov came in a mega 1993 draft-day deal along with three draft picks from the Hartford Whalers in exchange for San Jose's first pick, which was No. 2 overall. That meant the Sharks had decided to select players like Viktor Kozlov (sixth overall), Ville Peltonen (third round), and Vlastimil Kroupa (second round), and Makarov rather than 18-year-old defenseman Chris Pronger, whom the Whalers coveted.

That deal can be dissected in many ways, but it enabled the Sharks to lure an intrigued Larionov back to the NHL for a reunion with his former Soviet linemate and good friend Makarov. It was pretty shrewd planning, as the Sharks were also searching for a spark after finishing Year 2 with only 11 wins in 84 games. They were moving into their new jewel of an arena in downtown San Jose, and were looking for a way to attract and establish a new fan base.

The magic didn't happen overnight. Under rookie head coach Kevin Constantine, and with Larionov out with an injury at the outset of the season, the Sharks started 0–8–1. Instead of panicking, though, San Jose slowly chipped away while learning Kevin's system and were within two wins of breakeven at 11–13–5 by early December. Getting Larionov and Makarov on the same page, however, was another story.

Larionov and Makarov wanted to play their way—cycle the puck, retain possession, retreat, and reload if there wasn't a clear entry at the opposition blue line—and shoot only if the opportunity appeared high percentage. So they found themselves joined by young Swedish left wing Johan Garpenlov and swift-skating, puck-moving defensemen Sandis Ozolinsh (from Latvia) and U.S.-born Jeff Norton.

Remember, too, Kevin's plan was so structured because the team only had 24 points the year before. The hope was Igor and Sergei could provide some of that magic. And, as the year went on, Constantine saw they were able to hold possession of the puck, so it was a little bit different than, say, when Jamie Baker, Bob Errey, and Jeff Odgers hit the ice. And it also set them up to be more successful, too.

They'd jump on the ice with that five-man unit, and everybody's head would spin. All of a sudden the next group would come on, and Ulf Dahlen would make a move or have a little more space. Or Todd Elik would do something.

The five-man unit, led by Larionov and Makarov, played a style of hockey that was compatible to the way Silicon Valley fans saw the game. I think the fans observed and favored the effort—the physical part of the game—but I think they really appreciated the art of the way the unit played.

Larionov was more outgoing and curious by nature than Makarov, who was an intelligent man but not as social. If approached, especially by the media since he was in the midst of a team-leading 30-goal season, Sergei would often—if not always—respond with, "Always never talking." Igor was far more open with everyone, and while he didn't go overboard, let it be known he favored his way of playing hockey over Kevin's system.

You could see the dissension a little bit. Igor might say, "Yeah, I'm frustrated" with this or that, but he wouldn't say more than that. It's not so much a criticism of the other guys—he probably could see they couldn't play the style of hockey he played—as it was more about what his group of five were doing when they were on the ice.

I remember Kevin would hand out a sheet a paper to the guys and say, "Write down a couple goals you want to have for tonight." And Igor would just say, "Win the game." He didn't need to write anything down. Just win the game!

With Makarov (68), Ozolinsh (64), Larionov (56), and Garpenlov (53) representing four of San Jose's top six scoring leaders, the Sharks managed to finish eighth in the West with a 33–35–16 record to secure the franchise's first Stanley Cup playoff berth during its third year of existence. Not only that, but the Sharks upset top-seed Detroit in seven games and took the Toronto Maple Leafs to a seventh game in the second round before bowing out.

With the love affair in San Jose between the city's first major pro sports team and its adoring fans, a parade was thrown for the team upon its return from Toronto, despite falling two rounds short of any hockey team's ultimate goal.

As we got to know Igor and Sergei it was interesting to listen to them—well, Igor that is—talk about where they'd come from. The comments were often muted or guarded, but Igor and Sergei were a part of a major battle against an oppressive form of government—similar to goalie Arturs Irbe—and you can talk to them about that. They might answer it in different ways.

Realistically, they risked their lives standing up to those oppressive forms of government. You have to admire their courage. We take freedom of speech for granted. But if they were to say the wrong thing, they could be punished. And yet they managed to do that, but it was after they gained enough notoriety, of course. As young players they couldn't do that.

I'll also never forget that Larionov and Makarov were always on the bus at least 15 minutes before it was supposed to leave. They'd never cut it any closer. They were always first on the bus, sitting in their seats and talking to each other. They were always in Row 4, right side of the bus. Funny thing, I always try to sit in that row now.

Igor was the professor. More westernized than most of the early Russian players to join the NHL, Larionov was the guy who had the thoughtful exposition of why they were doing something. Makarov knew that and understood it, but he was more involved in the actual execution of what they were trying to do. They'd talk on the ice, but other times they'd just exchange glances and wouldn't even have to say that much to know what they were going to do.

Their second season together in 1994–95 was similar to the first, but both saw their offensive production slip. Makarov, now 36 years old, scored only 10 goals and 24 points in 43 games of the lockout-shortened 48-game campaign. Larionov managed four goals and 24 points. Both were important contributors in another first-round upset—this time in double overtime of Game 7 in Calgary when Makarov assisted Ray Whitney's series-deciding goal.

The band broke up early the next season after the Sharks got off to an awful start. Larionov was dealt to Detroit (where he would later win three Stanley Cups) in late October and an unsigned Makarov left via free agency to Dallas where he played the final four games of his NHL career.

I remember when Igor wasn't going to play for San Jose anymore. He was outside of Maple Leaf Gardens a week before the trade. The team had left, and he was on his own. I remember he was very emotional. I could see everything he had fought for flashed before his eyes. He was very emotional because he loved being a Shark, and he loved playing for the Sharks.

It was a joy to watch them play. It was less a game of brawn, and more a game of artisty. Watching them on the ice was like watching a work of art. It was special to see the way they thought through the game. It's not just the brute force, amazing speed, or incredible power of the shot, but rather the intelligence behind the act. When you see such intelligence and artistry at NHL-level speed, it's pretty obvious that greatness is in our midst. Such was the tenure of Larionov and Makarov in San Jose.

We talk about Patrick Marleau and Joe Thornton. We talk about Brent Burns and now Martin Jones. These are the iconic figures along with Arturs Irbe. But these two guys—Igor and

Sergei—are among the most creative and interesting hockey players and people you'd ever meet.

Mike Ricci and Jonathan Cheechoo

When I think of Mike Ricci, it really comes down to just one thought: he's a beauty.

I understand why fans flock his way. He had the long hair before long hair in hockey became fashionable. That gap-tooth expression on his face, especially when he scored a goal, was priceless. He wore his heart on his sleeve, and it was easy to see his passion and love for the game oozing out of every pore of his body.

Reech was one of the key acquisitions made by former Sharks general manager Dean Lombardi, who stabilized and gave the young organization a more clear direction after it searched for an identity the first five to six seasons of existence. Mike embodied everything Lombardi craved in a hockey player: grit, determination, leadership, skill, and an unwavering desire to win.

When the Sharks swung a trade a quarter of the way into the 1997–98 season with Shean Donovan and a first-round pick going to Colorado for Ricci (and a second-round pick that San Jose later dealt to Buffalo), he was less than two years removed from winning a Stanley Cup with the Avalanche. And while he was only 26 years old, Reech seemingly already had a career full of big NHL moments.

A native of Scarborough, Ontario, Ricci was Philadelphia's fourth overall selection in 1990. That's the same draft in which Owen Nolan went No. 1 to Quebec. Ricci and Nolan would soon be united for the first of three times in the NHL when Mike was part of the biggest and most debated trades in league history.

Mike Ricci (left) celebrates with right winger Owen Nolan after a 2002 playoff victory over the Avalanche. *(AP Photo/David Zalubowski)*

Just 20 years old, and after scoring a combined 41 goals in his two seasons with the Flyers, Ricci was packaged along with Peter Forsberg, Steve Duchesne, Kerry Huffman, Ron Hextall, Philly's first-round pick in 1993 (Jocelyn Thibault), $15 million, and future considerations to Quebec for Eric Lindros, who after chosen first overall in 1991, stood by his pre-draft stance and refused to sign with the Nordiques.

With an evolving Quebec franchise, Ricci fit right in with a young core that continued to ascend in the overall standings for the next three years before striking ultimate pay dirt in Denver in 1995–96 after the franchise relocated. Ricci had a breakthrough performance during the Avs' Cup run. He scored six goals and 17 points in their 22 postseason games, nearly matching his regular-season output, when it took him 62 games to produce six goals and 27 points.

Months earlier that season, Lombardi pulled the trigger on a trade that would help both teams immensely. He flipped young defenseman Sandis Ozolinsh to Colorado in exchange for Nolan. The Avs had an embarrassment of riches at forward when you consider this stable: Joe Sakic, Ricci, Nolan, Forsberg, Adam Deadmarsh, Stephane Yelle, and Rene Corbet along with the support of vets Valeri Kamensky, Scott Young, Mike Keane, and Claude Lemieux.

Since being chosen 30th overall in the Sharks' inaugural NHL entry draft of '91, Ozolinsh had developed into a unique risk taker from the blue line who created mismatches for teams trying to defend with his ability to join the rush and finish scoring chances. In the end, Ozolinsh was the final piece of the Avs' championship puzzle, and Nolan represented the first key building block for Lombardi and the Sharks.

Deals don't happen overnight, but clearly Ricci caught Lombardi's eye. San Jose was coming off consecutive last-place finishes, but heading into 1997–98 new head coach Darryl Sutter was brought on board to give the team a clear direction. Lombardi signed a number of battle-tested, high-character vets as well to support a young core of recent draftees.

Lombardi was able to strike another key deal with Avalanche president and GM Pierre Lacroix on November 21, 1997. Mike Ricci was now a San Jose Shark.

"I didn't think I was going to like it, to be honest," Ricci said years after his retirement. "I joked around that I was going to have to bleach my hair blonde. After a talk with Dean and Darryl, I realized these guys wanted me to be around here, and I've got to get my act together."

They did want Ricci around here. Badly. He was the guy the Sharks needed to break on through to the other side (apologies to The Doors and Jim Morrison). I remember Darryl Sutter and assistant coach Paul Baxter saying they had big plans for this guy. Ricci was a quintessential part of the Sharks strategy then and even today. And he brought something else. He brought a lot of personality.

Who could ignore the legendary tale of Ricci being named "Denver's Sexiest Man" at the same time a rather popular and handsome pro football quarterback by the name of John Elway was in the same town? One time Ricci was in a tavern minding his own business when he was approached and asked about his special moniker one time too many. Reech spit his false teeth into a mug of beer, flashed a wide-mouth smile, and asked, "How sexy do I look now?"

He brought a certain élan with him, too. It reminds me of how the legendary "Il Commendatore" Enzo Ferrari single-handedly transformed the Italian automotive industry, almost solely with the sheer force of his will. You could say that's what Mike Ricci did here, he transformed the character and the image of the San Jose Sharks. It was will over skill.

It was more than a coincidence that the Sharks became perennial visitors to the playoffs, and they did some damage in the postseason, too, under Ricci's watch. There was a seven-game ousting of St. Louis in the spring of 2000. The Blues were Presidents' Trophy winners, and the Sharks were seeded eighth after finishing fourth in the Pacific Division. Ricci, Nolan & Co. shocked the hockey world over those two weeks.

There was a feeling in 2002 that the team could reach the Stanley Cup Final. After a five-game win in Round 1 over Phoenix, the Sharks succumbed to Ricci's most recent team—Colorado—in a seventh game with a 1–0 loss. The fact that Teemu Selanne failed to score on a newly open–net wraparound would haunt that team and the franchise for years.

Bottom line, Reech was a tenacious competitor who absolutely refused to give up. He played through so many different things. He was fearless in front of the opponent's net, where his ability to tip pucks past the goalie was uncanny. He practiced that skill every day, and it was mesmerizing to watch.

He played the game far tougher than someone his listed height of barely 6 feet and weight of 200 pounds. He always found a way to be competitive even if he wasn't feeling 100 percent. As his wife, Beth, used to say, "As long as he's vertical and not horizontal, I'm okay."

Reech always looked good when he dressed up in a suit and tie, but that's not who he was. He liked to show up in jeans and flip-flops. And he didn't necessarily always look like a professional hockey player. Don't let looks fool you, though. Boy, when he got on the ice, he was a blue-collar, hard-hat, lunch-pail-style hockey player through and through.

Don't get me wrong, there was more to Reech's game than determination and passion. He had skill. And he was athletic. A standout soccer player as a youth, Ricci had a cousin by the name of Paul Peschisolido—a native Canadian international soccer star in his own right.

Once Swedish forward Niklas Sundstrom was acquired in a trade from Tampa Bay in the summer of '99, and rugged winger Scott Thornton signed as a free agent the following offseason, the new Sharks flanked on either side of Ricci. That is, in my mind, the best third line in team history. It's not even close. And that's if you call them a third line.

They had the tenacity to be successful and were a pain in the neck to play against. Ricci was a good enough faceoff guy to get control of the puck, and he refused to back down when things were going wrong. He lifted everyone else. Thornton, a physical bull, could protect the puck and was a smart player. He was a quadruple threat—he could score, fight, check, and play defense. Sundstrom was smart, didn't get credit for his physical play, and he had skill. When the others were intimidating you physically, Sundstrom could make magic happen.

I'll tell you what, I wish they had that third line a few years later, especially in the Stanley Cup Final against Pittsburgh.

Toward the end of Ricci's popular tenure in San Jose another fan favorite joined the Sharks—draft pick Jonathan Cheechoo. It was Ricci who helped the young man from Moose Factory, Ontario, get his feet wet in the NHL.

A member of the Cree First Nations group, Cheechoo came from a place that simply does not yield professional hockey players. Cheechoo grew up near the mouth of the Moose River, a locale you need to take a plane, train, and water taxi to reach—or a chartered helicopter when James Bay is frozen. Cheechoo figured he'd follow in the footsteps of his elders and become a trapper and hunter in his native village.

Despite starting the sport much later than most, Cheechoo developed and showed enough promise by the age of 14 that he left home in pursuit of the game he loved. Cheechoo was playing for the Belleville Bulls of the Ontario Hockey League by age 17 after scoring 35 goals and 76 points in 43 games in junior B hockey the year before.

The way San Jose got him was interesting, too. The Sharks had the No. 2 overall pick in 1998, and they may have led most to believe they were going to select center David Legwand, who was highly coveted by a young Nashville Predators franchise. So Dean Lombardi swung a deal with Preds GM David Poile to move down to No. 3 and pick up an additional selection at No. 29. Nashville took Legwand, and the Sharks next selected defenseman Brad Stuart, who I think was their guy all along, regardless of picking Nos. 2 or 3. Then they snapped up Cheechoo at No. 29 with the extra pick.

The Sharks knew Cheechoo's challenges. He would have to improve his skating skills to play in the NHL, but they didn't have concerns about any other portion of his game. They also loved his makeup. Cheechoo spent 137 games in the American Hockey League split between Kentucky and Cleveland before earning a promotion early in the 2002–03 season after the Sharks got off to a sputtering start. Cheechoo scored a modest 9 goals and 16 points in 66 games while toiling mostly on the third and fourth lines in what turned into a lost season for San Jose.

In Year 2, however, as a 23-year-old moved alongside Ricci and asked to provide more in terms of an offensive role, Cheechoo blossomed and scored a team-leading 28 goals (tied with Patrick Marleau) in 81 games as the Sharks rebounded to not only win the Pacific Division with 104 points but roll all the way to their first conference final before bowing out against Calgary in six games.

Ricci was gone via free agency the next time the Sharks would play—a full 18 months later since 2004–05 was a casualty of the NHL lockout—and San Jose didn't really have the perfect fit at center to play with Cheechoo. GM Doug Wilson rectified that with the three-for-one trade for Joe Thornton from Boston on November 30, 2005.

It turned out to be a match made in hockey heaven.

Cheechoo had seven goals and 15 points in the team's 24 games before Thornton's arrival. That included a season-long drought of eight straight without Cheechoo finding the back of the net. But it didn't take long to change when Jumbo Joe was instilled as Cheechoo's center with Joe's cousin Scott Thornton flanked opposite on left wing. Cheechoo scored two goals during Thornton's debut on December 2 in Buffalo, a 5–0 win that represented the first time the Sharks beat the host Sabres in 12 tries.

It was the start of a magical run for Cheech and Jumbo.

Every time they were on the ice you better keep an eye on them. Just like Brett Hull, Cheechoo could find a way to get open, and those quick hands with an accurate release meant no chance for the goaltender.

Keep in mind, too, that coming out of the lockout the league had a new standard as it looked to eliminate hooking and holding as a way to defend. Teams were still trying to figure it all out, and maybe there was just a little more space out there than before. Combine that with the fact that Thornton received more attention when he had the puck, and Cheechoo really benefited. He learned fast that there was nobody better at putting the puck on your tape than Jumbo.

Their numbers were astounding the rest of the season. With Thornton, Cheechoo scored 49 more goals in just 58 games. He enjoyed 13 multi-goal contests. His first career hat trick came in his eighth game playing alongside Thornton—a 4–2 win over rival Anaheim on December 20, 2005—and four more would follow before season's end. Cheechoo never went more than three straight games without a goal. And that mini-drought happened only once.

With a franchise-record 56 goals to go along with his 93 points, Cheechoo edged out Jaromir Jagr by two goals for the Maurice "Rocket" Richard Trophy. Thornton won both the Art Ross Trophy as NHL scoring champ with 125 points—an incredible 96 coming on assists—and the Hart Memorial Trophy as league MVP.

Cheechoo understood what his success meant to First Nations tribes throughout Canada and the United States. And it wasn't a matter of his celebrity. Cheechoo was modest and deflected attention like the rest of his hockey brethren, but he embraced the opportunity to share what he could with the people who were so proud of how far he'd come.

Cheech had cell phone numbers of every tribal chief in Canada. Any time they wanted to talk about anything, they had his number, too. He could contact anyone in a leadership role with any aboriginal or American Indian group. Think about all the pressure on him to be successful, and all the pitfalls he avoided to chase his dream, and respect for him goes way up.

It reminds me of Jackie Robinson and Major League Baseball, in that they both felt a responsibility for the ethnic group they represented, and did their best to fulfill it with excellence and class.

I can recall many a morning skate, especially in Canada, when Cheechoo would take the time afterward to meet with a group that traveled many miles just to have a 20-minute audience with their hero. And Jonathan never left them disappointed. He never lost touch with what was most important to him, and where he'd come from. You can't discount that.

Joe Thornton

There's a couple versions out there detailing exactly how Joe Thornton got the nickname Jumbo Joe. And, certainly, while one tale is more entertaining than another, one of them *must* be true.

Regardless of who hung the moniker on him, or how it was really derived, there's never been a more fitting personal tag for an individual than "Jumbo Joe." Everything about Thornton is big. He stands 6 foot 4 out of skates. He's 220 pounds. His game is large. The numbers he's produced are prodigious. His personality is colossal.

You get the picture.

So whether you believe it's because P.T. Barnum's circus attraction "Jumbo the Elephant" met its demise in 1885 just 200 yards from the rink where Thornton would play junior hockey more than a century later in St. Thomas, Ontario, or an unknowing teammate in Boston simply took one look and hung it on him, "Jumbo" fits Joe Thornton in a hockey sense every which way imaginable.

A product of the Canadian Junior Hockey League system, Thornton comes from a tight-knit family that means the world to him. His father, Wayne, and mother, Mary, still love traveling by car to watch their son play hockey, and Joe is nearly 40.

Joe is the youngest of three boys. His oldest brother, Alex, earned a Ph.D. in education at Boston University, and John, the middle son, is a lawyer who serves as his agent. There is a lot of talent in this family.

Jumbo's mind is very quick. He can joke with the best of them. Joe, however, is also compassionate and will listen intently to someone and display a foresight and wisdom that goes well beyond simply hanging with teammates in the locker room.

Joe's introduction into hockey is both a typical story and unique at the same time. Called Joey as a youngster, he played whatever sport was in season and whenever his older brothers wanted to include him. When his father took him to Maple Leaf Gardens to watch Toronto host Wayne Gretzky, his love for hockey was cemented.

Joe's room was filled with posters of the Great One, and he did everything he could on the ice to emulate Gretzky's style. Jumbo had another big influence early on, and it was someone in his own close family. His first cousin Scott Thornton was 8½ years older than Joe, who intently watched him first star for the hometown London Diamonds, then develop into a top prospect for Belleville of the Ontario Hockey League.

When Toronto made Scott a first-round pick—third overall, no less—Joe began to believe the dream of playing in the NHL could be realized. Fast forward to Jumbo's first game with San Jose—December 2, 2005, at Buffalo—and he took the opening faceoff with Jonathan Cheechoo to his right and blood-relative Scott Thornton directly to his left.

What a moment that had to be for the two Thorntons.

Scott played 10 years in the NHL with stops in Edmonton, Montreal, and Dallas after Toronto before signing with the Sharks as an unrestricted free agent in the summer of 2000. Scott was the strong and powerful winger the team desperately needed in the lineup as the Sharks were rebuilding toward respectability. Thornton, as it would turn out, was a perfect fit alongside Mike Ricci and Niklas Sundstrom. The effective two-way line gave San Jose the identity it wanted and so desperately needed under coach Darryl Sutter.

Scott Thornton enjoyed four good seasons with the Sharks before the arrival of his cousin from Boston. Scott scored a combined 67 goals and 126 points in 271 games. The 26 goals and 42 points he scored as a 31-year-old in 2001–02 represented career-high numbers. He was a good, hard-nosed hockey player the fans liked and who played the way Sutter and San Jose G.M. Dean Lombardi desired.

Thornton survived a number of significant changes in the organization once the Sharks' streak of four straight playoff appearances was snapped in 2002–03. Sutter and Lombardi were replaced respectively by coach Ron Wilson and G.M. Doug Wilson (no relation).

The Sharks ran all the way to the West Finals in 2003–04 under their new leadership, and then momentum was put on hold when the entire 2004–05 campaign was scrapped due to the failure of the players' association and ownership to reach a new collective bargaining agreement. What a travesty that was.

Back on the ice with a salary-cap system in place and a new standard of rules to crack down on hooking and holding, the 2005–06 season unfolded with the Sharks and Boston Bruins getting off to surprisingly slow starts. Doug Wilson was able to move three players to the B's for Joe Thornton in return, and the blockbuster deal finally united the cousins.

It was so cool when Jumbo came to the Sharks and got to play with Scott Thornton. It's interesting, too, when you stop to think about it. These guys were top draft picks—Joe was first overall and Scott was third overall with Toronto. Their fathers are brothers, and they're very close. But because Scott was that much older than Joe they didn't really get a chance to spend any time together until they were teammates in the NHL of all places!

Joe and Scott were together only for those final 58 games of the 2005–06 campaign and two rounds of the subsequent Stanley Cup playoffs. At age 36 in the offseason, Scott opted to sign a two-year, $3-million contract with the rival Los Angeles Kings, who had hired Lombardi as GM.

But I'll always remember this: Scott scored a goal and Joe got him the puck, and I could read Scott's lips. He said, "That was a helluva pass, Joe." He probably didn't have a chance to see those kinds of passes firsthand before because he was older and playing at different levels before Joe could get his career going.

Scott may have departed, but Joe was just getting started in San Jose. His incredible post-trade stats—92 points in 58 games—earned Jumbo both the Art Ross scoring title (125 points combined with his early-season numbers in Boston) and the Hart Trophy. Jumbo Joe thus became the only player in NHL history to be awarded MVP while playing for two different teams in the same season.

Here's the thing with Joe: he's one of those guys—and one of my favorite types of players to watch—you can see thinking on the ice. Typically players are simply reacting because the game is so fast and they're just doing what they can to stay with it. And they make plays because they're instinctively in the right place at the right time.

Well, Joe Thornton slows the game down. He takes control of the game as well as anybody. And you can see his mind working on the ice. There are very few players who are like that. Players like Adam Oates, Jean Ratelle, and Doug Gilmour. Wayne Gretzky and Igor Larionov are in that group, too.

These are guys whose hockey acumen you can really appreciate, and Joe's got that. Boy does he have that. And it's a pleasure to see it. You know, we're up in the stands, and we're high above it all. And the game is slowed down a little bit because we're farther away.

What you want to do is get down to ice level and you'll be impressed with the things he's able to create. Then you start to see the physical punishment he takes. The opposition's defenders aren't just letting him do what he wants out there. They're going after him, they're trying to stop him, and we're talking about the best players in the world.

My friend, and the team's long-time television play-by-play man, Randy Hahn has this description of Jumbo: "It doesn't get said enough how unselfish he is as a player and a person. To be that elite, and to carry it through to the way he makes others around him better, that's his greatest attribute."

Thornton's production as a Shark is off the charts. First off, the team reached the Stanley Cup playoffs in all of Thornton's first nine seasons in San Jose. And maybe not so coincidentally, Jumbo either led the Sharks in scoring—which he did six times—or was runner-up over the same span. Thornton scored 740 points on the strength of 173 goals and 567 assists during 675 games from his arrival through 2014. You don't find very many point-per-game players in today's game, and he averaged 1.1 points per outing over that time.

Now, you want to talk durability? Check these numbers out: the Sharks played 926 regular-season games from the day Thornton arrived through the 2016–17 campaign—a span of nearly 12 seasons. Thornton missed a grand total of 12. He appeared in all but two of the team's 127 playoff games over the same span as well. So, in all, Jumbo played in 1,039 of a possible 1,053 games.

Reminds me of what a couple hockey superstars had to say about Jumbo.

"Best playmaker in the game, bar none, and has been for many years," is how one-time teammate Jeremy Roenick described Thornton. "When you look at the best—Wayne Gretzky and Adam Oates—Jumbo is going to go down as one of the best two to three playmakers of all time."

And this from Patrick Marleau: "His passing is one of the best in the game ever. He sees the ice so well he makes everyone around him that much better."

Amazing.

Even more amazing when one discovers what he played through. He's one of the most courageous players I know. Just before the 2017 Stanley Cup playoffs, Jumbo suffered a torn ACL and MCL during a late regular-season game in Vancouver. Of course no one besides immediate teammates, coaches, trainers, and doctors knew of his exact diagnosis until after the playoffs. Thornton sure as heck wasn't going to tell anyone.

And, as it turns out, he sure as heck wasn't going to miss much time.

Jumbo missed the final three games of the regular season and the first two games of a first-round series against the Edmonton Oilers. He slapped a brace on the damaged left knee, skated just like nothing bothered him, and jumped back into the lineup for Game 3.

He logged ice times of 22:08 and 22:01 in Games 5 and 6 when his average ice time in 79 regular-season games was 18:04. So he skated four more minutes than his average when he was down to playing on one leg.

"I've never seen a guy play with a torn MCL and ACL," Sharks coach Peter DeBoer said at the time. "It's as courageous an effort as I've ever seen. Basically his knee was floating."

That seals who he is to me.

And that's not the first time he played through injuries in the playoffs. Go back to 2011 when the Sharks played Vancouver in the conference final, and Thornton played with a separated shoulder. Ironically, the injury was caused by a Raffi Torres hit. Torres would be a teammate of Thornton's in San Jose less than two years later.

A notorious hard-hitter who sometimes crossed the line with illegal contact, Raffi also suited up for only 16 regular-season games over two years' time with the Sharks because he was battling his own knee ailment. It turned out to be a career-ending injury. If Jumbo held a grudge against Torres for his hit in the 2011 playoffs, you couldn't tell by the time both were playing together in San Jose, that's for sure.

I remember that playoff year because I really, really wanted to see that Sharks team go to the Stanley Cup Final. Can you imagine the scene if it was Boston and San Jose for all the marbles? The minute San Jose's charter touched down at Logan Airport in Boston there would have been 50 cameras on the runway waiting for Joe to get off.

Boston hadn't won a Stanley Cup since 1972 at that point. "Oh, so you can't win with Joe Thornton, huh? Now you're going to have to beat him!" It would have been one of the most fascinating story lines in recent Stanley Cup history. It would have been something else. But, unfortunately, it didn't happen.

Then there was the time Jumbo played hurt in the playoffs with his former team, the Bruins. Captain of Boston at age 24, Thornton played a seven-game series against heated rival Montreal while concealing broken ribs. The Bruins were bounced from the first round with a 2–0 loss in the deciding game to the visiting Canadiens as Jumbo finished with no goals and no points in the series.

He was the target for much scrutiny in the Boston press. One prominent hockey columnist in New England went as far as to suggest Thornton surrender the captain's designation on the eve of the seventh game. Ludicrous suggestion. But that's where all this playoff criticism started: the misconception about what he is and who he is started right there. He does like to have fun, but boy, when it's time to drop the puck, he is all business.

Make no mistake, Joe desperately wants to win a Stanley Cup. He wants to win, period. One of the most satisfying things I ever saw was when the Sharks broke through and beat St. Louis to go to the Stanley Cup Final in 2016. When it was time for the national news conference, out walked Patrick Marleau and Joe Thornton. And they just sat there before the questions started. I could see the pride on both faces, but on Joe's in particular. You could tell he was satisfied with everything he had gone through to get to the point to play for the Stanley Cup.

Jumbo also wears his heart on his sleeve, but not in the same manner as other players do. Dan Boyle would wear his heart on his sleeve, too, but with Jumbo it's all about his teammates, and it's all about trying to win the Cup. He wants to make everyone better all the time. And I think that's just in his character to make people better.

I see in Joe somebody who is a real pro, a real team player, and who is courageous. He has a soft spot for children, too, which makes sense since now he's a family guy himself with a wife and two offspring. Having a family made him pay attention to other kids even more.

As he's gotten older he likes to pick his spots and spend time with his family on the road. His mother and father travel to see him play often, especially in Canada and some of their favorite American outposts, like Nashville.

Jumbo pulls everyone together, and they'll have team events. And Joe is usually involved with setting that up. That's the kind of guy he is. I wouldn't say he's always the Good Humor man, but he likes to laugh and he likes to have fun with his teammates. When it's time to play, though, he's all business. You have to expect that. He just wants to get in there and win once the game starts. And that's what matters to him.

Jumbo has a big heart. He's the first to greet and welcome a new member to the team whether it's a traded player, a veteran free agent, or a minor league call-up. He's always giving of himself because he wants to help the new player and the team. To him, that's the only way it works.

He befriends all his teammates. Douglas Murray is a good example. He made his NHL debut the very same early-December night in 2005 at Buffalo that Jumbo played his first game for the Sharks. Having played at Cornell and a native of Sweden, Murray didn't really know anybody on the team. He and Joe got along and are still very close friends. Jonathan Cheechoo is another player Joe took under his wing. He's good like that.

And it doesn't have to be someone on the team either. If Jumbo sees an opportunity to help someone, he makes an effort. Take, for example, the time he and one-time Sharks PR man Tom Holy were dining with a friend in Las Vegas. Thornton proposed a wager that whichever friend lost more weight would win a $2,000 cash award from him. Holy thought Thornton was joking until he and his wife, Tabea, showed up several days later at his door in San Jose with grocery bags full of healthy food.

"You just want to help people. They appreciate the help," Thornton said later. "It's such an easy thing to do if you have the means to do it. My wife's pretty nice in that way and I think I am too."

Then there was the time during the 2016–17 season when the team was in New Jersey for an afternoon matinee. During the game Thornton noticed a young boy wearing a Sharks jersey—sitting not far from the players' bench—and paying attention to the action throughout. Thornton thought about his young son, River, and how hard it would be for him to sit still that long.

Before the players exited the bench via a runway under the stands to the locker room, Thornton looked into the stands and asked the young fan and his father to join his victorious teammates. This is not something you see hockey players do every day. And certainly not from sure-fire future Hall-of-Famers.

"I don't know if he was even three years old," Thornton said later. "He was just such a big trooper, so I said come down and meet the guys. It was a pretty cool moment."

This, of course, comes as no surprise to his teammates.

"That's his personality. He cares about people, but it starts from his love of hockey," Brent Burns later said. "He's just a really special teammate and person. He loves the game and the people around it—from PR to the media to the training staff—he just likes to have fun and he just makes it special for everybody."

On a personal note he's just been great to me. When I was tabbed to be put into the Bay Area Radio Hall of Fame, Jumbo got together with me and gave me something nice. That's the kind of guy he is. He didn't have to do that. That's what this guy is all about.

On the ice, Jumbo is everything that Doug Wilson and the Sharks look for when adding someone to the hockey team. Thornton has all five qualities: (1) he has character, (2) he has hockey sense, (3) he has a love of the game, (4) he provides inspiration to make others better, and (5) he has the will to be at his best when it matters the most. The one we've always talked about over the last couple of years—being at your best when it matters the most—you can't say he hasn't been just that.

And don't overlook this, too, about Joe: he makes it possible for the team to be successful under the current rules of the salary cap. He's really thinking about his teammates all the time. Jumbo's been fair in that part of the business. I'd venture to guess he could have earned more term or even more salary on the open market when the deal was up several times in San Jose.

Loyalty is important to Joe. And that's just awesome. He wants to have a great team, and he's certainly not selfish in terms of contract demands. He just loves the game.

How cool is it that the top two picks from that 1997 NHL entry draft—Thornton and Patrick Marleau—could play together on one team for so long? When Joe came to the Sharks Patty was captain. In fact, Marleau and ex-Bruin defenseman Kyle McLaren were the two Sharks who went out to the Buffalo airport to get Thornton following the November 30 trade in 2005.

I don't know if people realized how great the combo was at the time. In their last few years before Marleau left for Toronto, Jumbo and Patty may only have joined together on the power play, but still to get players of that caliber to play so long for one team is rare these days.

I remember a few of my favorite calls involving Jumbo. The time he scored the series-clinching goal to end Game 6 against Los Angeles in 2011. I recall how he theatrically slid across the ice—a poor man's interpretation of Calgary's Theo Fleury celebration circa 1991 in the playoffs at Edmonton. Thornton was almost moving in slow motion on his back before he was mobbed at center ice by teammates.

Another favorite of mine was when Thornton fed Marleau on a 2-on-1 break in a 2010 conference semifinal series against Detroit. Marleau beat Jimmy Howard with the shot almost eight minutes into overtime, and the Sharks won inside Joe Louis Arena to take a 3–0 lead in a series they'd win in five games.

And, of course, the time Thornton struck the crossbar with a drive nine seconds into his first shift during his first game in Buffalo. He won the draw, got the puck back, drove the left-wing boards, and ripped one at the outset of an eventual 5–0 win, the Sharks' first ever in Buffalo after having failed in all 11 tries before Thornton came aboard.

Arturs Irbe

Arturs Irbe was far more than someone who simply played professional hockey. Deeply thoughtful, intelligent, and sensitive, Arturs was one of the first players I saw who really stepped forward to get involved with politics and what he believed in.

Hockey and politics became intertwined for Irbe shortly before he became property of the expansion Sharks of 1991. Irbe started playing professionally for Dinamo Riga of the Soviet Hockey League in 1987. Irbe was honored as the best goalie of the 1990 World Championships won by the Soviet Union team he played for, but things changed quickly thereafter.

Irbe refused to play for the Soviets in 1991 because their government attempted to use military force to stop Irbe's native country of Latvia from gaining its independence. And when the Moscow government sent tanks to Irbe's hometown of Riga, he joined the city's residents in the streets to place barriers to protect buildings, radio stations, television towers, and historical landmarks.

Irbe's country and the oppression that happened there was something that was truly important to him, just as hockey was important to him. Arturs was like a person painting the canvas of his life on the ice. He had a lot of courage and was very serious, on and off the ice. And in the midst of all that was somebody who loved hockey, loved his teammates, and loved to win.

Irbe came to the Sharks via the 1991 dispersal draft with the Minnesota North Stars, who had selected him in the 10th round of the 1989 NHL draft. Irbe was the only player of the 24 taken by the Sharks from the North Stars' list who was playing abroad. The other 23 were playing in the NHL for Minnesota, its International

Hockey League affiliate in Kalamazoo, college teams, or junior hockey.

After relocating to North America in the summer of 1991, Irbe appeared 13 times for the expansion Sharks during the inaugural season and 32 times for their top affiliate Kansas City of the IHL.

Unlike some players who came over from Eastern Bloc nations, Irbe had a working knowledge of the English language, more so than some realized. I recall very early on a funny story when he was going back and forth between Kansas City and San Jose. The Blades were in first place in the IHL and headed to the playoffs. And the Sharks, of course, were an expansion team at the bottom on the NHL's overall standings. A member of the media asked Irbe what was better: to be with a first-place team in the IHL or with a last-place team in the NHL?

After a pause to reflect, Irbe responded, "It's better to be a pauper in a rich man's house."

Understand how the context of a comment like that resonated with a young Kevin Constantine, who was frustrated to some degree when Irbe told the Blades' coach he didn't understand the adjustments Constantine was suggesting to try and make Irbe a better goalie. Kevin, a former goalie in his own right, was particular about how his players performed, and he couldn't always get Irbe to change.

Well, when the newspaper clips got faxed back to Kansas City (in those pre-internet days) and Constantine had a chance to read Irbe's articulate response, the two had a little sit-down chat about his obvious clear understanding of the English language. Irbe understood everything all along; he just pretended he didn't understand English as well as her did.

Irbe was one of those guys where you could see the intelligence seep out of him. He was pensive, very thoughtful, looking to put things into perspective all the time. He had a much larger perspective in his mind than simply answering the question you had for him. That's what I always liked about him. There was always a lot of thought behind what he was talking about.

Irbe hung in there those first two seasons of part-time play in San Jose before taking over as the team's No. 1 netminder at the outset of the 1993–94 campaign, and became was a workhorse that season. At the age of 26, he led the league with 74 appearances and 4,412 minutes played. Irbe became an instant fan favorite while posting a 30–28–16 record with a 2.84 goals-against average and .899 save percentage.

He was as big a key to San Jose upsetting Detroit in seven games of the first round in 1994 as anyone. And something that happened before the deciding Game 7 provided some additional inspiration for Irbe.

The way this story goes—after the Sharks and Irbe got blown out 7–1 by the Red Wings in Game 6—Constantine (having been promoted that year from K.C.) held a real blitzkrieg session in the video room afterward and before Game 7. He went on for 30 to 40 minutes and really let the players have it. Kevin ripped Larionov, he ripped Makarov, he ripped everyone. And he never really did that before.

Then Kevin went into the locker room just before Game 7, and he gave everybody a Sharpie and a puck. He started by explaining at the start of the year he'd talked about shocking the hockey world. And he said, "Right now you have a chance to go out there and shock the hockey world. You've spent years and years of your life just to get to this moment to play in a game like this. I want you to think about that one person who without him you couldn't get to this moment. I don't know if it's an uncle or an early coach. I want you to sign this puck right now and give it to that person after you shock the hockey world."

That apparently made a big impression on the guys, and of course that was something that really resonated with Arturs. That's the kind of imagery that Arturs responded to. While he had great humor and great intelligence to him, there was always this lingering aspect in the background with Arturs that this was bigger than just the hockey.

A couple weeks later after the team suffered a heartbreaking series loss to Toronto, Irbe's intelligence and ability to get to the heart of the matter shined through again. The story goes that in the visitors' locker room after Game 7 when no one was saying much Arturs stood up and said, "This is the best team I've ever played on." And everybody agreed. That was the kind of insightful nature that he had. It also said a lot about the character of that team.

And I'll always remember one statement he made during the Toronto series. Arturs got in front of the TV cameras and said, "Beeeeg mistake by me." I had to laugh. It was his style to wander from the net to play a puck that probably would best be left for his defense. He would take the risk, no different from his countryman Sandis Ozolinsh, like a riverboat gambler, and it was often an adventurous gamble.

Sometimes Irbe would give up the goal, but a lot of times he would make a spectacular save after scrambling back in the net thanks to his athletic ability. The home fans would chant "Irrr-bay, Irrr-bay, Irrr-bay." And meanwhile the coaching staff was pulling their hair out because he didn't have to do that. Irbe was just that kind of person. He was willing to take a risk for his teammates. And he was willing to take a risk for fun. It was just awesome.

The thought of Irbe strolling from the net popped into my mind more than two decades later when I was on the public address system calling a Sharks Legends game. Goalie Johan Hedberg came out, went for a little skate, and first I thought of Gary "Suitcase" Smith, who played for the California Golden Seals. A lot of people don't realize that the reason it's illegal for a goalie to skate past center ice with the puck is because of Gary Smith. He did it for the Seals back when nobody on his team could get the puck up ice. So he tried to do it himself.

On the play I was describing, Hedberg came out to try to play it and turned the puck over instead. He had to get back in goal as quickly as possible and I said, "There's a memory of Arturs Irbe right there." You couldn't help but think of him.

I'm not sure Archie was ever the same in San Jose after the Cinderella run of 1993–94. He played in all but 10 of San Jose's lockout-shortened 48-game schedule in 1994–95, but he struggled with a 3.26 goals-against average and .895 save percentage. He was replaced late in the first-round upset of Calgary by Wade Flaherty. His season-long slump really bothered him. He always tried to fight through that.

You wonder how much the offseason story of Irbe getting badly bitten by his beloved dog had to do with all this. There was always a question about what happened there. At one time the Russian mafia was threatening players. And you might wonder if something untoward happened behind that, but apparently it didn't.

Irbe explained to the team's newspaper beat reporters his large dog Rambo—a mix of Newfoundland and Labrador—suddenly attacked him after getting nudged from a sound sleep. Surgery was required to repair nerve damage and a severed artery in his left hand that Irbe sustained in trying to fend off Rambo. Irbe also fractured a couple fingers in the incident. The dog was subsequently put down. I'm not sure we have all the details. He seemed hesitant to divulge everything. But it was very emotional for him. Whatever happened, it bugged Irbe for a long time.

Finally, I was so happy Arturs was the first hockey player to gain entry into the San Jose Sports Hall of Fame. If you look at his numbers by themselves—57–91–26 record in five seasons with the Sharks—they don't tell the whole story. Irbe represented something much, much more.

His artistic style of play on the ice was unique, but he also had that willingness to stand up for what he believed was right. And Archie could convey his thoughts and beliefs in a constructive and positive way that was universally accepted and respected. He was a beauty. He was a pioneer, too.

Brent Burns

Try as I might, I may never learn exactly what all is in that backpack and rolling piece of luggage Brent Burns brings with him to the rink each and every day.

I do know this, however. Everything he carts around to morning skates, games, and on the road is associated with his complete and total commitment to being the best hockey player he can be. What is among his most secret possessions has something to do with training and diet because Brent has a desire that burns deep inside. He's totally committed to hockey.

Burnzie's importance to the organization can't be underscored enough. For years the Sharks took a stab year after year hoping to select a blue liner in the NHL entry draft who could develop into that special No. 1 defenseman that is so hard to find yet so necessary to a championship roster. It's even harder to trade for that player—hey, who wants to give that up?—but that's exactly how Burns ended up in teal.

When San Jose dealt forwards Devin Setoguchi, Charlie Coyle, and a coveted first-round pick at the 2011 NHL entry draft in exchange for Burns and a second-round choice, the Sharks weren't sure they were getting a future Norris Trophy winner, but they sure were hopeful.

It worked out pretty well, and credit goes to both the Sharks and Burnzie.

It's an interesting juxtaposition—the beard, the tattoos, the snakes—and the somewhat whimsical nature that people tend to see in Burns. Well, don't be fooled by that. The San Jose atmosphere sets him free and allows him to be himself. Under these conditions, he exhibits world-class creativity in ways that he doesn't always maximize under a sub-optimal level of freedom.

Selected 20th overall in 2003, Burns spent seven seasons with the Wild. His best season in Minnesota came in 2007–08 when, at the age of 22, Burns scored 15 goals and 43 points in 82 games. By the end of 2010–11, San Jose was searching for someone who could eventually replace the role 34-year-old Dan Boyle was adequately providing on the blue line.

The Sharks had enough of what Minnesota wanted to swing a significant trade. Boyle remained in San Jose for three more seasons while Burns continued to assimilate himself into a new city, a new organization, and a new role. After a season spent playing at forward necessitated by injury (more on that later), Burns became a cornerstone on the blue line with Boyle's departure following the 2013–14 campaign.

Burns is an athletic specimen—he's a beautiful skater and a powerful man. With the missing front teeth—that whole Bobby Clarke thing—he's willing to give everything to the team. Brent Burns wants to be the best at his position, and he's willing to do anything to learn and do the work that's going to make him the best.

By 2016–17 there was no doubt. He established a career high in goals (29) improved by one in points (76)—both franchise records for a blue liner. Burns cranked off 320 shots to lead the NHL. His biggest jump statistically, and it came from a lot work both physically and mentally, was posting a plus-19 rating. Burnzie was the first Shark to win the Norris, and he could have won it the year before, too.

Burns won the Norris Trophy because he led the league in shots and had 29 goals, and, yes, that got him attention. Beyond the statistics, Burns worked on being a little more compact in the way he plays. He knows himself better and understands when it's time to do something risky and when it's time to keep it within the 35 yard lines. He was magnificent.

I think that difference made him a better all-around player, and much more consistent. I think you have to give his defense partner Paul Martin credit, too. The Sharks inked Martin on the first day unrestricted free agents could sign in the summer of 2015. A top defender during his combined 11 seasons with New Jersey and Pittsburgh, Martin was seen as a perfect complement to Burns' style. Don't underestimate what Martin brings. He allows Brent to be himself, and he was an excellent mentor to young defensemen like Joakim Ryan and Dylan DeMelo. Martin was a true professional.

The other area Burns worked on to become elite was the mental side of the game. I think he benefited a great deal from assistant coach Bob Boughner, who after Burns' Norris-winning season was named head coach of the Florida Panthers.

Because hockey players have that burning desire to always be the best, sometimes they can become impetuous, almost like a teenager. I think Burns worked on being a little less headstrong and started to draw on his past experiences so he wasn't surprised by anything anymore. He made a commitment to be a great defensive player, which people don't always give him credit for.

Burnzie is a sensitive individual, and that's not a negative. He's a creative type. Creative people are sensitive. He has that side to him. That doesn't mean he isn't tough. That sensitivity allows him to be as artistically beautiful as he can be. He twists his body into a pretzel—nobody else can do that—and I've seen that happen a zillion times. I look over to broadcast partner Bret Hedican, who played the position at a high level for 17 NHL seasons, and he is continually amazed at how Burns manages to make the plays that he does.

Back to that 2013–14 season when Burns moved to right wing alongside good friend Joe Thornton. The move was necessitated because a hip injury prevented Burns from pivoting as a defenseman often needs to do. He could play the wing up and down the ice, and play it well as it turns out, while he waited to get the injury fixed in the offseason. Burns turned a lot of heads when he scored 22 goals and 48 points in 69 games. His ability to get in on the forecheck and create havoc in the corners was an intimidating challenge for the opposition to defend.

And while the Sharks made it clear Burns is a defenseman first and foremost, the truth is he is one of the very few players in the history of the game who has excelled at both forward and defense. Dustin Byfuglien is close, but not at this level.

Two others have been as good at both forward and defense. A lot of people forget Gordie's son Mark Howe started his career as a forward, and he was a really good forward. Then he became a top defenseman. Another one is Red Kelly. He was a defenseman who played with Detroit and won the Lady Byng as a blue liner. He was dealt to Toronto, where he became a center later in his career, and he was a really good one. That's how rare it is. Go back 60 years and you can find only a handful of them.

You can't talk about Burnzie without mentioning his off-ice interests.

A suburban home in St. Paul was nicknamed "Burns' Zoo" because of his collection of dogs, cats, and dozens of reptiles—mainly snakes—that he cared for.

Burns has great respect for the military. He has a tattoo on his left bicep that is a tribute to two generations of his family who served in the Canadian military. And Burns' admiration is authentic. He is sincerely impressed, and even humbled, by the sacrifices made by those in the military.

Burns grew his "lifestyle beard" and often put his long hair in a man bun, and then in 2013 he cut it all off to raise money for two charities close to his heart—Defending the Blue Line (enabling children of deployed military personnel to play hockey) and the Katie Moore Foundation (honoring the late wife of Dominic Moore and benefiting cancer research). Burns grew it out again to the point that he looks like Chewbacca on skates.

Off the ice, you can't mistake Burnzie in his flashy plaid suits, sporty tuques, and that ever-present camouflage backpack. He's a fitness freak, a big fan of mixed martial arts, a great father, and a doting father.

Rewarded early in the 2016 season with an eight-year contract extension, Burns has maximized everything here in San Jose because of his dedication to being the very best. He's been allowed to be himself, he's been appreciated for the values that he has and the contributions that he's made, and he doesn't get devastated on those rare occasions when things don't work. As far as I'm concerned, he's right at the top.

Teemu Selanne

Teemu Selanne never had a bad day in his two years as a Shark regardless of what happened. He might have had games he didn't like. Or there may have been practices he wished he could have skipped. But display any sort of bad mood, grumble out loud, or be any sort of a Debbie Downer?

Not Teemu. Not ever.

Everything with Teemu was always fantastic. Everything was always spectacular, or absolutely wonderful. Or absolutely true! He always used a lot of superlatives in his language, and he really felt that way.

It's ironic when I think about Teemu. You know, this is the guy who scored his first goal against the Sharks, and it was in the Cow Palace. He had two assists during his NHL debut while skating with the original Winnipeg Jets against Detroit on October 6, 1992. Two nights later, following a cross-country flight, Teemu potted goal No. 1 against San Jose goalie Jeff Hackett on the way to 684 career goals.

Selanne scored 76 goals and 56 assists for 132 points as a 22-year-old to win the Calder Trophy. Those 76 goals were only enough to tie Buffalo's Alexander Mogilny for the league lead. In addition, Selanne scored 24 power-play goals and registered 387 shots on goal, finishing sixth in the Hart Trophy balloting. The MVP that season was Mario Lemieux, who finished with 28 more points than Selanne to lead the league with 160. It was clearly a different NHL than we're used to today.

By the end of Selanne's 22-year career—20 of which were played with Winnipeg, Anaheim (twice), and Colorado—he scored more goals against the Sharks than any opponent with 51. It was special to see that kind of player come to San Jose. He scored 33 goals for the team that one year split between the Sharks and the Ducks, and he wasn't even fully healthy! And he never let people know about it either.

Selanne came to the Sharks at the trade deadline late in the 2000–01 season in the kind of deal you don't see very often in the NHL. Division rivals San Jose and Anaheim hooked up with forward Jeff Friesen, goalie Steve Shields, and a second-round draft choice going to the Ducks in exchange for the Finnish Flash, who was 30 years old at the time. Selanne had 26 goals in 61 games for the Ducks, who acquired his services from Winnipeg five years earlier in a blockbuster trade.

Teemu didn't deliver the desired impact in the postseason. He didn't manage any goals and was held to two assists during a first-round series loss in six games against St. Louis. Television cameras caught Selanne on the bench late in the series with a glove off and his right thumb heavily bandaged. When pressed for an answer between Games 5 and 6, Selanne admitted he broke the thumb on a slash in the opener, and hadn't been able to grip his stick fully. The injury definitely inhibited his ability to score goals and have any feel for the puck.

With the thumb healed in time for his first full season with the Sharks, Selanne was a productive member of the team. He scored 29 goals and 54 points in 2001–02 and followed up the next season with similar yet slightly better overall numbers: 28 goals and 64 points. And while he appeared in all 82 games both seasons, there were hints that he wasn't completely right. It's expected a player might lose a step, especially one who skated as well as Selanne, by the time he hits his early 30s. But with Teemu it turned out to be more.

"I don't know if he was always 100 percent when he was here, but he still loved coming to the rink every day, playing hard, and having fun," Patrick Marleau once said. "You could see that."

The 2004–05 season lost entirely over failure to arrive at a new collective-bargaining agreement couldn't have come at a better time for Teemu and his health, but more on that in a bit. The end of the 2002–03 campaign, one in which the Sharks missed out on the playoffs, signaled a time for change, and Selanne would move on.

Those two years were special for those of us who got the privilege of getting to know him. He was such a good team player, and a great guy to have around. It's unfortunate the thing we probably remember him most for is missing that wrap-around against Patrick Roy in Game 7 of a second-round series in '02. That was the most dramatic moment Selanne had as a Shark.

Let's get back to Marleau's comment. While Teemu was serious about his game and winning on the ice, he definitely liked to have his fun off it. And he wanted everyone else to have fun, too. Teemu had a lot of interests, and he was a big fan of other sports. But nothing got his attention like something that moved fast like automobiles and airplanes.

Selanne had quite the collection of exotic and fast cars at both his offseason residence in his native Finland and a gorgeous spread of property in Orange County's exclusive community of Coto de Caza. As they'd say, if Teemu Selanne showed up to buy a car, the dealer would automatically include 10 speeding tickets.

I remember the time, too, when Teemu went up with the Blue Angels. That was a big thrill for him. And I used to always talk about racing with him because—being from Finland—he was friendly with Finnish auto racers Kimi Raikkonen, Mika Salo, and Mika Hakkinen. We would sit and chat and call up the info in the latest race. He was really into it.

I remember another time when the team went out for a team-building event to a local go-kart racetrack. Nothing too crazy, but I'm sure management knew how competitive these guys can get, and they weren't going to tempt any undue risk. The people at the garage had to teach the players how to drive the karts. And Teemu was better than everybody else because he had done off-road racing in Finland. It was pretty funny to see him lap his teammates.

We found out early in the off-season before the lost season why Teemu appeared slow as a Shark. He underwent reconstructive knee surgery instead of retiring. And because some players were off the ice for basically 18 months thanks to the work stoppage, Selanne had full recuperation time and was 100 percent ready to resume being a productive scorer at age 33. Colorado signed him a one-year deal to reunite with Paul Kariya, but they couldn't strike the same magic they enjoyed earlier while with Anaheim. As it turned out, that's exactly where Selanne went to spend the final nine seasons of his incredible career.

The other thing that helped put Selanne's career back on track were the number of rule changes instituted to cut way back on hooking and holding as a way to defend once the 2005–06 season started.

He's one of the guys who benefited the most from the lost season. He was able to fix his problems. Then when he came back the rules were changed to benefit his game. With no more clutching and grabbing, he had a second life and that was special.

Of course he wasn't a Shark anymore, but this is the kind of impact he had on San Jose: even when he won a Stanley Cup with rival Anaheim, and you saw how he got so emotional, complete with tears of joy, I think it meant the world to anyone who was a fan of his that Teemu was able to win that.

You always feel good about guys like that who played in San Jose and went on to win the Stanley Cup just because you know them, you know how hard they work, and you know what great athletes they are. Selanne was one of those guys.

How many guys do you know who played over 20 years and never won the Stanley Cup? There are more out there than you might realize. While growing up, Jean Ratelle was one of my favorite players to watch. He played 21 years in the NHL and never won a Stanley Cup, even though he went to the Final on a couple of occasions. However, when he was done, he went straight to the Hockey Hall of Fame, where he belongs.

It's too bad that guys who had great careers like that never got to experience winning it even once. Marcel Dionne, Brad Park, Pat LaFontaine, Dale Hawerchuk, and Mats Sundin are a few examples of yore. All of these great stars really deserved to have it happen to them at least once, and that's only one way to show just how difficult it is to win the Stanley Cup.

Teemu finally won it with Anaheim in 2007, and that explains the tears of joy that he showed on international television when it finally happened. I wish that we'd got the chance to see him lift the Cup in Northern California, but it was still nice to see a friend get there.

In the end, Teemu is in the Hall of Fame. Realistically his chapter in San Jose was a much shorter part of his career, and it was at a tough time for him. I think, however, it was a good experience for him because it showed his perseverance and that he was able to take advantage of the time off to get healthy again. We watched him score a lot of goals against the Sharks, that's for sure. He loved seeing those uniforms.

Jeff Friesen

When it came to expectations for Sharks draftees, especially early in the franchise's history, players often came to the NHL for their debut with the tag "can't-miss prospect."

It's understandable. San Jose had a number of high picks in those early years. Scouts had pored over the talent, made their recommendations, and team brass made selections they were excited to announce. Those players had always displayed top skills, so the thought was with a little development and seasoning the same thing could happen in the NHL.

Well, it doesn't always work out that way. Sometimes your best players in a draft are the ones culled in lower rounds. The most pleasant surprise might be a fifth-rounder, or a player taken even later. And that first- or second-round selection might turn into a bust. Drafting 17- and 18-year-olds, and trying to project where they might be in three to four years, is definitely an inexact science.

Would you like some historic examples of hidden draft gems for the Sharks?

How about goalie Evgeni Nabokov, taken in the ninth round in 1994. Forward Joe Pavelski was chosen in the seventh round in 2003. Defensemen Marcus Ragnarsson, Jason Demers, and Douglas Murray were drafted, respectively, in the fifth (1992), seventh (2008), and eighth (1999) rounds.

So when Jeff Friesen jumped almost straight from the junior ranks to the NHL back in the lockout-shortened campaign of 1994–95, there was a renewed feeling of optimism that the Sharks would get what they needed and wanted out of the draft, especially from a high pick. San Jose made the native of Meadow Lake, Saskatchewan, the 11th overall pick in the 1994 draft.

Friesen played the final 25 games of his four-year term with the Regina Pats of the Western Hockey League while his future Sharks teammates were patiently waiting for a new collective-bargaining agreement so they could start the season. With 21 goals and 44 points in those 25 games, Friesen was feeling pretty good when the NHL started up and he found himself in San Jose's opening-night lineup.

It was a quiet debut for Friesen on January 20, 1995. He was scoreless with two shots on goal and a minus-1 during a 5–2 home loss against the St. Louis Blues. It wasn't so quiet the next night when the Sharks hosted the Toronto Maple Leafs with a big audience tuning in for *Hockey Night in Canada* CBC's national telecast.

Friesen scored his first career goal in dramatic fashion. It came on a short-handed break courtesy of an Igor Larionov pass at 18:56

of the second period. The goal not only broke a 2–2 tie, but held up as the game-winner. And nothing said it more than his first goal.

With all of Canada watching, Friesen blew by Kenny Jonsson, who was a highly regarded, young defenseman, and he was able to beat Leafs goalie Felix Potvin. That was a helluva play. It showed Freeze's tenacity, his skating ability, and that he could score short-handed in a pressure moment under the spotlight with all of one game of NHL experience. It was a great moment, and it brought hope and excitement to the Sharks fan base.

When I think about a young Jeff Friesen, I remember that he stood out in terms of his skating. He gave everybody hope and showed the direction the franchise was going. I think that was something everybody needed at that time. There was a lot of talk about how great these young players were. And then you see them, and it was kind of a mixed result. This guy was at a different level.

Friesen went on to lead the team in goals (15) and was second in points (25) to Ulf Dahlen's 34, but I think back on him giving everyone hope in that moment with the shortie. We were used to seeing a draft pick and knowing it was going to take three or four years for him to develop. And here he is, 18 years old, and stepping right in. It was impressive. What a difference one play can make.

A couple of interesting things happened to Friesen in his second season. First off, Jeff really loved Steve Yzerman. Friesen was given the number 39 the previous shortened training camp because as a young guy on the team at his first camp, he didn't get to pick his number, he had to take what he was given. But with No. 19 available the next season, and Friesen somewhat established after his strong rookie campaign, he asked to change to the same number his hero Yzerman wore.

Well, Friesen started his sophomore season slowly. And then he didn't score. So before long, he changed back to No. 39, and he started scoring again. Freeze pretty much said, "Alright, that's my number for the rest of my career." Now, isn't it weird? We've see other good players in the league with that number—Dominik Hasek and Doug Weight are two early examples.

Today, that number in San Jose is proudly worn by Logan Couture. You'd have to be a hard-core Sharks fan to recall the only other two players to wear No. 39 besides Friesen and Couture. They were forwards Ed Courtenay (1992–93) and Tomas Plihal (2007–09).

In his second year, Friesen matched the 15 goals he scored the year before, but it took him 31 more games to get there in 1995–96. He finished with 46 points, good for a tie for third among team leaders. But Freeze also finished with a minus-19 rating that actually was a fairly middle-of-the-road stat on a team that really struggled defensively.

He went through the inevitable struggles that occur when opponents scout tendencies and check a player a lot more closely. Freeze had to go through those adjustments, as all players do, and he finally won the Stanley Cup in New Jersey years later. It came in the 2003 postseason, when he scored 10 goals in 24 Devils playoff games.

Jeff ended up being kind of a third-line player on a valuable team. And he was valuable in that role. But, ultimately in San Jose, he was asked to play more of a top-six role as at that time the team definitely needed some skill and talent.

During his seven seasons in San Jose, Friesen scored 149 goals and 350 points in 512 regular-season games in which he averaged a hearty 19:24 of ice time. By the end of 2017–18, Friesen still ranked seventh on the franchise all-time scoring list.

Jeff went through a series of struggles off the ice, too. He may have had some concussion issues after he left San Jose. He gave it one last shot to extend a 14-year NHL career by attending a Sharks training camp as a tryout player in 2008. And that's when he hung it up.

Freeze made himself available to do a lot of things for the team off the ice, and that helped to endear him to the fans, too. For a short time the Sharks Foundation put on a number of offseason travel events. Friesen and Ronnie Stern stayed for a week at a Kaanapali Beach resort in Maui, Hawaii, spending time with the fans, going to all of the events. We had a great time.

Evgeni Nabokov

Surely you've heard this one before: goalies are a breed apart.

Usually that's used to explain some quirk or strange habit the guys have who wear the oversized protective gear and try to stop 100-miles-an-hour slap shots. And often that description is accurate. I've certainly known a goalie or two in my day who doesn't do things like others, or who simply isn't going to blend in with the group.

But some of the most interesting, intriguing, enlightening, engaging, and intelligent hockey players I've met are goalies.

Evgeni Nabokov falls in that category.

Nabby, as he would become affectionately known, took one of the most improbable paths to the NHL any player could imagine. Selected by the Sharks in the ninth round of the 1994 NHL entry draft, Evgeni didn't even know he'd been chosen until a friend showed him a newspaper days later in Russia.

The Sharks basically took Nabokov sight unseen. They went off reports from Konstantin Krylov, a native of St. Petersburg, who was part journalist, part hockey expert, and part fan of Russian hockey. Krylov was later hired by the Sharks to scout in Eastern Europe. San Jose trusted Krylov's recommendation combined with the fact they knew Nabby's dad was a professional goalie and Evgeni himself was property of Dynamo Moscow. The thought was if Dynamo was interested in Nabokov, he *must* be good.

A year later the Sharks sent the late John Ferguson Sr. to watch Nabokov play in the European championships, and the decision was made to ask Evgeni if he'd come to the United States and give pro hockey North American style a try.

After making the difficult decision to leave home, Nabby stepped off the plane in Minneapolis, Minnesota, and—before heading to the Minnesota Hockey Camps for evaluation—stopped at a hockey supply store with then-Sharks goalie coach Warren Strelow to get outfitted in gear. Nabokov didn't have any of his own.

Nabokov made a favorable impression, despite using gear that wasn't even broken in. He was assigned to Kentucky of the American Hockey League at a time the Sharks were also interested in two other top European goalie prospects they'd drafted in 1995— Miikka Kiprusoff and Vesa Toskala—who would be jumping over the big pond, too, shortly.

Nabby didn't know a word of English at the time either.

His acclimation to North American hockey, and simply living in the United States, was sped up during his time in the American Hockey League in Lexington, Kentucky, and in the IHL with the

Cleveland Lumberjacks. He met Tabitha Eckler, an American whom he would eventually marry.

She helped him with the language, and he was motivated to learn so he could not only have a relationship with Tabitha, but also fit into the American style of living. Nabby spent considerable time on assignment—33 games with Kentucky from 1997–99 before moving on to Cleveland in 1999–2000 to play 43 games before his eventual promotion.

Kiprusoff, who took over for Nabokov in Kentucky in 1999–2000, was one of six native Finns drafted of San Jose's 12 selections in the '95 draft, prompting Don Cherry to suggest on *Hockey Night in Canada* that the Sharks must have a scout with a girlfriend in Finland. Claiming Kiprusoff in the fifth round—and Toskala one round earlier—would turn out to be no joke, though.

The Sharks liked what they were seeing from Nabokov, and those impressions were further cemented when then-Detroit coach Scotty Bowman watched Nabby play a minor-league game and gave him his stamp of approval.

Nabokov's break came three months into his third pro season when he was promoted to back up Steve Shields, the Sharks' new No. 1 goalie after established veteran Mike Vernon was dealt to Florida in late December 1999. The rookie made two appearances in relief of Shields 10 days apart, but it was his first career start on January 19, 2000, that no Sharks fan will ever forget.

With the Sharks in Denver to oppose the perennial Stanley-Cup-contending Avalanche, Nabokov stopped all 39 shots Colorado fired on net while All-Star goalie Patrick Roy was asked to turn aside only 15 San Jose shots. The Sharks and Avs settled for a scoreless tie back in the day when the NHL still had ties.

In my mind that really sealed his bond with his teammates. Now they truly believed that this guy was the real thing.

Patrick Roy was pretty intense, too. But there was a certain coolness and calmness to Nabby in the midst of that intensity. I would compare that to Roy to a certain degree. When it was time for Nabby to play you could see him preparing and getting into that "zone" to compete. That gave his teammates confidence, especially in big games.

The other part was that competitive drive Nabby had. He wanted to be better; in fact, he wanted to be the best, and he had the skill to do it. I think because his command of the English language was a little better than most Europeans when he got to the NHL, he acclimated a little faster. Of course, his talent led him to becoming a franchise goalie.

As I said, goalies are some of the more interesting players on the team. Nabokov and early-franchise popular netminder Arturs Irbe had a lot in common—more than simply beating long odds to emerge from Eastern Bloc nations to play in the NHL.

They were both real pros, they were honest about their performances, and they were comfortable self-critiquing what they had done right and wrong. They were both good guys to have around, too. They weren't the kind of goalies to go off on their own and spend all their time away from the group. Instead, both stayed involved, whether the situation called for lively chatter or leadership.

One of my best memories of Nabby away from the ice and just being himself was when he'd sit behind Jamie Baker and I on the plane, and he'd have a running commentary of barbs going back and forth with Bakes. Some of it was in Russian, some in English. It was always good-natured and always made us laugh.

For whatever reason he warmed up to us quickly, and he was like that with the other guys, too.

With Nabokov having supplanted Steve Shields by late 2001, first Kiprusoff was promoted as backup when Shields was dealt, and then Toskala was knocking on the door a year later. At one point all three were on the roster, and the Sharks were forced to make a decision—Kiprusoff was traded to Calgary early in 2003–04, and Nabby went on to establish virtually all of the franchise goalie records with a 10-year stay in San Jose.

As fate would have it, the Sharks and Flames paired up in the Western Conference Final in 2004, and Kipper out-dueled Nabby in a six-game series that sent Calgary on to the Stanley Cup Final.

Don't forget, though, the deal to send Kiprusoff to the Flames yielded a high supplemental draft pick that the Sharks used to choose defenseman Marc-Edouard Vlasic. I think if the Sharks had it to do all over again, they'd have done the same thing. I know I would.

Joe Pavelski

Captain America is a pretty fitting moniker for Joe Pavelski.

All he's done since arriving in San Jose as a rookie just before midway through the 2006–07 season is show leadership. And lo and behold, just before the start of the 2015–16 campaign, Pavelski became the 12th captain in Sharks history. Not bad, especially considering there were two others still in the room, too—sure-fire Hall-of-Famers Joe Thornton and Patrick Marleau.

The interesting thing to me is he didn't really say too much about it. There's sort of a Midwestern sensibility about Joe. The native of Plover, Wisconsin, takes challenges in stride. It's one of his many strengths—when the heat is on, Pavelski is calm, and that's what you want in a leader.

He made the transition look easy, scoring more than 35 goals for the third straight year of his career. But think about it. Thornton lost the C after the Sharks were victimized by the Kings, who rallied from a 3–0 deficit in the first round of the 2014 playoffs to advance on their way to a second Stanley Cup in three years. After wearing it for four years, Marleau was replaced as captain by Rob Blake in 2009.

San Jose went with alternate captains in 2014–15, but Pavelski was the unofficial captain in that he met first with the media in postgame virtually every night. I wouldn't call it an audition for the job. It's just what came naturally for Pavs, and he certainly wasn't looking for any added attention.

On his captain's watch, the team did advance to its first Stanley Cup Final in 2016. So was it any surprise Pavelski would be named captain of the U.S. entry in the 2016 World Cup of Hockey Tournament? No surprise here.

When I think about Pavelski, I flash back to the first time I saw him play in person. It was a preseason game in Fresno. I'll never forget it. I looked at this kid and thought, *He's not going to be in the American League for long. He's going to be here this year.* Turns out he played 16 games with the Worcester Sharks. He scored eight goals and 26 points, so he was certainly productive after his two years spent at the University of Wisconsin.

He ended up playing half a year for the Sharks. I always think it's best you don't rush anybody. Sure enough, once he got recalled he never looked back. He scored 14 goals that half season and added the same number of assists for 28 points. His plus-4 defense rating was a portent of things to come.

Pavs finished as a plus player in each of his first 11 seasons in the league, including a plus-25 in 2015–16 and a plus-23 in 2013–14. Those numbers coincide with his two best offensive seasons—78 points including 38 goals in 2015–16, and 79 on the strength of 41 goals in 2013–14.

He was drafted in the seventh round, but obviously he could and should have gone higher. But it seems to fit him, too. Pavs comes from a family of workers, and you could say he's an underdog. Expectations weren't high: he was not the fastest skater, and he's not the biggest guy. Yet he has so much heart, so much will, and so much skill, talent, and intelligence. He's one of those guys you can watch think on the ice.

Look at how many goals he has scored the last five to six years. The number was 192 between 2011 and 2017 that included a lockout-shortened season of 48 games in 2012–13. Sure, it helped playing on a line with Joe Thornton, the game's greatest passer, but Pavs goes to areas on the ice where he knows he's going to have to battle for position and he could end up on his backside plenty. He's been known to jump back up and pot a goal when that happens, too.

He's the best in the NHL at tipping the puck, bar none. It's not even close. That comes from his good vision and an understanding of where the puck is going. He has great hockey sense, and that makes up for what could be perceived as a lack of overall foot speed. He's an NHL skater, but he's not Patrick Marleau. But he gets there almost at the same time because he knows where the puck is going five seconds earlier.

He plays the wing, and he can play center like he did with great effectiveness early in his NHL career. He takes faceoffs, and he plays the point on the power play. And, in that sense, he's a lot like Adam Oates. Oates used to do all that stuff, too. Pavs just makes others around him better.

Going back to Wisconsin, future NHLer Tom Gilbert scored the game winner that gave the Badgers the 2006 NCAA men's hockey championship. Pavelski passed him the puck. Along with future Sharks teammate Adam Burish, he had two assists in the game. He led Wisconsin in scoring. He always seems to be in the right place when it comes time to get things done, and it makes you want to have him on the ice when it matters most.

Don't forget, just before Sidney Crosby scored the golden goal in overtime against the United States during the 2010 Olympic Games in Vancouver, Joe had a really good chance, but he got stopped. It could have gone the other way. I would have loved to see that. Of course, with the NHL out of the Olympics at that time—and I don't think that's going to be permanent—he won't have a chance. But I hope he gets another shot.

I probably see the same thing fans see in Pavelski on the ice—he's got a quiet intensity about him. He likes to laugh, but not too much. He enjoys it, but to be that quiet leader who people follow, he draws the line. And he's a great father and family man, which has helped him develop his leadership capabilities. It really helps when you're dealing with your teammates if you're doing that every day at home.

It's always in a big game, always in a critical moment of the game, when he does something big. He's at his best when it matters. I think the world of him, too.

He's a real pro, and you can see that in how he approaches everything. The guys really like and respect him. Pavs has this quiet leadership ability that people really respond to. He'll play hurt. He loves to win. He absolutely hates to lose.

That's the other thing: if I had to pick two Sharks on the current team that hate to lose the most, I'd pick Joe Pavelski and Logan Couture. Of course, everybody hates to lose, but these two really hate it, and sometimes that makes a big difference in a pro locker room!

I'd like to see Joe Pavelski skating around with the Stanley Cup triumphantly raised over his head, because he is a winner. Mark it down: it's going to happen.

Chapter 2

Long Road Trips

Those of us who travel with a professional hockey team—whether as broadcasters, trainers and medical personnel, front-office staff, public relations types, or journalists—are very fortunate to do what we do.

You don't ever want to lose sight of that fact.

We are privileged with chartered air flights, five-star hotels, the biggest and brightest cities in the United States and Canada, great restaurants, and a bird's-eye view to the greatest game in the world. Don't forget, too, the opportunity to see great places all over the world. Over the years the Sharks have traveled to Tokyo, Japan; Mannheim, Germany; and Stockholm, Sweden, for regular-season games.

As a team based out of the Pacific time zone on the far West Coast, travel to an almost excessive level is part of the gig. National Hockey League teams in Vancouver, Los Angeles, and Anaheim know exactly what San Jose goes through on a yearly basis. The Sharks are not alone.

When you travel with essentially the same group all season, you get to know their quirks. You get to know who the bad fliers are. I'm talking about the white-knuckle, seat-clutching, floor-stomping travelers who don't like it when the ride gets a little bumpy. I have sympathy for them, but it can lead to some pretty funny stories along the way.

It didn't take long in the franchise's history to log a memorable trip well away from the ice. In fact, it was the first extended road trip during the team's inaugural season of 1991–92 that few who were a part of will ever forget. The Sharks played their first game ever on the road at Vancouver, and a week later embarked on a three-gamer in mid-October (more on that one later). But it was a seven-game, 14-night excursion to Hartford, Buffalo, New Jersey,

Long Island, Philadelphia, Quebec City, and Toronto from late October into early November that went down in infamy.

To back up a bit, the Sharks had lost seven of their first eight games, including the last six, on the eve of the trip. It wasn't a bad time to head out of town as the new group that was just getting to know each other could have the opportunity to bond. We were also checking off all cities that could be a challenge to travel to in winter months, considering we were going to beat the snow. And coaches often rationalize an early-season long road trip, saying it can go a long way in forming that team cohesiveness needed over the marathon NHL season.

Unfortunately for these teal-behind-the-ear Sharks, the trip itself felt like a marathon.

As the team assembled at the charter center in Oakland at a time when just a handful of teams were still flying commercial—hello, Edmonton Oilers—immediately we were told there would be a delay. It seems the pilot didn't have enough air miles, and while he was practicing touch-and-goes to meet the required minimum, a tire on the landing gear blew out.

Well, it wasn't a matter of simply changing a tire like a stranded motorist might do on the side of the road. The proper tool needed for the repair was over the bridge in San Francisco. And, once the jack arrived, there was the question of who was qualified to make the repair. I think it had something to do with another collective bargaining agreement.

As the eager traveling group began to get antsy, Dennis Hull—the team's first TV/radio analyst—headed onto the tarmac to tell the airline workers how to change the tire. He told me that they were arguing about it!

Players tend to make the best of situations like this. But not so much for California native Craig Coxe. The journeyman forward, who had the distinction of scoring the first goal in franchise history, found himself on the short end of a card game. Coxe managed to lose his entire trip's per diem before he ever got on the first flight. And, not to pile on, but Coxe scored only one more goal the rest of his career.

Another forward, Paul Fenton, passed out at the airport due to heat exhaustion, and was carted off to the hospital with a huge welt on his forehead after hitting the deck hard. Typical of the character-type players on that first-year team, Fenton scored 11 goals in 60 games in what would be the last of his seven NHL seasons. Not surprisingly, he's gone on to a successful executive career in the league, recently becoming the general manager of the Minnesota Wild.

Once in the air, following a 14-hour delay, we landed during the early-morning hours in lovely Hartford and realized there was one last travel hurdle to overcome. There was no bus at the airport to take the team to the hotel. Why? Because Drew Remenda forgot to reschedule the bus for a later pickup once we knew our arrival would be delayed.

In those days, scheduling bus transit on the road was the responsibility of an assistant coach. That would be unheard of these days. And the lovable Drew, who would be a great addition to the broadcasting booth in years to come, was an assistant coach those first couple of years with the Sharks.

At 5:45 AM we finally pulled into our hotel, directly across the street from the mall that housed the Whalers' home rink. Hartford goalie Kay Whitmore stopped all 33 shots the Sharks managed

Longtime general manager Doug Wilson scored the final 12 goals and 48 points of a 16-year playing career and served as the Sharks' first captain from 1991 to '93. (Graig Abel/Getty Images)

in a 3–0 Whalers win later that same day. Strike up the "Brass Bonanza."

Following a 3–1 loss in Buffalo, San Jose pulled into the Meadowlands to face the New Jersey Devils on the second night of back-to-backs. The game stands out because it was Randy Hahn's television debut with the team. Joe Starkey was the team's first play-by-play announcer, but when he had conflicts with San Francisco 49er telecasts, Randy would step in before he became the full-time TV voice.

Randy will never forget his first game in the booth. The Sharks lost 9–0. Future Shark David Maley, playing for New Jersey, dropped the gloves with the legendary Link Gaetz. I called the game all alone from the halo at the Meadowlands, miles from the ice. It was a lonely perch that night.

And how did the rest of the trip turn out? The Sharks lost every game to sit dead last in the overall standings at 1–15 exactly one month into the season.

The Sharks had another three-game trip early on, and inaugural team captain Doug Wilson made his first return to old Chicago Stadium where he skated on the Blackhawks' blue line for 14 seasons.

Doug gave our expansion franchise instant credibility when he agreed to a trade from the Original Six team that had drafted him sixth overall in 1977. He was a star in Chicago where he scored 225 goals and 779 points in 938 games. A six-time All-Star with the Hawks, Wilson won the Norris Trophy as the league's best defenseman in 1981–82—a year he scored 39 goals and 85 points in 76 games.

If nothing else, the Sharks wanted to support their captain as best they could in a special game that came just 24 hours after losing the trip opener in St. Louis, 6–3.

Wilson may have had admiring fans awaiting his return, but the Blackhawks were in no mood to be congenial hosts. They racked up 72 minutes in penalties, which represents one of the highest road totals in almost three decades of Sharks hockey, while the Sharks pushed back with 44 minutes of their own.

The Blackhawks beat the Sharks 7–3 in a game marred by those 116 penalty minutes. Wilson provided the primary assist on San Jose's first goal—the second of the early season for Perry Berezan—to tie it 1–1. Chicago, however, poured it on and led 4–1 at the first intermission. Wilson finished with five shots on goal and with the one assist.

The Hawks had two players ejected—John Tonelli and Steve Thomas—both for spearing. The only game misconduct earned by a Shark—goalie Brian Hayward—was for leaving the crease to jump into a fracas as he saw San Jose was outmanned after future Shark Jeremy Roenick instigated a fight with Kevin Evans.

"Hazy had to go in there," was the comment from teammate Steve Bozek after Hayward tried to intercept Chicago defenseman Chris Chelios. Funny thing, too, Hayward and Chelios were pals from their time together as teammates in Montreal.

When the normally mild-mannered Hayward skated off the ice, television cameras caught him wildly swinging his goal stick and narrowly missing a fan heckling him in the stands before he descended down the stairs to the visitors' locker room.

As it turns out, Hayward's wife, Angela, was entertaining neighbors in their new South Bay home while the scene was playing out on television.

"My wife tells me our neighbors were in shock watching all of this," Hayward said years later. "She told them, 'He's really not like this.'"

And, if that wasn't enough, the Sharks had a third memorable event on the road that first year, too.

We had a flight scheduled from Minneapolis—where, at the old Met Center, the Sharks lost 7–4 to the North Stars, who had yet to relocate to Dallas. We were headed to Winnipeg, where the original Jets played prior to their relocation to Phoenix. It was just after the holidays in early January, and the die was pretty much cast on what was going to be a losing season as the team sat at 9–32–3.

We were coming into Winnipeg after the matinee game in Minny, and, in a place I never would have expected, there was dense fog. The approach seemed to take forever, and you couldn't see anything. Pea soup everywhere.

Someone from the back of the plane, (I think it was Jayson More) asked, "What is that sticking out of the clouds?" Someone suggested it looked like a TV antenna. And indeed it was. It was the roof of somebody's house. The pilot had missed the runway. And, at that very second, the engines fired up and the plane climbed sharply, our heartbeats racing at warp speed.

Unable to land in Winnipeg, we flew to Fargo, North Dakota. Because we had returned to the United States, and crossed back over the border, we had to pick up our luggage. This was before 9/11, but security was none too thrilled with what happened next.

Despite all the losing that first season, we had a roster full of good-natured guys. One of them was Jeff Hackett, a promising goalie the Sharks plucked the previous May with their first pick in the 1991 NHL expansion draft from the New York Islanders.

Hackett jumped on the conveyor belt, scrunched up, and moved along as if he were a piece of luggage. Everyone was laughing. Well, everyone accept security, who were going cuckoo. When they set out to find him, Hackett grabbed one of his teammates' leather jackets and put on sunglasses. Security couldn't recognize Hackett.

At that point the pilot came to us and said, "It's dark in Winnipeg now, so the landing lights on the runway are on. We'll probably be able to see them. So if you want to try it again, let's go."

"Try it again?!" I thought. It didn't sound very reassuring.

Back over Winnipeg, we couldn't see anything again. All of a sudden, we realized that the plane was about 100 feet off the ground, and we saw the dim glow of the landing lights through the thick fog. I couldn't believe that we tried to land.

For a moment, a feeling of relief engulfed the plane, and I remember hearing the sound of a few hands clapping, as if to commemorate the end of our adventure. But that was only for a moment. Suddenly, about 50 feet over the ground, we hit a heavy gust of wind. The plane slammed into the ground and tilted precariously, but the capable pilot regained control, straightened us out, and landed the plane.

I remember that this was the flight that Brian Mullen asked the pilot on his way out if we had just landed or if we were shot down.

Describing the scene a little later, Ken Hammond remarked, "I thought that we were going to be at nine wins and holding forever."

Given how much winter travel the team does, it's remarkable that there are relatively few incidents like that. Of course, when there is such an issue, it becomes a trip to remember. The one that got me, and that topped the foggy landing in Winnipeg, was going to and returning from Dallas after the Sharks were eliminated in

Game 5 of a second-round playoff series in the spring of 2000. San Jose was coming off an epic seven-game upset of the Presidents' Trophy–winning Blues in the first round, but ran into a veteran Stars team that won the first two and last two games after San Jose managed a 2–1 victory in Game 3. It wasn't a close series.

The traveling party is typically larger in the postseason as teams take more people, including front-office staff and medical personnel. So we needed a second plane to get everyone there and back. The players flew on the usual big charter while I was on a smaller plane with the other broadcasters, front-office staff, scouts, and doctors. We'd refuel in Albuquerque, New Mexico, because our plane didn't have the capacity to reach Dallas on one tank.

It started with our departure from San Jose. We were gaining altitude when all of a sudden one of the windows cracks, and all of the oxygen masks deploy. Guess whose window it cracked next to? Drew. Of course. Deservedly loved universally by Sharks fans for his fine work on television and radio, my good friend Mr. Remenda was not a fan of flying. He pretty much detested the experience anytime anything was amiss on a flight. The slightest turbulence was enough to set him off.

When the oxygen masks came down, he was ready to take a parachute and jump out.

Next, we got a message from the cockpit: "Yeah, we saw that, no problem, we'll get to Dallas." It reminded me of that scene in *Apollo 13* when one astronaut says to another, "You think they're going to tell us if there was anything wrong?"

We were flying so low over the Sierras it felt like we were about to scrape the top of the mountains. The pilot popped on and said, "You might notice we're flying a bit low. That's because we want to make sure with the loss of cabin pressure we don't fly too high."

What he left out was if we flew too high, we'd all pass out. So that was inferred.

We got to Albuquerque, and we were bouncing all over the place. Same thing going from Albuquerque to Dallas. Then we lose and are eliminated a night later, and it's time to return home on the same small plane.

That was the bumpiest flight I've ever been on in my life. It was a roller coaster all the way home. Food was flying around. At some point super-needling veteran forward Dave Lowry calls out two of our less-enthusiastic fliers—Mike Ricci and Stephane Matteau—and shouts from the back, "Die like a man!"

We lost in the playoffs. Now what else were we going to lose?

I missed a third hairy flight while recovering from an auto accident in November of 2000. On a team flight from Dallas to St. Louis a bird somehow knocked out the hydraulics for the plane. I don't know how that happened, but they have an emergency plan in place for it. They have cables, which had just been tested a couple months before. For the pilots, it was no big deal. They took off from Love Field in Dallas and landed at nearby Dallas/Fort Worth International Airport, but during the approach and landing fire trucks and emergency vehicles lined up on both sides of the runway.

Enough with the negativity, though. Most trips are fun. Many trips take you to historic spots in two countries. On some trips, history is made.

When the schedule comes out, the first thing broadcasters do, and I think the players, too, is look at is the road trips. Where are we going and when? The heck with the home games. It's just the way it is. I remember Fred Cusick was nearing the end of his long career doing television play-by-play for the Boston Bruins—first from 1971 to 1997 for WSBK-TV and then from 1984 to 1995 with NESN. In an effort to lighten his load as he approached his 80th birthday, Cusick was asked if he wanted to do either home or road games. He picked the road. I'm sure the network thought he'd pick the home games.

A few years back the Sharks had the road schedule oddity of playing at Chicago, at St. Louis, and at Chicago again with two or three days off between each game. The coach at the time, Todd McLellan, decided the team would return to San Jose after its first trip to Chicago, then fly to St. Louis a day before the Blues game before moving on to Chicago again.

The joke at the time was if the Sharks stayed in the Midwest with all that free time, they could go practice at Notre Dame or something, but they'd all end up back in Chicago. With that much time on their hands, a couple of the players could have married, had a kid, and then gotten divorced before the trip was over!

Anticipating the sojourn, the broadcasters put their heads together, and made other plans. Instead of returning to San Jose after the first game, we stayed in the Chicago area for eight days and nights. We took in some great music, wives joined us, and some of us visited family.

Another season, when Ron Wilson was coaching, the Sharks played a game at Washington, and a stop in New York was next. But getting an appropriate practice ice in the Metro New York area to jibe with the Sharks' schedule was proving difficult. So Wilson opted to have the team swing by the U.S. Naval Academy in nearby Annapolis, Maryland. The team practiced on their ice and joined the midshipmen for a meal in the dining hall where Sharks players were paired with Bay Area midshipmen. It was a great experience for the players, and a big thrill for the cadets.

We had to take their word for it, though, because it took the broadcasters about five seconds to decide we'd hop on the train instead and spend an extra few days of freedom in Manhattan!

When the Capitals finally moved from Landover to downtown DC, it allowed for long walks around the historic buildings in our nation's capital. What I found really cool is now with many of the streets blocked off around the White House for security purposes, roller hockey games were breaking out all over the place as kids were playing in the streets. I thought the Capitals were really having an impact there!

Speaking of history, I'll never forget that first trip to Dallas after the franchise relocated from Minnesota to Texas for the 1993–94 season. We flew into Love Field, and as we were driving into Big D to our hotel next to Reunion Arena, I recognized the triple underpass and knew we were about to go right by the Texas School Book Depository where it's believed the gun was fired that killed President John F. Kennedy on November 22, 1963. All the guys were talking, and it was late at night. Then somebody said, "There it is, the grassy knoll!" You could hear a pin drop, as all heads turned toward the intersection of Houston and Elm Streets, and observed the scene in person for the first time.

And then there was 9/11. September 11, 2001, coincided with the first day of training camp. And my childhood favorite team—the New York Rangers—was scheduled to be at the hotel near the World Trade Center. The Sharks played the Rangers at Madison Square Garden on October 22, not quite six weeks after the terrorist attack. I remember thinking *Where are the towers?* as our plane descended on New York. I knew they were gone, but it was so strange to look at that skyline and not see them.

What happened barely a month earlier was on everybody's mind. A couple guys got a chance to go to the site, and while they were there, a body was discovered. I went home and visited my family. That was a very spooky trip. Everything had changed. Everything was so fresh. Everybody was very pensive and quiet.

I knew five people who died on 9/11—two ex–St. Lawrence hockey players that Jamie Baker knew, too, a person who was in my graduating class at St. Lawrence, and a guy who grew up down the street from me in my hometown.

The fifth person was another story that takes some explaining.

Back in San Jose at a time when our broadcast location was literally in the front row of the second deck—a great vantage point from which to call a game—it was also easily accessible. Fans stopped by to say hi or wave all the time.

One couple, who had met at games and married, had season tickets in the upper bowl but always made the effort to stop by and say hi. They always had their radios with them so they could listen to the broadcast.

As I was setting up at Madison Square Garden for the post–9/11 game, the very same couple from San Jose came up to the booth. So many people were avoiding travel to New York shortly after the tragedy, and I told them how good it was to see them at the game and that I was glad they didn't change their plans to see the game.

The wife, who normally was very talkative, didn't say anything. Instead, her husband said, "We didn't plan on being here." Upon hearing that my heart sank. Their daughter worked at Cantor Fitzgerald's corporate headquarters with the others I knew who also perished in One World Trade Center. The grieving couple was in New York to clean out her apartment.

That trip really got to the guys. It didn't matter if you were an American, Canadian, European, or from Mars. It affected everyone.

On the ice, the game had a memorable moment in club history, too: Vincent Damphousse scored a goal when the Sharks were two men down. It's the only 3-on-5 goal in franchise history to date.

Chapter 3

Dean and Doug

They came from very different backgrounds.

One was American. A deep thinker, analytical in nature, who sought out a law degree after leaving his playing days behind. He never played in the NHL. The other Canadian. Born to play the game. He excelled at the NHL level, and enjoyed a long and productive playing career. The leadership he displayed on the ice translated to business, and eventually to the front office of an NHL team.

Both Dean Lombardi and Doug Wilson have left indelible marks on the San Jose Sharks. Their accomplishments and longevity in the general manager's seat are nothing short of impressive.

Lombardi grew up in Ludlow, Massachusetts, 10 miles from Springfield and 80 miles west of Boston. Dean wasn't a bad hockey player in his own right. He was honored as an All-Western Massachusetts forward at Ludlow High School during his junior season of 1974–75.

That success served as a springboard for Lombardi's senior season when he was a member of the Wallace Cup champion Springfield Olympics of the New England Junior Hockey League. He played for Gary Dineen, who was a top developer of hockey talent. Dineen coached future NHL star and ex-Shark, Bill Guerin, too.

Lombardi continued to play a couple more seasons for Dineen and eventually was selected to the All-America junior hockey team. Lombardi began his college hockey career at Elmira, but transferred to the University of New Haven in Connecticut. Always the studious type, in addition to his ambition to play hockey, Lombardi captained the Chargers his junior and senior seasons when he was named a scholar athlete before eventually graduating third in his class.

As we would learn much later, Dean always had a plan. And his plan after graduation was to find a way to continue to be involved in hockey somehow. Lombardi attended Tulane University where he specialized in labor law while earning another degree. He initially became a player's agent under the mentorship of Art Kaminsky, who boasted a stable of young American hockey players—many from the 1980 "Miracle on Ice" gold-medal winners.

The son-in-law of Hockey Hall of Fame winger and longtime NHL executive Bob Pulford, Lombardi joined the management team of the Minnesota North Stars, where he served as assistant GM from 1988 until 1990. The expansion Sharks developed partially from the North Stars' organization, so it only made sense that the Minnesota front office would move West, too. And Lombardi followed San Jose's first-year general manager Jack Ferreira to the Bay Area, again as assistant GM.

Lombardi was given more responsibility immediately after the conclusion of the team's inaugural season, during which the Sharks went 17–58–5 to finish last in the Pacific Division with 39 points. Ferreira was fired, and Lombardi was joined by Chuck Grillo (director of player personnel) and George Kingston (head coach) as a vice president at the top of the Sharks' food chain. The three shared the office of general manager in what was viewed around the hockey world as a unique and proactive approach. Others simply termed the trio as "the three-headed monster."

After Kingston was let go following a miserable 11–71–2 second season, the GM seat was shared by just Lombardi and Grillo, and they would see good and bad times over a rocky 2½-year arrangement. All seemed good on the surface when the Sharks rebounded with a record 58-point improvement in Year 3—the first in San Jose's new downtown arena—to not only reach the

Stanley Cup playoffs for the first time, but to knock off top-seed Detroit and take Toronto to a seventh game in the second round.

The upset-minded Sharks did not stop there. Again finishing under .500, and this time during a lockout-shortened 48-game campaign, San Jose beat division champ Calgary in double overtime of Game 7 in the first round before getting spanked in four games by Detroit in Round 2.

Disagreement over how to build the roster bubbled to the surface early in 1995–96. Grillo was eager to see his high picks, many of European lineage, given a chance at the NHL level. Grillo had a keen eye for distinguishing talent and innovative ideas for player development. He owned the Minnesota Hockey Camps, where many of the young Sharks' draftees saw a lot of ice time.

Lombardi often favored a mix of grit and skill on his roster, and he understood the importance of developing draft picks so they would be accepted by the veterans in the locker room. He did not want to risk a fractured workplace, because the perception was draftees were rushed into the lineup where they'd take the job away from a vet before his time.

Lombardi's vision won out as Grillo departed in March of 1996 during the season in which young head coach Kevin Constantine was let go and team president Art Savage also left. Lombardi knew he had a tough task ahead, and while he didn't have all the answers, he knew where he could get help.

Lombardi went back to school in the most practical sense.

He studied and met with the most successful builders of pro sports teams of the time. The distinguished group included Lou Lamoriello of the New Jersey Devils, Pro Football Hall of Fame GM Ron Wolf of the NFL's Green Bay Packers, and head coach Bill Walsh of San Jose's backyard dynasty San Francisco 49ers.

"He not only read about all the builders of sports teams, but leaders that were political figures, too," said Wayne Thomas, who during 22 years with the Sharks was an assistant coach and key member of the front office. "He never stopped trying to learn. He never stopped trying to push us in that direction, too, to create knowledge and to get better."

Dean wasn't afraid to put it all right out there during his initial press conference.

"One good thing about this is there's no more 'Grillo's guys,'" he said. "From now on, if there's anybody on this bus, it is because of Dean Lombardi. If a player is here, it's my call. We're going to do it like every other team where coaches coach and managers manage.

"We all know who's the target right now. Now it's, 'You're the GM. Oh, by the way, you'd better get it done.' We're not going to have a dramatic change in philosophy in what we're trying to build here."

Dean was focused and detail oriented. You could see how his legal training had an effect on the job, and he always talked about the influence of Lamoriello on his career. He had an idea of how he wanted his team to play, he made a plan and stuck with it, and he wanted to get players to do that, too. He was stubborn, but that was his philosophy. Once you have that plan you want to see it through, he figured.

I think a lot of the way Dean managed went back to his roots. There's a very tight hockey community in Boston, but he was from the outskirts of that. He was from Massachusetts, but he wasn't of the Harvard pedigree. He didn't have a lot of connections. And yet he accomplished a lot more than "Harvard guys" because of his hard work. He just willed his way to do it.

Dean also had a lot of ability. He didn't go to a Division I school. He went to the University of New Haven. He went to Tulane University for law school. A different path took him where he wanted to go. Even though it wasn't considered orthodox at the time, now all these analytical types are becoming general managers.

The first hire he made was Al Sims, who was a top assistant in Anaheim under expansion Mighty Ducks coach Ron Wilson. A defenseman, Sims had played for the Boston Bruins for six of his 10

Executive vice president and general manager Dean Lombardi poses for a portrait on September 1, 2002, at Compaq Center in San Jose, California. (Getty Images/NHLI)

NHL seasons. He even was Bobby Orr's blue line partner for two seasons.

But as a head coach, it just didn't work out. Not at all. The Sims-led Sharks were no better than the dysfunctional group of the year before. San Jose finished 27–47–8 and dead last in the Pacific again.

Dean learned a lot by then. That was a tough year, and a tough year for him, too. That was when Dean's faith in himself and his confidence were being severely tested.

Dean made the change he had to make with the coach: Sims was out and Darryl Sutter was brought in. That was a big defining moment for Lombardi.

Dean should get a lot of credit for building a team that was tough to play against. Think about it: new team president Greg Jamison saw the need for the hockey department to have one leader, and Dean was the guy he chose. I think Dean's focus and his resolute approach helped him draw up a blueprint of what he wanted the Sharks to be. Under him, the Sharks became a hockey team with a definitive character.

Lombardi didn't differ from Grillo in his belief that a hockey team's enduring success is best achieved through the NHL entry draft. The key, Lombardi believed, was turning that young talent into dependable and responsible players who would accept the mantle of winning at the NHL level. What the Sharks didn't have was those veterans who would pass the mantle to the youth.

So Lombardi scoured opposing rosters in search of veteran players whose pedigree included winning, who possessed strong character traits, and who were ready and willing to accept a mentoring role on a team while getting one last kick at the can.

Lombardi knew, too, he might have to overpay in the free-agent market to lure that kind of player to rebuild San Jose. Lucky for Dean this was all before the financial restrictions posed by the salary cap system.

The team's doomed 1996–97 roster included seven players the Sharks selected in the first or second rounds of a draft—Shean Donovan, Jeff Friesen, Viktor Kozlov, Vlastimil Kroupa, Andrei Nazarov, Mike Rathje, and Ray Whitney—in addition to lower-round picks Marcus Ragnarsson and Michal Sykora, who had developed into regulars.

In addition to hiring Sutter to lead the team in 1997–98, Lombardi set out to surround the promising young core with the veterans who possessed the qualities Lombardi sought. Dean managed to sign Kelly Hrudey, Tony Granato, and Marty McSorley, all Los Angeles Kings teammates the year before. Vets Ron Sutter, Tim Hunter, and Todd Ewen also signed to join a roster with experienced holdovers Bernie Nicholls and Todd Gill.

Dean was fiercely loyal to the people he drafted, and to the people he worked with. He went out of his way to help guys who went the wrong way, and I think that showed the compassion he had for people. I don't think he always gets credit for that, but there's no doubt he really cared about his players. Sometimes that may have slowed progress, but he wanted to wake up, look himself in the mirror, and feel good about what he did. That was a big part of it for him.

Dean met journalists at the Keyes Club, a cocktail bar in downtown San Jose. Those were legendary nights, where Lombardi could turn a five-minute conversation into a two-hour marathon. And no one went away feeling like they'd wasted their time. Dean was a bit uneasy around the media in those days if the cameras were rolling but generous with his time and much more at ease with the small groups at the Keyes Club.

I never went to the Keyes Club, but there were some similar outings on the road. I remember going to the Anaheim White House, an Italian steak house. Dean got into a good-natured but intense argument with the owner of the restaurant about who was more Italian!

Dean was intense. Every once in a while he'd go into the bowels of an arena, and you could count how many cartons of cigarettes he'd smoked. We joked that was the Pulford influence.

Dean really got into a game, and he was one of those guys who lived and breathed a team. He lived and breathed the stride of every skate. That was the kind of guy he was. He wanted to do everything in his power to win a Stanley Cup—and sure enough he won a couple in L.A years later.

Dean's plan in San Jose was starting to gain momentum once Sutter guided the Sharks into the playoffs in 1998. It started a run of five straight visits to the Stanley Cup playoffs. At the start of that first season under Sutter, more veterans were on their way just in time to help support four more first-round picks—Patrick Marleau, Alexander Korolyuk, Marco Sturm, and Andrei Zyuzin— and Shawn Burr, Murray Craven, Stephane Matteau, Mike Ricci, and Mike Vernon all came via trade.

And that's not all. Dave Lowry and John MacLean were acquired in November and December. Then Bryan Marchment and Joe Murphy came aboard in deals at the March trade deadline. Just a month before, while the NHL took a break for the Olympic Winter Games in Nagano, Japan, Lombardi gave his okay to an idea for the team to hold a mini-camp in the Canadian resort town of Banff, Alberta.

"Wow, did we bond," Kelly Hrudey said years later. "We practiced hard, and enjoyed each other's company away from the rink equally as well. I was 37 years old and really in a different place than those kids. You don't often see guys 36 to 37 hanging around with guys who were basically 20 years old."

I think what he learned when he counseled with Lou Lamoriello was really taking hold. Dean was seeing the early stages of his plan unfolding successfully. That was a step forward for him. He knew exactly how he was going to do the job.

Dean didn't ever want anybody to hold back. If you had an opinion, especially one that differed from his, he wanted to hear it. He wanted you to get out there and say it and disagree with him if that's what you wanted to do. He was good with that. And, in fact, once he felt that was happening in his organization he felt comfortable because he knew he was getting the best advice from all the people he trusted.

Lombardi continued his pursuit of quality veterans to fill holes in the roster while keeping the youth movement going forward. It became easier to recruit, because outsiders saw what Dean was doing and that it was working. They knew, too, with a coach like Sutter at the helm, the team would have an identity and play hard every night. They also knew there was a legitimate chance to annually compete in the postseason.

Doug Wilson smiles during the news conference to introduce him as the new general manager of the Sharks on May 13, 2003. *(AP Photo/Paul Sakuma)*

Six vets either retired or moved on after 1997–98, and free agents Jamie Baker, Bob Rouse, and Ron Stern were signed while Vincent Damphousse was acquired at the trade deadline as the Sharks reloaded for another run to the playoffs.

"And all of us guys were great about it, no egos, let

the kids play and help them with things," Hrudey recalled. "And it was really a cool dynamic because there was just such good chemistry between all of us."

During Lombardi's seven full seasons as the team's sole GM, no less than 10 of his chosen vets concluded what had been long, multi-year careers in San Jose, including Craven, Damphousse, Ewen, Granato, Hrudey, Hunter, Nicholls, Bob Rouse, Ronnie Stern, and Gary Suter. Five more—Burr, Lowry, Matteau, Ricci, and Ron Sutter—played for only one more team before hanging up their skates.

Dean's tenure ended after a disappointing 2002–03 campaign when the Sharks missed the playoffs for the first time in six seasons. With new ownership, Lombardi was forced to make a coaching change. Sutter was let go two months into the season, and the team could never right the ship afterward. Lombardi was relieved of his duties days after the trade deadline late in the season.

His replacement wasn't named immediately, but speculation the job would go to Doug Wilson was confirmed on May 13, 2003, when the team's first captain and director of pro development for the previous five years became the general manager and executive vice president.

"Doug's work with us, in addition to his experience with the Canadian Olympic team and the NHLPA, displays the diversity necessary for an NHL general manager," said Greg Jamison, San Jose's president and CEO at the time. "He also knows talent, which will always be the most important element for a general manager."

While there were most certainly a number of qualified candidates inside and outside the organization, promoting Wilson was a no-brainer. As Jamison's comments suggest, it's hard to imagine an individual could bring more to the table in his first opportunity as general manager at the NHL level than Wilson with his wide range of managerial experience, knowledge of the game—both past, present, and into the future—and his vast contacts in the hockey world.

Before Wilson filled the Big Seat, he enjoyed a long and successful NHL career that ended in San Jose. He spent his first 14 years in Chicago. And what a run he had with the Original Six Blackhawks.

The sixth overall pick in 1977, Wilson was coming off three outstanding seasons playing for legendary coach Brian Kilrea and the Ottawa 67s of the Ontario Hockey Association. Ottawa, of course, is Wilson's hometown, too. He scored a combined 80 goals and 254 points in 156 games for Ottawa. Wilson was also drafted fifth overall in '77 by the Indianapolis Racers, the World Hockey Association team that would add a kid by the name of Wayne Gretzky to its roster a year later.

Wilson jumped into the established Blackhawks lineup as a 20-year-old rear guard, and he was assigned to room on the road with Stan Mikita. Wilson's defense partner for a short time his second season was the great Bobby Orr, ex-Boston Bruin who retired from hockey at the age of 30 after playing only six games during the 1978–79 season with Chicago.

Mikita, a future Hall of Famer, had a profound effect on Wilson's early development. Wilson would lean heavily on Mikita for paternal advice and guidance, especially after Wilson's father died when Doug was only 25 years old.

A smooth skater with a cannon for a shot, Wilson's offensive production improved at a modest rate until his fifth year in the league when he put it all together like no other defenseman that season. Wilson scored a career-high 39 goals and added 46 assists for 85 points to win the Norris Trophy as the NHL's top blue liner in addition to finishing ninth in the Hart voting as league MVP.

Wilson played nine more full seasons with Chicago to give him 14 in all while wearing that distinctive Blackhawks' logo. He finished his time in the Windy City with 225 goals and 554 assists in 938 regular-season games. His 779 points are still tops among all-time Chicago defensemen.

As the summer of 1991 progressed, Wilson was told by Blackhawks management that he would be dealt before the start of the upcoming season. With many options available to him, Doug chose to accept a new start in a new city with a new team, and so, in close consultation with his family, he chose to move to San Jose and begin the next chapter in his life.

"Doug has a vision few people see in the game," said his older brother, Murray Wilson, a four-time Stanley Cup champion with the Montreal Canadiens. "He wants to help the game grow."

If there was one thing that Doug Wilson brought to the Sharks immediately, it was instant credibility. The cost was a player, Kerry Toporowski, who would ultimately never play a game in the NHL. A defenseman, Toporowski was selected in the fourth round of the 1991 Draft by San Jose, and after earning six fighting majors in four preseason games with the Blackhawks, he wound up spending 12 seasons and 481 games in the AHL, IHL, ECHL, UHL, and Russia.

Joining the team a couple days into that first training camp held at the Cow Palace, Wilson explained he wanted to be in on the ground floor in building a new franchise. And as the team's first captain, he brought the Sharks instant credibility anywhere they went. A lot of those early-franchise players were terrific guys, and it was really fabulous to go to a place like Madison Square Garden and see how positively the Rangers fans were reacting to the likes of Kelly Kisio and Brian Mullen, for example.

Arturs Irbe, Jeff Hackett, and Brian Hayward were all legitimate goaltenders, too. But Doug Wilson was an NHL All-Star, and former Norris Trophy winner. He was the first truly top player that the Sharks franchise ever had. Thus, it wasn't too much of a surprise to see him become the team's lone representative at the 1992 NHL All-Star game in Philadelphia, where he and his Campbell Conference teammates beat the Wales Conference, 10–6.

But Doug Wilson was an All-Star. He was the first top player that this team had. He was, in fact, the Sharks' lone representative in the 1992 NHL All-Star Game at Philadelphia where Wilson's Campbell Conference beat the Wales Conference, 10–6.

"With the Detroit Red Wings, it's Gordie Howe. With the Boston Bruins it's Bobby Orr. With us, it's Doug Wilson," said Lombardi, at the time the team's director of hockey operations.

Wilson scored nine goals and 28 points that first year in San Jose, but he struggled to stay healthy. Out 17 games with injury and illness in the first half of the season, Wilson scored 15 points over a 16-game stretch but then suffered a knee injury and missed the final 19 games. Still, though, he led in blue line scoring.

The highlight of another start-and-stop second season with the Sharks came November 21, 1992, when San Jose hosted Wilson's old team, Chicago, at the Cow Palace. The occasion was Doug's 1,000[th] career game. He became the 77th player in league history to reach the milestone at the time.

My co-author recalls writing a 100-inch feature published in the *San Francisco Examiner* to preview Wilson's milestone. And when he asked Wilson's wife, Kathy, about her husband's accomplishments, she broke down and cried. That spoke to the sincere love and respect Kathy and Doug have for each other.

Creation of the Doug Wilson Scholarship Foundation to provide assistance to worthy college-bound Bay Area students was announced during a pregame ceremony. Not surprising, Wilson was the team's nominee in each of his two seasons for the King Clancy Memorial Trophy, awarded annually for leadership and humanitarian contributions both on and off the ice.

"We lost 2–1, but we gave them their money's worth. The team played hard for our captain," goalie Arturs Irbe recalled. "The look Doug gave me, and the embrace, it was more telling to me than later reading what 1,000 games in the NHL meant."

The Cow Palace was a unique venue for many reasons, but one thing that stands out was the loading dock between the two locker rooms where the two teams would congregate afterward and where they were joined by Sharks players' families. That never happens anymore.

You'd see all the guys hanging out with their wives, kids, and everyone. The image I'll always remember is Doug, Kathy, and their four young children walking out together as a family. And that's how he sees everything. That family is very important to him. And that group at work around him is very important as well.

I'm guessing if Doug ever had any regret it was that he didn't play a third year for the Sharks—the team's first in downtown San Jose. His body didn't allow him to play the third year. He didn't announce his intentions to step away from the game he loved playing so much until the eve of training camp.

In an ideal world, that pioneer player would have played in the new building in San Jose, but, unfortunately, he just wasn't healthy enough to keep going. He wanted to spend time with his family and hang out with his kids instead of being in a bad medical position. I can't say I disagree with his decision, as tough as it may have been.

In all, Doug finished with 1,024 games played—and isn't it appropriate he went 24 games over 1,000, since that's the number he wore his entire 16-year career whether in Chicago or San Jose? He scored 237 goals and 827 points, was an All-Star seven times, put 3,293 shots on goal, and even collected a hat trick—a rarity for a defenseman. It happened during his last season in Chicago on January 26 against visiting Toronto inside the fabulous old barn on Madison Street.

Wilson scored another 19 goals and 80 points in 95 career Stanley Cup playoff appearances. The Blackhawks missed out on the postseason in only one of Wilson's 14 seasons with Chicago. Doug missed the 1988 playoffs due to shoulder surgery. Otherwise he visited the postseason with Chicago 12 times. To this day I firmly believe Wilson deserves entry into the Hall of Fame as a player. But—who knows?—he might go in as a builder someday, too.

Wilson started his management career almost as soon as his playing days ended. President of the players' association his final season and a vice president for eight seasons with the NHLPA as a player, Doug began a tenure with Hockey Canada first by being a consultant for the nation's entries in the 1994–97 World Junior Championships. Those four Canadian representatives all won gold medals. Wilson continued his contributions to Hockey Canada by serving on the board of the Canadian Hockey Association.

A stint outside of hockey with Coca-Cola followed and gave him experience in the business world. And by 1997, four years after retiring as a player, Wilson was ready to return to the Sharks.

He was hired as director of pro development, where he evaluated talent at the pro levels while getting involved with personnel issues and contract negotiations.

By 2003, Wilson was qualified and ready to take the reins of a franchise that had established an identity under Lombardi. When you think about Dean you think about his loyalty and his work ethic. With Doug, it's the same thing. Let me use a racing analogy: Dean stuck to his guns much like Italian driver Luigi Musso, who would grit his teeth around each corner at the Italian Grand Prix. Wilson was more like Argentine star Juan Manuel Fangio, who made auto racing look effortless. Both had success, yet had a different way to get there.

I can't say I've seen Doug have a bad day. He always looks at the positive, which is important for a general manager. He tries to make people better around him all the time. And I think he largely succeeds at that.

Wilson began his first year as GM in 2003–04 looking to rally the Sharks back into the postseason after the team missed out the previous spring for the first time in six campaigns. Doug was inheriting head coach Ron Wilson—no relation—but the bench boss had a good idea what the roster had and didn't have as he coached the final 57 games of the previous season. The combo proved successful as the Sharks went all the way to their first Western Conference Finals appearance by year's end.

Along the way, Doug did what he felt he needed to do and didn't worry about what people said. He was pretty superstitious, too. And the two notions joined forces during the second half of that initial season, making for a pretty funny and unique anecdote.

With his team struggling through two periods at old America West Arena, the original home of the Phoenix Coyotes, Doug plopped himself down between the two traveling newspaper writers—one of whom is the co-author of this book. The Sharks rallied in the third period to win, and a new tradition was born. Wilson made it a point to sit between the same two writers for a majority of the remaining 16 road games, over which time the Sharks had a winning record to reach the playoffs.

"Doug does things his way and doesn't worry about what others say," said former Sharks executive Wayne Thomas, who spent 22 years in the organization. "And it's hard to argue with his track record."

It didn't stop there. Wilson continued his superstitious habit all the way to Game 3 of the third round before realizing the visiting press box was not a good place to display emotion in an emotionally charged playoff moment.

Sit with Doug for a game and you learn he's very intense. A lot of GMs have that superstitious streak. I think it's a way to get through the game. All players are like that, too, especially great players. They do something and have a really great game, and then they just want to repeat it. They want to eat the same thing for breakfast and go to bed at the same time. They want to have their routine and feel good about everything. That way they have a lot of confidence. The story my co-author shared didn't surprise me.

After the labor dispute wiped out the 2004–05 season, and just after the quarter-pole of 2005–06, Doug left an indelible mark on the franchise with this three-for-Joe Thornton trade. The trade shocked the hockey world and changed the Sharks' franchise for the better going forward. Doug got the call from his old teammate, Boston GM Mike O'Connell, who knew he was putting himself in a tough spot to trade Thornton. O'Connell felt he could at least get a trustworthy deal with Doug.

Significant trades at key moments helped the team sustain a streak of 10 straight playoff appearances in Wilson's first 10 years as GM. In addition to Thornton, he acquired defenseman Dan Boyle in 2008, defenseman Brent Burns in 2011, goalie Martin Jones in 2015, and forward Evander Kane in 2018.

Each acquisition was a very good deal for the organization. You can see why the other teams did it, too. The process of looking to make a deal to fix something reinforced the philosophy he had, which was to draft great players and take advantage of every opportunity to acquire good young talent. It's better than having a free agent come for a lot of money and not work out. And it's better than having to get a rental. The Sharks had a few rentals that didn't work out.

In his first 13 seasons in charge of the Sharks, who reached the postseason 12 times in that span, Wilson guided the franchise to its most successful era. The Sharks reached their first Stanley Cup Final in 2016. They captured a Presidents' Trophy in 2009. They won five Pacific Division titles and advanced to the Western Conference Final four times. Throw out the lockout-shortened 2012–13 campaign, and Wilson's Sharks averaged 104 points per season from 2003–17 and posted four 50-win campaigns along the way.

Do you know what he's really good at? In the current salary cap era, he is an outstanding money manager. Doug knows the deal that's both good for the player and the organization. He's also loyal—when he moved players like Douglas Murray to Pittsburgh and Ryane Clowe to the Rangers during a time of transition in 2013, every single one of those guys moved to a place where they could succeed.

Take Andrew Desjardins as an example. He went to Chicago and won a Stanley Cup. For him and others, he was helping his team and helpful to those who now were no longer part of the future here. I don't think a lot of general managers do that or even think about that. Who knows? Maybe it's a stroke of luck. But I think he puts a lot of thought into things like that.

Doug approaches everything with balance. And no stone goes unturned whether it's managing money or thinking about the future. A lot of that is because he has great people around him, and he's trusted them. He's brought people in who excel at their jobs. And that's the mark of a successful manager. It engenders confidence and allows people to be themselves.

In more recent times you can see, too, that Doug lets his players have their fun, yet expects them to be serious when the time calls for that, too. Look at something as simple as Brent Burns and Joe Thornton with their crazy beards. Lou Lamoriello would never have allowed that. And George Steinbrenner wouldn't have either. And that's fine for other teams. But Doug doesn't want his players to feel manipulated. He wants them to feel they can express themselves. That's the way Doug handles it.

You have to look at the whole body of work. Great player, got into management, nurtured contacts, took advantage of his opportunity to advance, made San Jose a great place to play, and always kept family close. Wilson is a very smart hockey guy. He knows people. As Dean did, Doug has a real vision for how he wants his team to play. He gets players to do it.

That's the good news. The Sharks have been in great hands for more than two decades with just two general managers— Lombardi and Wilson. Ownership hires good people and sticks to them. Doug joined an extremely elite group along with Bobby

Clarke, Bob Gainey, and Bob Pulford in January of 2017 when Wilson became the fourth individual to play in 1,000 NHL games and to serve as GM on an NHL club for at least 1,000 games. I truly hope that Doug lands in the Hall of Fame someday soon, either as a player or a builder, and I will also be very happy to see him bring the Stanley Cup home to San Jose.

Chapter 4

Coach's Chalkboard

As broadcasters and members of the media, our job is to interview, gather information, and keep our fingers on the pulse of what's significant, serving as a conduit for passionate fans of the team we follow. And, as an additional perk of the job, we get to know the players and coaches on a personal level.

Our access serves as a window into their lives, and it allows us to learn so much about the game and so much about the dedication and perseverance it takes to not only reach the pinnacle of their sport, but remain there, too.

When I think about the coaches the Sharks have employed throughout the years, I'm struck with how knowledgeable they are about the game and how passionate they are about getting the absolute most out of players for the betterment of the team.

Whatever you do, don't ask me to pick a favorite!

Looking back at the impact coaches had on this organization, the five and a half years Darryl Sutter spent behind San Jose's bench established a tone for what Sharks hockey was going to be. The coaches who preceded Darryl—namely George Kingston and Kevin Constantine—had the challenges of taking an expansion franchise from ground zero and building it up. The Sharks had endured growing pains, surprising postseason success, and sudden disappointment again during the six seasons—including one lockout-shortened—before Sutter arrived to right the ship.

Darryl was an important hire for general manager Dean Lombardi, since his decision to go with former Anaheim assistant Al Sims the year before did not turn out well. The Sharks were coming off consecutive last-place finishes and felt far removed from a pair of magical early-franchise seasons in Years 2 and 3 when they recorded impressive first-round upset wins in the Stanley Cup playoffs.

While Lombardi was furiously tinkering with the roster to put the right blend of seasoned, character vets around the franchise's drafted prospects, he needed the right leadership at the top. And when he paid Darryl a visit on the Sutter family farm in Viking, Alberta, he knew he'd found his man.

A popular ex-captain of the Blackhawks, who had his eight-season NHL career cut short by injuries, Sutter needed to be convinced his next job was a good fit. He had stepped away from the coaching rigors for two seasons after spending three from 1992–95 behind Chicago's bench.

Everyone was familiar with what the Sutters represent. The family sent six brothers to the NHL to play a combined total of nearly 5,000 games and win six Stanley Cups, and they all displayed the trademark characteristic of hard-work ethic.

There's an old saying in hockey that there's no tighter group of people than the Sutter family.

What attracted him to the San Jose job, besides the challenge of building up from the ground floor, was the fact that the South Bay region had special needs schooling and professional care for his young son, Christopher—born with Down syndrome—that proved to be a pre-requisite for the Sutter family.

Sutter knew turning the Sharks around would be a big job. And he had a couple newspaper writers who covered the team on a daily basis laughing when in the middle of first-day training camp drills that featured a bloated roster, he bluntly stated, "I'm not here to run a hockey camp." As we got to know Darryl better, we learned with 100 percent certainty he wasn't trying to be funny.

I remember him saying at the outset he was not only coaching the squad, but he had to be captain of the team, too. He talked

Darryl Sutter calling out instructions, while Stephane Matteau (left) and Mark Smith look on during a 2002 game against the St. Louis Blues. *(AP Photo/Paul Sakuma)*

about why he was brought here. He was here to change the culture of the team, and he had to change it fast.

The Sutters are all about hard work, and maybe there wasn't enough of that in what the Sharks had been doing in the recent past. There was no question the team had drafted skilled players who would one day assimilate into the league and be successful. But the element of working hard, and establishing a mindset that starts with keeping the puck out of your own net, needed to be ingrained into San Jose's game.

Darryl was sternly critical of that part of his analysis, but he was usually right in terms of what the team needed. He would express himself in short bursts and never beat around the bush. What he said wasn't necessarily a personal shot, it was just what he determined was necessary for the team. They would take the still shots of the guys and put them on the video screen over the ice at center. And when they took them of Darryl he looked so serious, like he was ready to tear somebody's head off.

And yet the other side of him would usually come out in the meetings with only us present and where he would always show his humanity.

I do a popular Sharks radio segment called "Coach's Chalkboard" that aired minutes before every opening faceoff. Those interviews were generally recorded following that day's morning skate or several hours before if the team had an optional workout.

When I occasionally interviewed Brian Sutter, Darryl's brother, the tenor of his quotes had a slightly more energetic cadence to them, whereas Darryl was a bit more soft-spoken in his delivery. But Darryl's honesty and insightful analysis made our segment a must-listen for all Sharks fans.

One interesting observation: Darryl sometimes seemed more open and relaxed when the team was on a three-game losing streak than his more terse delivery when the team was on a roll. It was because he wasn't reacting to what was going on at the time. He had a lot of forethought. He knew where he needed his team to be, where it was headed, and what he needed to do to help.

The pieces started to come together as I got to know Darryl. It was certainly a relief considering my first recollection of him.

I remember I first met him when he was coaching Chicago. It was the day of a game between the Blackhawks and the Sharks in San Jose. He was sitting in the stands watching the end of our morning skate just before his team would take the ice for theirs. I walked up to him, introduced myself, and he did not want to talk at all. He was focused.

I was thinking to myself, *What the heck is it with this guy?* But he was busy. He was there for a reason, and he was watching. That's something I understood better years later after he joined our organization.

Surprisingly, Darryl got the Sharks to play the way he wanted fast enough that they reached the Stanley Cup playoffs in his first season behind the bench. San Jose didn't have a winning record—34–38–10—but managed to finish fourth in the Pacific Division and eighth in the conference.

The Sharks were 14th best out of 26 teams in goals against. That's why they made the playoffs. San Jose ranked third worst in goals surrendered the year before, and dead last in goals scored. Darryl had them thinking defense first. The mindset and the culture were changing. A veteran Dallas Stars team, headed for a West showdown with Detroit, needed six games to beat the Sharks in the first round.

The first year was really something because the team went through so many struggles, adversity, and change during the previous two years. Darryl quickly established a new tone and a new culture. He got the veteran players, who were in that corner, to say "I'm all in," which meant all the younger players were in, too.

Darryl was multifaceted: there was the nose-to-the-grindstone work ethic that he demanded every day, but he also had another side. He liked to be around the guys and be around the team, too. That human side sometimes got overlooked.

I remember the team was enjoying a private event around the Christmas holidays, and Darryl had momentarily lost sight of his son, Chris. My wife, Karen, said Darryl was almost in a panic, like, *Where's my son?* When he saw Chris was with one of the players, Darryl relaxed and everything was fine.

He had a very special bond with Christopher, one of both love and concern at the same time. He laughed with his son, he had Chris talk with the team in the dressing room, he had him around all the time. That happened more when Darryl went to coach the Kings in Los Angeles because Christopher was older then. Darryl is a family person first. But second, he understands people from all walks of life, and it makes him a very empathetic person.

You never know what's going on with a coach away from the rink. He had a lot on his mind as a father. He was married and had a teenage daughter at the time, too, and another son, Brett, who in later years reached the NHL. And being a guy from a small town and living in a much bigger city, I think Darryl felt more comfortable in San Jose.

The night of November 25th, 2000, right after Thanksgiving, the Sharks were hosting the New Jersey Devils. I was in an auto accident that afternoon, was in the hospital having surgeries and missing the game. My wife was walking out at night with others from the office because the hospital was closing.

The small group got outside and noticed a vehicle parked by itself across the way. A couple of people, including team president Greg Jamison, walked over to the car. Sitting inside was Darryl Sutter. He had driven to the hospital after the Sharks had lost a one-goal game to the Devils, and was waiting for someone to come out to report on my condition.

Karen and I will always appreciate that gesture. You're not going to get much better than that.

A little more than a month later, and with my recuperation well underway, I rejoined the club on the road. It was an emotional trip for several reasons as we flew into Chicago. My father-in-law was in a hospital near the United Center, and he wasn't going to live much longer. It was the last time I saw him, in fact. I spent at least six hours at the hospital on an off day—a lucky break in the schedule.

I felt really good as we traveled from Chicago to Nashville, and then to Minnesota, winning two out of three. Getting off the plane after returning to San Jose, Darryl looked to me and asked how it felt at the end of my "first" road trip. I appreciated the fact that he took the time.

I'm sure that Tony Granato can relate to this story. A gritty and talented winger, Granato was signed before the 1996–97 campaign after he missed the final 33 games of the previous season with Los Angeles, having undergone emergency brain surgery on Valentine's Day, 1996.

Granato developed a blood clot that was causing pressure and bleeding from his left temporal lobe. Teammates, family, and friends didn't recognize the symptoms until weeks after the injury occurred in Hartford on January 25. Memory loss and slurred speech tipped off teammates that he needed to go to the hospital immediately, and the surgery likely saved his life.

At age 32, married and the father of four children, Granato was at a crossroads in his career. He wanted to leave on his own volition, so he chose to sign with San Jose when GM Dean Lombardi made an offer he couldn't refuse. His remarkable comeback season included 25 goals in 76 games with San Jose, an All-Star appearance, and was capped by winning the Bill Masterton Trophy for perseverance and dedication to the game of hockey.

Now, just 14 games into season No. 2 with the Sharks for the final game of a five-stop trip, Granato was close to his own goal defending when St. Louis Blues defenseman Al MacInnis wound up for a shot from the blue line. MacInnis wasn't just any old NHL defenseman. He possessed one of the hardest shots in league history. His blast caromed off the shaft of San Jose defenseman Doug Bodger's stick right into Granato's face.

Tony went down like he'd been shot, and it was serious. Later we found out he broke his jaw in several places. And there's always concern about a concussion. Luckily, Granato had been wearing a special custom helmet that was lined with additional padding since returning from his brain surgery.

We were flying home right after the game—a tough 2–0 loss that was the team's third straight setback on the trip—and Tony was all wrapped up, sedated, and cleared by the medical staff to return. We were boarding before takeoff, and Darryl sat in his customary front-of-the-plane seat. Everyone was talking about Granato's injury, and Darryl said something along the lines of, "Ah, he's lucky, it could have been worse."

Coincidentally, Sutter suffered two injuries to his head—one as a player and another as a coach. Darryl had a cheekbone shattered and suffered damage to his left eye early in his career when he got struck—get this—by a Doug Wilson slap shot in the face. San Jose's initial captain and later successful executive, Wilson was a teammate of Sutter's in Chicago. Sutter cracked his skull when he experienced a bad fall on his farm during his coaching days.

So when Darryl made that tongue-in-cheek comment—no pun intended—there was a hint of bravado and the tough guy coming out. Then, after the plane took off, Darryl made his way to the back where Tony was sitting. And Darryl spent at least three-quarters of the flight making sure Granato was okay.

Yes, Darryl could be tough on the team, especially with players who he didn't think were serious enough during the game. He'd wear that death stare on his face as he's looking at those guys at the back of the bus or plane, and he looked like he was ready to kill somebody.

But at the same time he cared for his players and the people around him. He respected everyone. He had that understanding of the people around him regardless of the job they performed.

The Sharks reached the Stanley Cup playoffs in all five full seasons Sutter coached. San Jose went out in the first round each of their first two tries, but upset St. Louis in Sutter's third year behind the bench to meet Dallas in the second round. The Blues were the NHL's best team in the regular season while the Sharks made it as the eighth seed in the West, but managed to win Game 7 on the road to advance past the Blues.

The Sharks moved on to Round 2 during two of Sutter's final three seasons with the team. When San Jose got off to a slow start in 2002–03, and under new ownership, Sutter was let go by early December. Not before his indelible mark, however, was left on the organization.

Mike Vernon was in his first year with the Sharks, too, in 1997–98, and hung the most appropriate nickname of "Big D" on Darryl. It encapsulated everything about Sutter—his determination, grittiness, dominant voice in the room. It captured everything about him.

Most of the guys complained when Darryl was tough just like they would with a father who was being hard on them. But there was never any doubt that their coach cared about them. Maybe there were a few times he went over the line, but I think everyone knew Sutter was just trying to figure out how to say the right thing and to get the team headed in the right direction.

In the years B.D.—or Before Darryl—there was George Kingston, Kevin Constantine, and Al Sims behind the Sharks' bench trying to guide the team from its earliest days of expansion toward respectability and eventually into Stanley Cup contention.

To suggest there were a few bumps in the road is putting it mildly.

The team's inaugural coach, George Kingston, was the professor. Sporting a distinguished look complete with a pretty fair mustache from the halcyon days of hockey, Kingston came to the Sharks after assistant coaching stints with Calgary and Minnesota as well as 16 years as head coach at the University of Calgary.

He was also a volunteer assistant for 10 years with Hockey Canada and had international coaching experience. Kingston was a bright, educated, positive, forward-thinking leader who, while competitive in his own right, also knew what he was getting himself into.

George was the guy who knew the team was going to be in a world of hurt given the roster, given the league, and given everything else. But he was always trying to find the positive angle for the guys, even though it was hard. He wasn't anything but genuine. He knew he had to try and build a small foundation for whatever was to come.

I felt like that first year no matter what was happening the coaches were always talking about Link Gaetz. Link was a supremely strong and talented hockey player who had issues off the ice. Link appeared in all of 48 games that first and only year with the team. And he led San Jose in penalty minutes with 326. It's a penalty record that may never be broken in San Jose.

On one team flight into Vancouver, we saw Royal Canadian Mounted Police cars with their lights on, approaching the plane after we landed. Somebody said, "Link, they're coming to get you." Just about then a cop came on board, and all he did was look at George Kingston and say, "Link Gaetz."

Kingston and his coaching staff did what they could with a revolving-door roster in Year 2, the final campaign before the Sharks moved from their temporary first home of the Cow Palace in Daly City to their new digs in downtown San Jose. George was let go after the Sharks won a combined 28 out of 164 games their first two seasons.

George was different from all the other coaches. He was very competitive, don't get me wrong, but he was supposed to emphasize teaching and be the man who developed the somewhat undermanned group into a cohesive team. He was able to do just that, in spite of the win-loss record.

Up next, Kevin Constantine was more of a marine drill sergeant on the one hand, and a character out of *Dumb and Dumber* on the other. Director Peter Farrelly and his brother, Bobby Farrelly, were his buddies, in fact, from Rensselaer Polytechnic Institute, where Constantine played briefly in goal. Kevin's name is even in the movie credits, even though he doesn't appear in the movie. That's because of some of the wacky stuff they did at RPI inspired scenes in the hilarious flick.

Kevin was very rigid, structured, and demanding of the players—he wanted them to play his system. He'd had success on all levels—including a Turner Cup won with the Kansas City Blades of the International Hockey League in 1991–92. But he had to deal with Igor Larionov, Sergei Makarov, and that whole group of skaters who didn't want to do it his way.

The proud Larionov was outspoken against Constantine's desire to dump and retrieve the puck while putting a premium on defense. Makarov coined the famous line, "Best defense offense yours," as the two Russians were insistent on an attack that featured circling with the puck, passing, and maintaining possession. If entry into the attack zone was blocked, there's no way they were going to dump it in. They simply skated back, regrouped, and tried again.

Frustrated with a handful of skaters' resistance, Constantine took Larionov's advice and put him together with Makarov, Johan Garpenlov, Sandis Ozolinsh, and Jeff Norton. The idea was that this top group would be able to play their way, while everyone else would play Kevin's way.

As it turned out, the "OV" line with Ozolinsh and Norton on defense proved to be one of the more creative, dynamic, entertaining groups of five skaters in the entire NHL that season.

They also proved key to an incredible first season in San Jose that not only opened a new arena, but also ushered in a new era in Sharks history.

Kevin's upstart Sharks made the playoffs in his first two seasons in San Jose, reaching the postseason party with losing records in each campaign. However, as Sharks fans certainly know, it was in the playoffs where the team was at its best, as they upset the Detroit Red Wings in seven games, then handed Calgary a similar fate in double OT of Game 7 a year later.

The slaying of the Red Wings during the Sharks' inaugural season in San Jose Arena, and the push of the Maple Leafs to the brink, served as inspiration for a citywide parade thrown in the team's honor. That's right, a parade for *losing* in the second round!

A native of International Falls, Minnesota, and drafted by the Montreal Canadiens, Constantine didn't support the idea of a parade but put on his best face for the adoring crowd. That's not to suggest the Red-Haired Fist—as he was affectionately nicknamed by a San Francisco sports columnist—didn't let his guard down and show a sense of humor now and then.

Daily newspaper beat writers noticed Constantine had a habit of pinching a bottle of water supplied at postgame and post-practice Q&A sessions. He'd give thoughtful and analytical answers to what he was being asked, all the while seeing how close to the top of the bottle he could make the water level rise before occasionally taking a quick swig.

One day, with the good graces of somewhat reluctant public relations staff, a writer topped off Constantine's water with whiskey. Sure enough, after Constantine squeezed the bottle a few times, he took a swig. And, no reaction.

Then, after the media session ended and as he was walking out of the room with the journalists, Kevin stopped and shot back, "Next time make it a little stronger."

Classic.

When the Sharks got off to an awful 3–18–4 start in 1995–96, Constantine was a casualty of front-office dysfunction that led to chaos on and off the ice. Jim Wiley finished off the season as interim coach, and former Boston Bruins defenseman Al Sims got the job for 1996–97.

Al was one coach I couldn't figure out. He was more distant. And he was totally different from what I remember of him as an assistant coach in Anaheim. Sims was more open and jovial then, working under Ducks inaugural coach Ron Wilson, and the weight of the world wasn't on his shoulders.

I think it had a lot to do with what he thought could be done, and what happened on the ice because things just didn't go well. It just wasn't the right fit. Lombardi knew he'd made a mistake when he heard it first-hand from the players. They weren't on board with Sims, and it wasn't going to change.

As a player Sims spent two full seasons as the defense partner and skating alongside Bobby Orr from 1973–75 when the game's greatest defenseman scored 122 points one season and 135 the next (both Norris-winning campaigns). Sims played with a lot of the Bruins' greats, including Phil Esposito, Ken Hodge, Wayne Cashman, and John Bucyk.

Cashman was even Sims' top assistant his one season in San Jose. But they couldn't bring the Boston magic to the West Coast, and the Toronto native Sims was gone following a 27–47–8 record that landed the Sharks in the cellar of the Pacific Division for a second straight season.

To be fair, I think that Al had some good ideas as to what needed to be done, but it just didn't translate on the ice, and it didn't work with his players. It simply wasn't the right fit.

It was a very difficult year, but out of that dark cloud, a very important silver lining emerged from inside the same coach's office. It's often forgotten that one of the more important people in Sharks history, Roy Sommer, was part of that same coaching staff. Born and raised in the Bay Area, Sommer had been very successful as a player and as a coach at every level that he had played, including some summers of roller hockey in San Jose, where he won a Murphy Cup championship with the San Jose Rhinos in the now-defunct Roller Hockey International.

Since that year on Sims' staff, Roy became head coach of the Sharks' AHL team, where he has excelled at producing well over 130 NHL players for the big club. The coach with the most wins in the history of the American Hockey League, Sommer's contribution to the Sharks organization continues to be absolutely essential over two decades later.

The Sutter era followed, and Ron Wilson was next when Darryl was fired in early December of 2002. The thing I'll remember about R.W. was that he was a real cerebral coach. He really understood the game, and he understood his team pretty well, too.

Wilson was the product of strong hockey influences. His father, Larry, and uncle, Johnny, each played for the Detroit Red Wings in the 1950s and won Stanley Cups. A standout defenseman at Providence College, Ron Wilson played under the tutelage of coach Lou Lamoriello. Once his playing days were over—parts of seven seasons in the NHL with Toronto and Minnesota along with five abroad in the Swiss League—Wilson applied his knowledge and experience in the game as a fine coach.

A combined nine seasons in the NHL with Anaheim (five seasons) and Washington (four) preceded his hiring in San Jose. Ron understood what was wrong and what needed to be done to fix it. And he didn't sugarcoat his opinions.

Wilson was the guy in the $2,000 Armani suit. He was the coach ahead of his time in terms of mixing technology into his coaching. Wilson was among the first to use a laptop or tablet on the bench for quick replays. He had area software developers work on statistical analysis long before fancy stats became the rage. If there was a new gadget or piece of technology on the market he thought he could use, Wilson was all over it.

And he had a wicked sense of humor, too.

An avid collector of hockey memorabilia, Wilson had a little fun at the expense of Teemu Selanne. Late in the 2006–07 season, Wilson received a signed hockey stick of Selanne's to congratulate him on his 1,000[th] game coached in the NHL. Wilson had coached Selanne in Anaheim, where they became close.

Ron looked at the stick, realizing that Teemu had grabbed it from the pile of sticks that he was using that season. Examining it, he thought that it looked illegal, and getting it measured, he realized that the blade of the stick was slightly more than the maximum three inches in width, which calls for a penalty in a game.

Less than a month later, on a night Selanne's Ducks had a chance to eliminate the Sharks from possible Pacific Division title contention, the game was tied 2–2 after regulation as the visitors were about to start overtime with a power play. Wilson, however, called for a measurement of Selanne's stick. The blade measured more than the maximum three inches in width, resulting in a minor penalty that nullified Anaheim's advantage. The Sharks went on to beat the Ducks 3–2 in the shootout.

I'll never forget the sheepish grin that suddenly appeared on Selanne's face in the penalty box, as he realized where Wilson got the idea to call for a stick measurement. As it turned out, no one scored in overtime, but the Sharks' Ryane Clowe got the game deciding goal, and San Jose picked up the win and the two points in the standings.

Of course, RW who was willing to gamble Selanne's game stick would match the one he was given a month earlier, had a good laugh afterward. Meanwhile, Selanne shot back, joking that Wilson "wasn't my favorite coach anymore."

Ron had another personal tradition that few knew.

During the anthem before every game he coached, Ron Wilson would stand alongside his players, reach into his pocket, and pull out his father's hockey card. It was a tribute to the man who died when Ron was only 24 years old and playing his final American Hockey League season with the New Brunswick Hawks.

Following a 152-game NHL career spent with Detroit and Chicago, Larry Wilson was set to become the first coach of the expansion Adirondack Red Wings for the 1979–80 season. Out for a jog just before the start of training camp, Wilson suffered a fatal heart attack at the age of 48. His brother, Johnny Wilson, was often seen inside the Sharks' locker room when San Jose visited Joe Louis Arena. Ron Wilson, coincidentally, turned 50 in the middle of his four and a half seasons with the Sharks.

San Jose kept knocking on the door during Wilson's tenure, but a third straight second-round bow-out spelled his doom. San Jose lost in a franchise-record-long, four-OT game at Dallas. GM Doug Wilson termed it "a time when the classroom needed a new professor."

The Sharks then turned to Todd McLellan, who had spent the three previous seasons as an assistant to Mike Babcock in Detroit, and was part of the Wings' staff that won the Cup in 2008.

Todd was great with everyone inside and outside the organization. He was always approachable and became friendly with everyone he got to know. He wanted to win, and worked very hard at implementing his systems into the team. The results brought the Sharks ever closer to the Stanley Cup during his tenure.

San Jose won the Presidents' Trophy with a club record 53 wins and 117 points during McLellan's first season in 2008–09. But the Sharks were eliminated in six games of a first-round series against rival Anaheim, which came into the playoffs firing on all cylinders.

Two more Pacific Division titles followed, and the Sharks advanced to the conference finals each time, only to get swept by Chicago in 2010 and to lose in five to Vancouver in '11. A third-place finish sandwiched by two second-place showings followed, and the Sharks lost in the first round twice and the second round once.

Todd had a definite idea what was needed. He got the team to a certain point, but a pretty successful non-playoff finish in 2014–15 spelled McLellan's fate after seven pretty successful seasons.

Now the Sharks have Pete DeBoer, and he's one of the best coaches in the game. He is a little less likely to be joking around with us, but he does do that in his own world, with the guys on the team and with his fellow coaches.

Pete is all business, a button-down kind of guy. His personality comes from holding two law degrees, his time coaching the Devils when Lou Lamoriello was in charge, and his years in junior hockey where he was GM and coach. He had to wear both of those hats and deal with 16-to-20-year-olds, and that's a different dynamic.

He may be the best bench coach the Sharks have ever had. He has a good feel for who should be on the ice at any given moment. And he's not afraid to sit a guy, or make a change if it's needed, and it's hard for other teams to adjust to that.

It is for these reasons, and many more, that the Sharks advanced to their first Stanley Cup Final in 2016. Under DeBoer's steady guidance, the Sharks have made that next step, and all that is needed now is to bring the Cup home.

Each of the last four coaches behind the Sharks' bench have been among the very best in the entire NHL. They're all different, but what they have in common is a burning desire to bring a Stanley Cup to San Jose. They're also part of an organization that provides the tools and the trust that are so important to reach that ultimate goal. It's really a privilege to work with these fine men.

Chapter 5

The Parade

Anyone who has followed the Sharks for some time, and especially those who tuned in during the early years of the franchise, are aware the city of San Jose hosted a parade after the team's return from Toronto in the late spring of 1994.

That's right. The Sharks were honored with a full-blown parade after *losing* in the second round of the Stanley Cup playoffs to the Maple Leafs. On the surface the idea of celebrating a "nice try" for an underdog team that may have captured the imagination of a new audience grates against the sensibilities of the hard-core hockey fan.

But, really, that's not what it was all about.

To back up and put the season in context, you have to go back to the start of the regular season some eight months earlier. That's when the doors of San Jose Arena opened for the very first time—the bright, sparkling new home of San Jose's first entry into the world of major pro sports. It was a glorious time of innocence and anticipation for the growing city.

The expansion Sharks played their first two seasons from 1991–93 in the venerable old Cow Palace located 50 miles to the north in Daly City, California, while the team's permanent home—situated in downtown San Jose on the corner of West Santa Clara and North Autumn Streets—was being built.

The team was led by rookie head coach Kevin Constantine, who had been promoted from the team's top development affiliate Kansas City of the International Hockey League. That's where Constantine guided the Blades to the Turner Cup in 1991–92 during Kansas City's only second season of existence. The energetic, red-headed firebrand renewed the Sharks' optimism after San Jose managed a combined 28 wins out of 164 games its first two seasons.

But hold on—the third-year Sharks' team, which had undergone a number of additions and subtractions to the roster and had some early-season injuries to contend with, was still searching for its first win several weeks into the season. San Jose stood 0–8–1 when Constantine offered these uncertain words: "We're on the verge of something. What? I'm not exactly sure. But I know we're on the verge of something."

The Sharks got one key piece back for Game 10 as legendary Russian-born center Igor Larionov returned from injury to score a goal as San Jose finally broke through with a 3–1 win over Edmonton. Larionov had missed all but one of the team's first nine games. The one he appeared in was the only one San Jose managed a point in during a 1–1 tie against Boston.

Larionov and close friend Sergei Makarov were inspirational catalysts and offensive leaders who sparked a remarkable turnaround. The Sharks rallied from that winless nine-game start to an NHL record 58-point improvement from one year to the next by season's end. San Jose went 33–27–15 from October 26, 1993, to April 5, 1994—the fifth best record in the entire league— to finish eighth in the West and secure their first Stanley Cup playoff berth in franchise history.

Regardless of their fast finish and youthful enthusiasm, the Sharks weren't given much of a chance against the Detroit Red Wings in the first-round matchup. An experienced team coached by the legendary Scotty Bowman, the Wings won the Central Division and were the only team in the West with a 100-point season. And the Original Six franchise played in an intimidating old barn whereas inside Joe Louis Arena San Jose was already 0–5 as a franchise. They were outscored by a combined 28–10, including 5–3 and 2–0 losses during the 1993–94 campaign.

Well, a funny thing happened to Detroit on the way to the second round. They never got there.

San Jose served notice with a 5–4 win in Game 1, then rallied from a 2–1 series deficit with wins on home ice in Games 4 and 5. Detroit knotted the series with a convincing 7–1 triumph in Game 6, but the Sharks shocked the hockey world two nights later with a 3–2 series-clinching win in Game 7 at Detroit.

The Sharks teammates celebrate their 3–2 victory over the Detroit Red Wings in Game 7 of the Western Conference playoffs on Saturday, April 30, 1994, in Detroit. *(AP Photo)*

Round 2 meant a meeting with yet another Original Six opponent three time zones away as the Toronto Maple Leafs were primed to continue a playoff run in the hopes of ending a Cup drought that spanned back to 1967.

The Sharks were more than holding their own, leading the series 3–2 as Game 6 went into overtime inside historic Maple Leaf Gardens. San Jose had several golden opportunities to win and advance—one being a potential winner off the stick of Johan Garpenlov that instead struck the crossbar—before the Leafs got a season-saving goal from Mike Gartner. Host Toronto won 4–2 two nights later to move on and send the Sharks home disappointed.

The skies were overcast and it was cold after a cross-country flight and a day of rest, but more than 10,000 fans braved an unseasonably ugly mid-May day to gather at Guadalupe Park for a raucous celebration that included the parade.

I had a weird feeling about it. I don't want to say I felt left out, but I was just there. The organizers sort of threw it all together. Football player Dana Stubblefield, a rookie defensive tackle for the 49ers, was on one of the floats, and I wondered, *What the hell is he doing here?*

While feeling a bit odd about a parade for a second round loss, there was a method to the madness. It was simply a case of a community's expression of love and appreciation for its team, and it was another way to let the rest of the world know that another step forward had been taken in the city's cultural development.

Some history would be helpful here. Matt Levine, a prominent early-franchise executive who successfully marketed and helped promote the team, identified the three types of supporters the

Sharks had from the Cow Palace years to the opening of the new building.

The first group were called "Seals Pups." These were people who were kids when the California Golden Seals were playing in Oakland. They went to see the Bay Area's first NHL venture from 1967 to 1976 for bargain basement prices to watch Bobby Orr and other NHL greats from that era, and were among the small-but-dedicated group of fans in the region.

It was an affordable activity, it was fun, and these kids grew to love the game. Fast-forward to the 1990s, and these "Seals Pups" grew up, became successful, and more often than not, lived and worked in Silicon Valley. With the arrival of the Sharks, these fans thought, *I had a lot of fun going to those Seals games. I have a lot of good memories of that, so I'm going to buy Sharks season tickets. I can't wait for the NHL to get back here.*

This group of fans, who also had come to see a number of NHL exhibition games that had been staged in the area in the interim period, proved to be among the most rabid Sharks fans those first few seasons. Many of them have remained loyal season-ticket holders for over 25 years.

When the Sharks organization celebrated the 50th anniversary of NHL expansion, they paid tribute to the Seals during a January game in 2017, and the "Seals Pups" were there in abundance. It was tremendous, one of the great things that the Sharks have done over the years. The Seals' alumni on hand couldn't believe the length of the lines for autographs, and the ovation that they received when they were introduced and recognized at center ice before the opening faceoff.

Another group Levine identified that really supported the team, especially when they moved to San Jose, were called "South

Bay Patriots." Demographically, sports fans in the Bay Area primarily come from the South Bay, the Peninsula, the East Bay, and the Tri-Valley Area, with Contra Costa and Alameda counties figuring in significantly. That's where people with the necessary disposable income to buy tickets to sporting events reside.

In sheer numbers, there are more people in the Sharks ticket-purchasing demographic who reside in the South Bay than in any other region of the marketplace.

The "South Bay Patriots" didn't have the vivid NHL memories that the "Seals Pups" did, but they had something else. "You know," they said, "the NHL is the first of the four major pro sports to move to San Jose. This team is going to be called the San Jose Sharks. I'm going to buy season tickets because I'm proud of where I live, and I think it's about time that San Jose got major league recognition and a top level arena."

These people came that first year with no real expectations as to what they might witness, but by the end of the year, they had picked up the game very quickly and had fallen deeply in love with the whole atmosphere.

A third group of fans those first few seasons were transplants from places like Chicago, Philadelphia, Detroit, Boston, New York, and Toronto who were now living and working in Silicon Valley. These were the people who would arrive on the scene in another team's jersey.

There is still an element of that today, as is the case in all NHL arenas, but this group is decidedly smaller than the earlier years. This group learned to love the Sharks, and it probably isn't surprising to note that many of its members still keep a Toronto or Pittsburgh jersey hidden in their closets at home.

These three distinct groups of people cemented the early success of the Sharks franchise, and the parade was a chance for them to celebrate together and say, "Hey, we're here. We're a major league city. We have our own identity. We're not living in the shadow of San Francisco or anywhere else, and we love hockey."

The parade was a big party for San Jose. People were taking pride in where they live. That is why you have a sports team—to encourage those feelings and bring people from different backgrounds, cultures, and world views in one place, not focusing on those differences, but bonding over what they have in common. That commonality is represented by the team.

We have people from all sorts of backgrounds at Sharks games, representing all races, languages, nationalities, and creeds. All find common ground and friendship by cheering together for Sharks hockey. They put aside their differences and through the exploits of their favorite hometown hockey team, realize that we all have more in common than not.

To me, that part of it is really cool, and although you'll never see the public streets closed off for a parade anywhere again after a team loses in the second round, I think that's what the 1994 Sharks parade was really all about.

Chapter 6

Jumbo Trade

Everything seemed normal at 5:00 in the press dining room, deep in the bowels of Dallas's American Airlines Center. Well, as normal as you could expect, as the sputtering Sharks were hoping to avoid losing for a 10th straight game.

The start of the 2005–06 season wasn't going as planned. In fact, it was getting frustrating. Everyone was eager to get off to a good start, especially considering the entire previous season was scrapped because the union and the league's owners couldn't reach a new collective-bargaining agreement.

A lockout that started on September 16, 2004, continued until the season's drop-dead date of February 16, 2005. Horrifically, the NHL became the first North American professional sports league to lose an entire season over labor strife. For the first time since 1919 when a Spanish flu pandemic canceled the playoffs, the Stanley Cup was not awarded.

But back for a full slate of 82 games starting in October of 2005, the league restarted as teams operated under a new salary-cap system, which was previously the bitter and contentious sticking point that players didn't want to accept. Regardless of who felt like they won or lost, it was time to finally play hockey again, and everyone was ready for it.

Fast forward two months and the Sharks found themselves with a last-place 8–11–4 record despite an 8–5–1 start. This was a similar San Jose roster that fell two wins shy of its first Stanley Cup Final when it last skated in the spring of 2004.

What had happened?

I noticed Niko Dimitrakos and Jim Fahey—a young forward and a similarly young defenseman—eating in the dining room, too, which made sense since they were expected to be the two healthy scratches. That jibed with what I saw in the morning skate. And they were expected to be upstairs in the press box where the extra players sit during the game.

Then they were not, although I hadn't noticed that, yet.

We were handed the game sheet that lists the eligible skaters and two goalies for each team. Nothing appeared out of order. But I did see coach Ron Wilson call the referees over to the Sharks' bench just before the opening faceoff. I made a comment on the air: "You know, that's happened before where the coach filled out the lineup wrong and that player is ineligible."

Then they dropped the puck. The Sharks immediately changed lines, and I heard myself say on the air, "Fahey passes the puck to Dimitrakos." And as those words are coming out of my mouth, I thought, *Wait a second, I just saw them eating dinner at 5:00— something's going on.*

I turned to Jamie Baker—it was his first year in the booth— and I asked him to count the bench. See who is here and who is not. We determined Keith Primeau, Brad Stuart, and Marco Sturm were missing.

"Ladies and gentlemen, there's been a trade," I said. Then we started scouring the internet. I remember the Dallas PR guy, Rob Scichili (the Shick Dog) came over. He said, "Check Sportsnet, they often have the story first." The team's two traveling beat writers had noticed the switch-a-roo, too. But this was in the pre-Twitter era. Nowadays someone would have spilled the beans on social media. And, after dispelling the possibility that maybe food poisoning was running through the lineup, the writers pored through the rosters of Eastern Conference teams that might make for a trade partner.

I checked Sportsnet, and they had the scoop: "Joe Thornton coming to the Sharks."

Joe Thornton reacts to a question during the news conference announcing his trade to the Sharks. *(AP Photo/Don Heupel)*

I went on the air and credited Sportsnet with it. Normally we don't do that, but this was too big. It was the biggest trade in Sharks history. We had it 10 minutes before anyone else in the building.

It would be a while before we could confirm or interview Sharks brass. General manager Doug Wilson and assistant Joe Will were downstairs with the departing players. They were contacting families and making sure the league had all the proper documentation.

Eventually the team's top management made it upstairs and held court about the deal. It made sense. Both the Sharks and Bruins were off to bad starts with still a lot of season left. It was a blockbuster. But you know what they say. The team that gets the best player usually gets the better end of the deal. Everyone was very excited.

The late-night flight postgame was predictably quiet in light of a 4–1 decision that went the Stars' way. That was 10 straight losses. And it was low-key because the team had lost three popular teammates. Somewhere, though, there was an air of relief and expectations about what would be waiting for the team in Buffalo.

It's not as if the players didn't know what they were getting. In fact, Sharks forward Scott Thornton and Jumbo Joe were first cousins. Suddenly, San Jose was in possession of the Nos. 1 and 2 picks from the 1997 draft, as top-choice Thornton joined next-pick Patrick Marleau, who was serving as the Sharks' captain. And they were both in the prime of what would be long and successful careers.

Thornton arrived in time on the off day between games to participate in a brief presser in a conference room at the team hotel. When Jumbo slipped on that No. 19 teal and white jersey for the first time, I could never remember another Sharks player who looked that great.

It wasn't long before Thornton made an impact.

On the second day of December of 2005, the 6-foot-4 hockey artist from London, Ontario, took the opening draw, accepted a pass on the left boards, and rang a slap shot off the crossbar, all within the opening nine seconds. Thornton contributed two assists to a 5–0 drought-busting win that not only was the team's first in 11 games, but was its initial win in Buffalo ever. The Sharks were 0–11 as a franchise in Western New York before Thornton arrived.

Thornton's debut overshadowed two footnotes. It also marked the first career game for defenseman Douglas Murray, one of the more popular Sharks in history. It was also the seventh and final game for goaltender Nolan Schaefer, who got into action during the final minutes when starter Evgeni Nabokov went down with an injury.

Schaefer would never play in an NHL game again, but Thornton would appear in many, many more.

Chapter 7

The Characters

ecause we are as much hockey fans as broadcasters, we tend to get excited watching and describing the great stars make all of those amazing plays each night. However, we also focus on the larger picture of a team's full body of work over the course of a season, with all of the implications for the present and future, and what the subtleties are in that magical process.

Is a team contending for a division title? Who might get traded? What's the magic number to get to the playoffs? What does the free agent list look like? Who are the unsung heroes? What are the human interest stories? Our lives are certainly comprised of a series of questions.

One of the benefits of working closely with a team is that it's possible to really to get to know the players and observe how they handle their journey through their careers. No two players are alike in terms of personality, and everyone is unique in the way that they approach preparing for a game. We also get to see how much work that the coaches, trainers, and support staff put into providing an environment where the team can be successful.

Every locker room has its characters, and the Sharks have had theirs over the years. They certainly know how to keep it light in what can be on otherwise long season, and they're all business when the puck drops and action begins. Some of those characters stand out in my mind.

Let's begin with Al Iafrate, a hulk of a defenseman who possessed one of the hardest shots the NHL has ever seen. Al came to the Sharks at the end of his career, acquired from Boston for a popular, heart-and-soul Shark, Jeff Odgers. Toronto made Iafrate the fourth overall pick in 1984, and he played 10 years for the

Maple Leafs, Capitals, and Bruins before arriving in San Jose as a 30-year-old who was battling a variety of serious injuries.

We liked to call him "Big Al." I swear that he always seemed out of action with one serious injury or another, and he had a unique way of expressing the graphic details of his medical chart.

According to Al, he never had any bumps or bruises, and he never "hurt" or "injured" anything. No, it was always a little more dramatic, say, "I ruptured my back," or "I shattered my knee," or "that can cause a compound fracture." He was very descriptive.

These strains, ruptures, lacerations, abrasions, and other impairments limited Iafrate to 59 games in two seasons with the Sharks before he announced his retirement at age 31.

The first time I saw Iafrate was in Washington while he was in the prime of his career with the Capitals. This was in the early 1990s. Back then the workout facilities were rudimentary. Teams hadn't yet invested in state-of-the-art training rooms that accompany a practice rink today. At the old Cap Centre in Landover, Maryland, the rink had those old-fashioned exercise bikes at one end of the building. Al was riding a bike while listening to heavy-metal music, completely naked.

We were inside Reunion Arena in Dallas, when he was with the Sharks. The visiting locker room was at one end. These older buildings don't have as much security or ways to keep the players isolated from the public. And, like a number of players from that old-school hockey fraternity, Al smoked. He lit cigarettes with the blow torch used to prepare hockey sticks.

So there was Big Al, cigarette in hand, working on his sticks, totally naked, standing just outside the Sharks' locker room. The area was semi-private, but the end of the corridor opened up to a

Injuries conspired to limit hard-shooting defenseman Al Iafrate to only 59 games with the Sharks in what would be the final two seasons of his 12-year NHL career. (Claus Andersen/Getty Images)

public area, and those fans walking past into the building could see where Al was standing if they glanced in that direction.

Sensing a problem, a Reunion Arena security guard rushed in Iafrate's direction, a serious, determined look on her face. "Sir!" she exclaimed sharply, as Al peered back at her with his trademark, deadpan stare. "There's no smoking in the arena!"

I guess that being naked in front of the fans was fine with this particular security guard, but smoking was absolutely out of the question.

Along with his coaches and teammates, Al was frustrated with his absences from the lineup, especially because the Sharks desperately needed offense from the blue line. During one post-practice media scrum, Darryl Sutter was asked how the team's patience was being tested with Big Al's injury situation. In typical Sutter style, he replied, "They'd like to pile his equipment in the middle of the room and burn it."

Biting sarcasm aside, I think that Al had a very good influence on his defense partner, Mike Rathje, who was playing under a lot of pressure back then. He took Rathje under his wing and shared that relaxed attitude that always seemed in abundance.

Another time, we were in Vancouver, and Al was out with an injury again. I was broadcasting a number of games alone back on those days, and I'd be joined occasionally by players who weren't in the lineup. On this particular night, Al jumped on the radio with me, and by the middle of the game, he decided that it was time for a cigarette. There was no smoking in the arena, of course, but the gondola in Vancouver is separated from the rest of the press area and is somewhat contained, so Al lit up.

Suddenly, on the ice, the wheels fell completely off the cart for the Sharks. The Canucks flew up the ice with ease against very little defense, there was a nice move at the blue line, and the puck was in the back of the net.

As I finished calling the play, Big Al took an audible drag on his recently lit cigarette, blew out the smoke, and said, "I'm baffled, Dan." It was all I could do to avoid bursting out in laughter on the air.

A native of Dearborn, Michigan, Al was definitely a Detroit guy. He said that he always wanted to go hunting with Ted Nugent. He was like an earlier, rougher-around-the-edges version of Brent Burns, complete with the size, skating skill, shot, physical play, and a variety of tattoos that were always noticeable in the locker room. He had one tattoo of Crazy Horse that he described to a reporter as a "reminder that we are all on Indian land."

Dale Hunter, his former teammate with the Washington Capitals, told us on Sharks Radio once that Al "was always talking about the ozone layer." We aren't sure if he meant the offensive zone or the layer of the stratosphere that absorbs most of the ultraviolet radiation that reaches the earth.

On the bus and on the plane, Al always took the time to stop by where the broadcasters were sitting, and not only would he talk to us about anything, he would usually say something that was entertaining. One time, he came by and said to one of the traveling P.R. guys, "You know, I was watching one of those late-night TV shows, and they were advertising this product you spray on your head to hide your bald spot. Would you think less of me if I bought that?"

Al could be a cut-up, and he could be intensely serious. Sometimes, both qualities would bubble to the surface like an active volcano. At another game in Dallas, the guys on the bench were chirping at each other. As the story goes, the Stars' Mike Modano accused Al of being lazy. Al looked back at him. Stone-faced, he replied, "Well, at least I can take a check, so shut the f--- up."

As a few players on both benches feigned laughter, Dallas coach Ken Hitchcock sauntered over from his spot behind the bench to see what was going on. Al glared at him. "What are you going to do about it, Alfred?" he blurted out.

I knew that Hitch was an excellent director of NHL talent from behind the bench, but that was the first time that I had ever heard him compared to the man who guided Cary Grant, Grace Kelly, and James Stewart through their legendary performances in *Rear Window* and *To Catch a Thief.*

Of course, it was all forgotten the moment the game was over. I remember at a later game, Iafrate and Hitchcock walked past each other. They both said hello and smiled.

Al had a way of disarming people and making them smile or laugh, even if they were in a lousy mood. It wasn't just the people around the hockey world, either. He would talk to anybody, always eager to learn about and communicate with people in any walk of life.

Once, we were in Detroit, and Al was injured, of course. He and I stepped into the elevator to go up to the press box at Joe Louis Arena. After about 5:00 in the afternoon on game nights, an elevator operator manned the controls, and on this occasion, the lady pressing the buttons was clearly in a downright grumpy mood. She sat staring and scowling, as if nothing positive had happened to her all day. It certainly didn't seem as if she wanted to be assigned to elevator duty.

Al wasn't going to let this slide. Looking her straight in the eye, he put on a falsetto voice and said, "How's it going, sugar?"

The elevator operator instantly perked up, smiled, and all of the grumpiness was gone. We made conversation on our ride upstairs, all because Al took the time to be nice to her. She wished us a good night on our way out.

Another short-time Shark was Ed Belfour, and he was quite the character as well. He is ultimately remembered by Sharks fans as someone who didn't want to stay in San Jose, and who became a villain when he left via free agency for Dallas for less than what he had been offered in the Bay Area.

I've never seen a reaction to a visiting goalie like that from the home crowd except for Philadelphia's Ron Hextall and Islanders' legend Billy Smith. Belfour drove the trainers crazy because he was very particular about his skates. He was obsessive about how his skates needed to be sharpened, and often put his nose to the grindstone himself. Much of that came from his extraordinary desire to be the best, and some of it was attributed to the fact that he was a goalie.

You'll have to remember that few thought that Belfour would make it. He went undrafted and had a stellar season at the University of North Dakota before Chicago took a chance on him as a pro. The rest is history.

Belfour not only made it, he had a fantastic career that put him in the Hall of Fame. Already a star with the Chicago Blackhawks, he arrived on the scene in a January 1997 deal that cost the Sharks Ulf Dahlen, Michal Sykora, and Chris Terreri. When he arrived after the huge deal with the Blackhawks, his ex-Chicago coach Darryl Sutter was quoted as saying, "I'm glad he's here."

Most of us thought that it would all work out and Belfour would sign a long-term deal to stay in San Jose, but unfortunately, that didn't happen. Belfour departed for Dallas after playing in only 13 games in a Sharks tenure that was marred by a couple of nagging injuries. Once he took the Stars' offer, he promptly joined the Sharks fans' "Most Hated List."

In contrast to Belfour, the late, great Gaetan Duchesne was one of the most beloved characters in early Sharks history. He was a "Good Humor Man," one of the more mischievous Sharks players ever. Appearing in 117 games over the course of two seasons with the team from 1993–95, "The Duke" always had something to say from the back of the bus, the media scrum in the locker room, or at a club charity event.

One particular group always in his sights were the P.R. and Team Services guys such as Tim Bryant or Ken Arnold who took care of all of their needs on road trips. Gaetan's attention would perk up if there were a travel snafu, such as a delayed flight. If Tim were on the trip, Duke would yell out, "Nice job, Tim, this wouldn't happen if Kenny were here." If Ken was on the road, the inevitable "Tim's way better than you, we never have these problems when he's with us!" would ring throughout the locker room.

When something went right, Duchesne was also there with a word of encouragement. His was, "Attaboy!" He yelled that out so often that we couldn't help but blurt out, "Attaboy, Duke!" whenever it made sense to do it.

Another time, Gaetan noticed that I had a genuine shirt from the 1994 Swedish World Cup soccer team that I had picked up in a trade with a team member's relative who was at a game played at Stanford Stadium. Well, it wasn't just *any* game, it was a quarterfinal match between the Swedes and Romania, a see-saw battle that wound up in a 2–2 tie, and Sweden won, 5–4 on penalty kicks.

The Duke saw the shirt, and immediately asked if he could borrow it. Wearing it in the back of the plane, he put on a show, claiming Swedish citizenship and asking Ulf Dahlen how the shirt looked on him. Ulfie was acting as if it were an affront to his country, but he was laughing the entire time.

I'll always get a smile on my face whenever I recall some of his meetings with the media. With his effusive personality and French Canadian accent, he always had a crowd around his locker stall.

During the 1994 playoff run, the news departments started to follow the team. CBS-TV's Dan Rather actually put in a short note on his national newscast during the Detroit series, so after Game Seven, it was no surprise that CNN would also show up.

In the locker room in front of the CNN camera, Gaetan had a look that smacked of joy, fatigue, and amazement that the Sharks had just beaten the top team in the NHL in a first-round series. With that marvelous accent, he said what everyone else was thinking: "It feels like we won the Stanley Cup!" That memory always puts a smile on my face.

Duchesne played in his 1,000th regular-season game wearing a Sharks uniform when he was 32, and he was honored by the team at a game. Afterward, it was an honor to be invited to the legendary San Jose banquet Hall, Lou's Village, for some post-game shenanigans.

Gaetan and his wife, Gina, were quite a couple, and whenever they were together, it was obvious that they loved each other very much. Their son, Jeremy, was drafted by the Philadelphia Flyers in 2005, and I'm sure that his parents were very proud on that day.

Sadly, we don't have the Duke around to spruce up our Sharks Alumni Association events. On April 16, 2007, we were all shocked to hear that while working out at the gym, he suffered a heart attack and died suddenly. He was only 44 years old, had been an athlete his entire life, and would never get to see Jeremy play in his only NHL game, on April 1, 2010, for the Flyers.

When we think of Gaetan Duchesne today, we do so with a smile, and every once in a while, I'll drag out that Swedish soccer shirt.

Bob Errey enjoyed two stints with the Sharks after winning a pair of Stanley Cups with the Pittsburgh Penguins. A captain from 1993 to 1995, Errey was the perfect kind of galvanizer for that team. Just before the '94 playoff series against Detroit, he was having lunch after practice, and trying to crystallize a few keys for post-season success. Pulling out a pen and jotting his thoughts on a napkin, he wrote "16 Points for Playoff Success."

We still refer to those 16 points on occasion during our broadcasts, because they still apply to anyone looking to focus his energy on what it takes to win. It wasn't rocket science, as you can tell by point No. 1: "It takes 16 wins to win the Stanley Cup."

Errey listed such things as "never take anything for granted," "one shift is as important as 20," "never dwell on the past," "throw stats out the window," and "you're never out of a game." All were basic thoughts designed to prepare his teammates for the ups and downs of a long playoff run.

Todd Harvey was another character. Acquired from the Rangers midway through the 1999–00 season, Harvey scored an empty-net goal in Washington to complete a hat trick on December 18, 2000. That was one of the very few live Sharks' games I've watched on

TV because I was home recovering from my auto accident. I'll always remember the camera focusing on Darryl Sutter laughing on the bench because Todd was at the end of his shift, huffing and puffing with absolutely no gas left in his tank. He could barely get to the puck to knock ito into the net, but he did that, and the Sharks got the win, too.

Claude Lemieux was a great story more than anything else. It was amazing that a 43-year-old who had not played in the League for six years could possibly find a way to get back to the NHL. It was more of a one-off story for us, but it was a fascinating experience to call the 18 games that he played toward the 2008–09 campaign.

Lemieux dropped hints of making a comeback attempt just before NHL training camps started up the previous September. He went to the China Sharks of the Asian League where he could train and get back on the ice. He signed a two-way contract with Worcester, San Jose's AHL affiliate at the time, and after 14 games there, he earned a promotion to the Sharks in mid-January. He was a solid guy, and the way he was off the ice and in the locker room belied his previous reputation on the ice. In the final analysis, he left the game on his own terms, with dignity and honor, and that's the way that all warriors want to see it wind down.

Ryane Clowe was another man of high quality and character. Even though he was never the team captain, Clowie was one of the better leaders that the team had in many ways. He came from humble beginnings, worked his way to the top, and earned absolutely everything that he got out of the game.

A native of Fermeuse, Newfoundland, Clowe played a lot in far eastern Canada, and once he got his chance to play in the QMJHL in front of top talent scouts like Tim Burke, he took advantage of it. He was tough as nails. He was not only an excellent fighter, he could also really play effectively, and he had that intangible will to win that is so important to the fortunes of any team. He was a member of a long line of important Sharks who were extremely difficult to play against, and he was usually at his best when the stakes were at their highest.

Ryane scored some big goals during his eight seasons in Teal. He had a good touch around the net, was tough physically, and was also a fantastic teammate. If you have to go to war, you want Clowie in your foxhole.

But sometimes, you just need him on your bench. On April 5, 2012, the Sharks were in Los Angeles for an important 81st game of their season against the Kings. On that date, the Kings were leading the Pacific Division and the Sharks were in the eighth and final playoff spot in the standings.

Clowe had long been a thorn in the side of the Kings. In the 2011 playoff series against L.A. won by San Jose in 6 games, he picked up 3 assists in Game 1 and scored a pair of goals in both Game 3 and Game 4.

On this particular April night, the Sharks fell behind 3–1, but roared back to tie the game, 3–3 on an unassisted Clowe goal at 1:10 of the third period. Down 3–1 in the game, San Jose roared back to tie the game with Clowe notching the tying tally early in the third. After Justin Williams and Patrick Marleau exchanged goals, Clowe assisted on a Martin Havlat goal that put the Sharks in front 5–4. Given the fact that Clowe had engaged in two fights with Matt Greene and Kyle Clifford earlier in the game, the assist gave him his third Gordie Howe Hat Trick in his Sharks career.

The lead didn't last. Williams, one of the great clutch players ever, picked up his second tally of the game with only 3:31 remaining in the game to tie things 5–5, and it looked as if both teams would batten down the hatches until overtime.

But with 2:45 remaining and with a Marleau penalty giving the Kings a power play, the unthinkable happened. Longtime Sharks nemesis Jarret Stoll rushed the puck up the right wing side, with Logan Couture in pursuit.

As Stoll skated past the Sharks bench, it looked as if Stoll wouldn't be caught, but a lightning stick got a piece of the puck along the right wing boards, and Stoll was unable to regain control. Couture poked the puck back into his own zone, but three Kings sticks raised in the air, their direction focused on the officials.

The Kings insisted that the stick that made contact with the puck had come from the bench, but none of the officials on the ice saw anything untoward, due to their positions on the ice. Had one of the officials seen it, it would have given Los Angeles a 5-on-3 power play, and that seemed significant, since seven power play goals were scored in this game.

With 10 goals already in the net, the overtime and shootout turned into some sterling moments for goaltenders Antti Niemi and Jonathan Quick. Already with a Gordie Howe Hat Trick in hand, Clowe's shootout chance was stopped by the L.A. netminder. The game was decided by a Joe Pavelski goal in the shootout, and the Sharks took home two important points, 6–5.

After the game, reporters swarmed around Clowe, asking if his stick came off the bench to touch the puck. "I have no idea," he said. "I'll have to see the video or something. Show me on video."

Well, video showed that it was, indeed, Clowe's reactive play without thinking on the Sharks bench actually did reach out and nick the puck with his stick.

I guess that we can all laugh about it now, because Los Angeles would eventually go on to win the Stanley Cup that year, and a repentant Clowe never reacted to a puck coming toward him on the ice again unless he was actually on the ice. But with his Gordie Howe Hat Trick and his late game shenanigans, Clowie did find another creative way to stick it to the Kings.

Speaking about personalities, how about Bernie Nicholls?

I picked him up right after he signed with the Sharks on August 5, 1996. We drove directly from San Francisco International Airport to the Olympic Club for a charity golf tournament. It was a non-scramble tournament, but it the rules of the day didn't matter to Bernie. He just wanted to play at the Olympic Club.

The event was held at the Lake Course, where the U.S. Open would be waged. Our first hole was No. 18—one of the most famous holes in golf. First, we attended a clinic that Ken Venturi conducted. Bernie was fascinated. Venturi was surrounded by people and calmly hit balls right through the crowd, with full confidence that he would not hit anyone. He made it look effortless.

We walked to the 18th hole to start, and Bernie took a couple of practice putts. I'll never forget what happened next—on that day, he shot a 72. He actually went par on that challenging and unfamiliar course after only a few practice putts. Now, that's

Bernie Nicholls is surrounded by his teammates as they celebrate his 1,000th NHL game on November 2, 1996. *(AP Photo/Paul Sakuma)*

something! I'm the only one other than Bernie who can attest to this fact, but I was there to see it. That's the kind of athlete he was.

In just his second game, Bernie and fellow ex-King Tony Granato were playing for the first time back at the Forum in Inglewood against their former team. Tony had a hat trick and an assist for four points. Bernie scored a goal and added three assists for a four-point night. The Sharks won 7–6, and it was a satisfying night for the two ex-Kings.

Bernie was one of those guys who is a borderline Hall of Fame candidate. He scored 475 career goals—too bad that he didn't hit 500—and those great hands that paid dividends on the golf course made him very skilled offensively when he was on the ice.

Here's another one of his special qualities: He was a star player who was able to adjust his game to remain effective in a lesser role as he approached the 18th hole of his NHL career.

Nicholls found a way to do that. We know older players have to find a way to change the way they train because their bodies at 36 are different from when they were 26. They have to become more dedicated in terms of proper diet, a good night's sleep, and general physical fitness. I think that in Bernie's case, he added all of those things, along with penalty killing, faceoff proficiency, and using his prodigious hockey intelligence to add a few more clubs in his hockey bag. Because of that, his career was extended to 1,127 games and 1,209 points.

Jeremy Roenick was certainly a character. As is the case with a couple of others we've talked about, he came to the Sharks at the tail end of a long and successful career, and by the time it ended in a San Jose uniform, it was in a bright place and on his own terms.

His greatest individual performance as a Shark was one of the most incredible in Sharks' history, and it came against his old coach, Mike Keenan, who was behind the Calgary Flames' bench for Game Seven of a 2008 opening-round playoff series against the Sharks at SAP Center.

J.R. had had a couple of terrible years, and he wasn't even expecting to get any interest from a team for the upcoming season. He had veered away from the hard skating, hard hitting, big scorer that made him great in Chicago, becoming a kind of side show for a couple of years in places like Phoenix and Los Angeles. I credit Doug Wilson for going to him and saying, "Look, we have an opportunity here and if you do this right, you can really help us. But you're going to have to change some things. You're going to have to train more seriously. You have to be all in."

Roenick agreed, and when he showed up in San Jose, he was not only in shape, he was revisiting some of the ways that made him a household name earlier in his career. The first sign that Doug's words were being heeded came on the day that we saw what number that J.R. would wear in San Jose. Instead of No. 97, which he donned during the side show years, he took No. 27, the number that he wore during his glory years in Chicago. From that day, one could see that J.R. was filled with purpose.

There's no doubt that J.R. is a showman, but he had a great balance of fun and focus while he played for the Sharks. Number 27 played old-fashioned Roenick hockey, adjusted for the changes in age, wear, and wisdom. During that first season in a Sharks uniform, J.R. scored his 500th career goal on November 10, 2007, against his old Coyotes teammates. In a tip of the cap to his showmanship, it came on a dump-in from center ice that bounced off the end boards, ricocheted off goaltender Alex Auld, and into the net.

Of the 14 goals that he scored during the season, an incredible 10 were game-winners, which ranked him second in the NHL to Washington's Alex Ovechkin.

But then, it was time for the playoffs, and Round One against the Flames. With a 3–2 series lead, coach Ron Wilson elected to keep Roenick out of the lineup for a critical Game Six at the Saddledome, and after former Sharks Owen Nolan (one goal) and Mikka Kiprusoff (21 saves) played critical roles in a 2–0 shutout, Game Seven was forced upon SAP Center on April 22, 2008.

Following Coach Ron Wilson's mantra, J.R. was "intense without being tense," as he had been for so many big games in his career. The Sharks had prepared for over 300 days together to be ready for a game like this one, but Roenick gathered all of his previous experience and played this one as if it would be his last.

Two goals and two assists later, SAP Center was magically transformed into the "Kingdom of Roenick." J.R.'s four-point extravaganza under the most pressure-filled conditions imaginable proved to be one final moment of glory for the U.S. born hockey master. The Sharks outshot Calgary 41–22, bested the Flames 5–2, and advanced to Round 2 against Dallas. It was a magnificent performance.

Jeremy Roenick was a great player. He scored more than 100 points in three straight years for the Blackhawks, the first U.S.-born player to ever do that. He was a great representative of the very best American players. He scored 500 goals. He had that amazing Game 7 performance against his old coach. Finally, when it all came to an end, I'll always remember Roenick's emotional retirement ceremony at SAP Center, where he was very thankful, very forthright, and very professional. It was typical J.R., because it all unfolded on a national NHL Network telecast.

Mike Vernon and Kelly Hrudey were two good, experienced goaltenders, and they were funny characters, too. They were a very important tandem in 1997–98 to get the Sharks back into the playoffs after a two-year drought. They could put everything into perspective for the younger guys on the team, and even though Vernie was thought to be the champion of the caustic remark, Kelly could come up with some good zingers when the chirping was zipping across the dressing room.

They were also good at balancing out Darryl's intense style by taking the edge off, or, at least repurposing it.

I'll always remember asking "Mr. Goalie," the great Glenn Hall, who he thought the best goaltender in the NHL was. Without hesitation, Hall replied, "Mike Vernon," the netminder he was working with in Calgary at the time.

Vernie certainly had some big games in San Jose. He was one of the better puck stoppers of his era, and he had that Glenn Hall endorsement to back it up.

Kelly Hrudey, too, was someone who was still an important contributor toward the end of his career. We remember him for the winning goaltender in the 1987 "Easter Epic," a four-overtime classic between the New York Islanders and the Washington Capitals. Later on, he wore that custom mask with the "HOLLYWOOD" sign during his years with the Los Angeles Kings. I always said, since he was coming to Silicon Valley, Kelly should have painted it to say "Intel Inside" and sell the company a sponsorship for it.

That never happened, but many other great things did, and they all really helped the Sharks get better fast. For instance, Hrudey took an 18-year-old Patrick Marleau under his wing, and had him live with his family during Marleau's rookie season. That was an act of kindness, class, and true leadership from a great veteran.

We have a few more quick impressions of a couple of other characters. Darren Turcotte played 74 games over two seasons from 1995 to '98 with the Sharks, and missed six weeks because he poked his ear drum out with a Q-Tip after warm-ups and right before the start of a game. He was a late scratch, literally!

In addition, let's not forget the late Shawn Burr, another player who spent portions of two years as a Shark. Once, he required surgery to replace a torn ACL. Doctors took a tendon from a cadaver to repair Burr's knee. He said that he hoped the deceased donor was a "fast guy." What a piece of work!

When Burr knew that his career was coming to a close, he very kindly took the broadcasters out to dinner on a road trip in Montreal. He retired to his home in Michigan, and sadly, he died in August of 2013 after a fall in his home caused massive brain trauma.

Another favorite character from Sharks days of yore is defenseman Marcus Ragnarsson. One night, he separated his shoulder and went off the ice with his arm balanced up in the air because he couldn't move it. He got it reset, and came back to play in the same game. He was a rugged man.

"Rags" wasn't a huge fighter, but he was strong and he was great in both ends of the rink. He was a two-way defenseman when you consider the balance between his offensive skills and his shut-down abilities in his own end. He and Mike Rathje became one of the best defensive pairs in the game while they were together, and they didn't always get a lot of credit for that.

Rags piled up some pretty big points. He's still sixth in all-tie scoring on the blue line for the club, and he played in over 500 games for the Sharks on defense. He was also popular in the locker room. Like so many of the Swedish imports—Douglas Murray was another—he was just a great person and fabulous teammate. Not bad for a fifth-round draft selection.

Murray is another one of those characters. His maternal grandfather, Lasse Bjorn, represented Sweden in the Olympic Games and World Championships in the 1950s. Taking a different path, Douglas came to the United States and played on Long Island before going to Cornell University for four years.

I first saw him play on an off-night during a road trip. We got into the car in Columbus with assistant GM Wayne Thomas and John Ferguson, Sr., the legendary Montreal Canadien. Murray was working on his foot speed in those days, but every time he got on the ice, it was easy to see his high hockey IQ, and his tremendous body checks that brought Ferguson out of his seat in the press box.

Douglas had a technique where he disguised his intent, then finished off his opponent with what he called "the Old Classic Chester." He wound up employing that technique in over 500 games for the Sharks, and he's simply one of the better people that's ever worn Teal.

Those are only a few examples of the many characters who have graced the ice at SAP Center all these years. I could go on and on about the likes of my friend Jamie Baker, for instance, but then again, we'd have to write another book!

Chapter 8

The Owners

When you think about Sharks ownership, you have to trace it back to the very start. If it weren't for George Gund's foresight, the NHL's second venture into the Bay Area might have ended like the first. San Jose had no desire to last less than a decade as had the Seals, who played nine seasons in Oakland from 1967–76.

I remember so much about George, who unfortunately died at the age of 75 in 2013. I admire him and his brother, Gordon, and their families so much. I thought when they owned the team they were the best in the NHL. They let their employees do their jobs, and they supported them. They didn't get in the way, and they just loved the game.

While Gordon remained mostly in the background, George was very much the face of ownership. And he went about his business in a very unassuming and friendly manner. I first met George at the Cow Palace—the Sharks' temporary and antiquated home in Daly City for the first two seasons—before the first game was ever played.

I saw a guy approaching on a motor scooter while wearing an all-leather Sharks varsity-style jacket. Of all the early-franchise merchandise that flew off Bay Area shelves, I'd never seen that sharp article of clothing before. George had a distinctive look with a chiseled jaw, a full head of hair, and eyebrows that in length might qualify for the Guinness Book of World Records.

And then there was Gund's manner of speech. I don't want to suggest he mumbled. That might come off as sounding disrespectful. He had a very soft-spoken manner of verbalizing his thoughts to you. And he used an economy of words to express himself. One of his favorites was "yeah." And "yeah" could mean a great many things depending on his inflection for the number of times he repeated the word in succession, which he did often.

Those who conversed with George often understood his habit of saying, "yeah," and didn't find it all that odd after a while. Others, however, who might be talking to George for the first time could be fooled. There was a time when George was asked by a news outlet for his reaction to a rumor that a players' strike was going to end the following day late in the 1991–92 season.

Caught a bit off guard, George started his response with, "Yeah, yeah," before elaborating to more accurately suggest the end of the labor dispute was *not* imminent. The news crew heard only "Yeah, yeah," and went with that on the air. Oops!

Robert Redford used to tease Gund for his soft-spoken style of speech. Yes, *that* Robert Redford. And more on their relationship later.

George was clearly a very smart guy. He loved the game, he loved the team, he gave everybody the time of day, he treated everybody the same. And what an interesting background he had! A native of Cleveland, Ohio, George Gund III was the youngest of six siblings who were bestowed a large inheritance and corresponding responsibility from their father, George Gund II. He was a philanthropist and the head of the Cleveland Trust Company when it was the largest bank in Ohio.

The younger George dropped out of high school and joined the Marines at age 18 in a stroke of fate that would lead him to San Francisco. After his military service, Gund attended Menlo College but never graduated. Instead he began bringing—dare we suggest smuggling?—Eastern European films and, as a member of the San Francisco Film Society, he distributed them around the

Greater Bay Area and portions of the United States. He wanted to see great work finding its audience.

Gund's early passions included independent filmmaking, studying American Indian history, cowboy poetry, high art, and Japanese calligraphy. As he has been described, and to which I completely attest, George was never one to flaunt his wealth or social status.

Most importantly, he loved the sport of hockey.

It's interesting to note that before George and Gordon were granted NHL expansion rights on May 9, 1990, to what would become the San Jose Sharks, the brothers nearly saved the aforementioned California Golden Seals—another expansion franchise renamed several times. The Gunds became minor investors in the Seals' ownership group that had hopes of moving across the bay and into a new arena planned for San Francisco. But the arena project was scrapped after a mayoral election went the wrong way for hockey fans. As a result, the NHL dropped its previous rejection for relocation, and the Oakland franchise was transferred to the Gunds' hometown of Cleveland.

Relocated and renamed the Cleveland Barons, the franchise continued to hemorrhage cash due to poor attendance and sponsorship, so after only two seasons there, it was agreed that the team would literally merge the team with the Minnesota North Stars, move to Bloomington, and retain the North Stars name. The Gunds went all in with the Minnesota merger, and George became chairman.

Gund was universally respected in the hockey world as his résumé would later include membership in the International Council of USA Hockey, representing as chairman and trustee of the U.S. Hockey Hall of Fame and a trustee of the USA Hockey Foundation. And he did not hide his intentions to return hockey to the Bay Area, as the Gunds asked to relocate the North Stars in the 1980s but the league denied it.

Coincidentally, and at almost the same time, an investment group led by former Hartford Whalers owner Howard Baldwin was working with the NHL to expand to San Jose, where there were plans to build an arena. All parties were satisfied when the league allowed the Gunds to sell their majority share of the North Stars to Baldwin's group in exchange for an expansion team in the Bay Area that would begin playing in 1991–92. The Gunds paid $50 million for the new franchise and were allowed to select 14 skaters and two goalies from an unprotected list made available by the Minnesota North Stars to start to build the Sharks' initial roster.

I wasn't there to witness it, but there's a humorous story that came out of one of the early board of governors' meetings. Most of the other teams' governors weren't familiar with the Gund brothers yet. They knew that one of them, Gordon, was blind, and they knew the other, George, could be a little eccentric. Well, here came the Gunds, one brother pushing the other in a wheelchair. Somebody who had noticed it said, "Boy, that's really nice. His brother is blind, and George is just making sure they get there quickly and safely."

What they didn't know was that George had thrown out his back shortly before the meetings, so *he* was the one in the wheelchair and Gordon was pushing it. Along for the ride, George was directing Gordon by saying, "left...right...straight." He probably threw in a few "Yeah, yeahs" for good measure, too.

George Gund III (right) shares a laugh with hockey legend Gordie Howe after unveiling the team's colors and logo at a press conference in Cupertino, California, on February 12, 1991. *(AP Photo/John G. Mabanglo)*

I have so many great recollections of George in those early years, especially during the team's inaugural season.

Long before the 1991–92 season started, the Sharks hosted an event to unveil their popular initial team jerseys. George Gund was joined by the great Gordie Howe to model a uniform! George wore the team's white jersey, which was primarily worn at home that first season. Howe, who didn't have any affiliation with the Sharks other than being an acquaintance of the Gunds, proudly displayed the popular teal-colored look.

The elaborate press conference was the brainchild of the team's initial marketing guru, Matt Levine. It was held at a local rink, complete with portable bleachers set up on the ice, and it attracted the national network attention of CNN, ESPN, and CBS, along with a host of local affiliates. The cameras were rolling as 300 invited guests, who had all suggested "Sharks" during the name-the-team contest, filled the makeshift bleachers.

Late in that inaugural campaign, collective bargaining negotiations were not progressing, and there was talk of an actual players' strike. In that incendiary atmosphere, on the night before an all-important NHL Board of Governors meeting scheduled in Chicago, the Sharks were in Winnipeg to take on the Jets.

As a frame of reference, we were in the glorious old Winnipeg Arena, and the franchise was the original Jets club that had emerged from the World Hockey Association in 1979 and eventually wound up in Arizona. It was a cozy building that had a giant painting of Queen Elizabeth II hanging from the rafters.

It was the middle of the first period between the Sharks and Jets during one of the games I did alone on the radio. All of a sudden, the door to my broadcast booth opened, and in walked George Gund. Remember, it was the day before the big meeting, and George was nowhere near Chicago. I said, "George, what are you doing here?"

He replied, "Hi, Dan, can I hide in here? The media is hounding me about the negotiations, but I just came to watch the game."

It got even better. He sat down next to me in the booth, along with our radio engineer. He put a headset on so he could listen to my broadcast while he watched. He had popcorn in one hand and a drink in the other, and he was all set to enjoy the game.

On the ice, the Sharks were flying. They made a great play and scored a pretty fantastic goal. I was calling the action, and George got really excited. The chairs that we were supplied were office chairs that have rollers on them. George got the wires from his headset tangled in the chair somehow. And, when he jumped up, the chair rolled a bit away, and he fell on his back just as the goal went in! Popcorn fell all over him, and he was looking straight up with a big grin on his face. All he said was, "Yeah." How many times has that one word had such a poignant meaning?

Here's another story that I heard. The Gunds have a number of well-known friends from all walks of life, but this one goes a little beyond the characterization of celebrity. Apparently they had been invited to the White House for an event, as they had known the Bush family for a number of years.

As the story goes, both Gordon and George were at the White House. With everyone gathered waiting for the event to begin, George noticed some artwork he liked down a hallway, so he strayed off to look at it. That put Gordon all by himself, without George to guide him in this unfamiliar place. Hearing that the event was starting, and in a mildly frantic search for his brother, he called out for him. "George! George!"

Well, according to the story, it just so happened that the President, George H.W. Bush, happened to be walking by. Sensing the presence of someone near him, the younger Gund exclaimed, "Where the hell have you been?"

Oops, wrong George.

Of course, the Secret Service found George down the wrong corridor, and they were trying to figure out who he was and how on earth he had gotten there. They brought him back to the event, and all proceeded smoothly from there.

Sometimes, George knew exactly where he wanted to go, even if no one else did. One year, he joined his team's scouts in Prague to observe the World Championships. As the story goes, he told the Sharks' first-ever general manager, Jack Ferreira, "Meet me for dinner," giving a very early time to convene in the hotel lobby. Thinking that it was an odd time to have dinner, Ferreira went along, as George was the boss.

Ferreira soon found out what George's idea of an early dinner in Prague meant. A car took them to the airport, where they boarded George's personal plane and flew to Reykjavik, Iceland to dine at one of his favorite restaurants.

When they got there, the restaurant was closed! So, George called the owner, who was more than happy to open up the place just for him.

Perry Berezan was a member of the Sharks for the final two seasons of his 10-year NHL career. He recalled a bunch of team members retiring to the home of Brian Mullen late after eating at a restaurant following the final home game of that inaugural season. Long after 1:30 or 2:00 in the morning, the iconic Sharks van—complete with a likeness of S.J. Sharkie painted on its exterior—pulled up with George in his leather Sharks jacket at the wheel. He went into the house, sat down at the kitchen table with a beer, and quietly listened to the players' stories.

Another time in Year 1, George offered his yacht for the team to tour the popular San Francisco tourist destination of Alcatraz. Brian Lawton, the former No. 1 draft pick of the Minnesota North Stars, remembered everyone was on the boat except George. Where was George? Then, around the corner, here came George on his motor scooter, and he hopped on board just before the yacht departed for the former federal penitentiary located in the water a couple miles offshore.

George could show up anywhere at any time. He enjoyed that type of lifestyle, and he could afford it! One thing he'd never miss, however, was the team's annual holiday party, usually hosted on the home-rink ice, where George played the part of Santa Claus. All dressed in red, except for maybe one year when he donned a teal and white Santa's hat, George enthusiastically welcomed those children invited to open gifts he bore.

I have been fortunate enough to enjoy the privilege of emceeing the annual private event, and I liked to have a little fun with George as he filled the Santa Claus suit. I would say, "Santa, how was your trip from the North Pole?" He'd reply with something like, "Yeah, well Dasher was giving me a little trouble, and Dancer needed a rest, so we vectored in once we got over the border and stopped in Minnesota for a few hours." He'd get going with some aviation jargon, and he'd have everyone laughing.

During those years, my family's annual Christmas card included a picture of us with Santa Claus, and it was always George!

Another annual event George wouldn't miss was the team picture. Though to say he never missed it might be a stretch. Let's just say he wasn't always on time. I was never in the picture, but I was around for it. If George was late, the team got somebody to pose as him, and they would crop George's head on top. That happened a couple times.

George simply had no clock in life. He came and went when he pleased, and if he was struck to do something at a certain time, he wouldn't hesitate. He might get in the mood to go for a skate at 1:00 in the morning. I recall a time he was at a resort in Sun

Valley, Idaho. He took that first-year team there for a New Year's celebration, and it shows you what kind of a man he was.

He owned the ice rink in Sun Valley, and when he showed up after hours to skate he was met by a security guard who didn't recognize him. He told George, "Rink's closed, you can't come in." And George said, "Okay." He didn't say, "I own the team," or "I own the building." He was just like anybody else. He left.

George didn't have that problem at the Cow Palace or at the new arena in San Jose, where it was a common sight to see him either skating on his own or in a game of shinny hockey between the morning skate and before a game that evening. Kevin Constantine, who coached the Sharks for just over two seasons in the new arena, related a funny story. Often when George was done skating, he'd ask Kevin if he could use the coach's private shower. Almost chagrined, Constantine said, "I always found it funny the owner of the team would ask."

George loved the game and loved being as close to it as possible. And at old Maple Leaf Gardens in Toronto, he could do just that. There were seats for fans right next to one end of the visiting players' bench. Sometimes the backup goalie might have to get up and maneuver a bit just to allow a seat-holding fan to sit down.

I recall broadcasting a game from inside the historic building. I looked down, and I saw George opening and closing the door to the visiting bench for the guys. He was opening the door with one hand, and he had his phone to his ear in the other. And I realized that he had called the listen line to hear the broadcast. So I said hi to him on the air, and he turned around, looked up to the press box, and grinned!

Late in the Gunds' tenure as owners—they would sell in 2002—George helped me in a big way. It's one of my very favorite personal tales about George, and that's why I saved it for last.

My parents were celebrating their 40th wedding anniversary in a couple days, and we had a game in Dallas on a Saturday night to end a three-game trip. We didn't have another game until Wednesday against Phoenix four nights later. It was just one of those quirks in the schedule that would work perfectly for my family.

My brothers and sisters planned a surprise party for my parents in Connecticut for late Sunday. I walked into the locker room afterward to see Darryl Sutter, who was in his second year coaching the team. I said, "Darryl, I'm not going back on the plane to San Jose because I'm flying to New York tomorrow. The party is tomorrow night. I'll get there in time, we'll spend a day or two, and I'll fly back and see you in San Jose." And Darryl said, "Okay."

George was standing nearby and heard this. He came over, sidled up to me, and said, "I'm going to New York tonight. Do you want to come?" And I replied, "Sure!" We boarded his private plane and flew to Teterboro Airport in New Jersey. On the flight I realized, *How am I going to get where I need to go from there?* I phoned my uncle, who grew up in northern New Jersey, and asked, "Do you know where Teterboro Airport is?" Of course he did. He picked me up at 2:00 in the morning.

George and I had a great conversation. It was just the pilot, the co-pilot, and the two of us on the flight. We talked about a lot of things, not just hockey, and it turned into quite a memorable trip. As it turned out, this surprise party turned out to be the last time that all five kids in my family were at the same place at the same time, with both of our parents, due to the death of our sister a number of years later. Because of George's thoughtful charter service, our family got an extra day together, and I'll always be grateful to him for that.

George, too, had to also deal with the death of a close relative. He went through a terrible tragedy when his son, Greg, was killed.

Greg was something of a free spirit, more the rebel type. All of a sudden, he fell in love with flying. He started a business taking people on tours in Costa Rica. I don't know what happened, but reports are he was piloting a small plane with five passengers near Tamarindo, Costa Rica, and crashed. All six perished, including two children. Greg was just 32 years old. I remember it was so terrible for George and the entire family.

We will all miss George Gund for so many things. I'll never forget his memorial service, held inside San Francisco's historic and beautiful Grace Cathedral on Nob Hill, after his death following a cancer battle. There were so many people who I knew that were there. In the same room—and this is an extreme example of the wide range of people he knew—were actor Robert Redford and politician Nancy Pelosi. What a contrast!

Gund and Redford were familiar with each other from the Sundance Film Festival held annually in Park City, Utah, and the Sundance Resort. It's the largest independent film festival in the United States. Married to Iara Lee, Gund produced many of his wife's movies, including one I watched with him titled *Synthetic Pleasures*. That was one wacky, crazy film.

I'll cherish the time I spent with George; he really was a special guy.

Told by his financial advisers they recommended selling a majority of his holdings, Gund requested then-Sharks president and CEO Greg Jamison locate a group of local investors to purchase the team and keep them in San Jose. By late February of 2002, Gund transferred ownership to an 11-member group billed as San Jose Sports & Entertainment Enterprises. Gund retained a small interest in the team until his death in 2013.

The main investors included Kevin Compton, Hasso Plattner, Gary Valenzuela, Stratton Sclavos, Greg Reyes, and Harvey Armstrong. It was this group that guaranteed that the team remain in Silicon Valley. The ownership group kept the focus on the team, and as was the case with the Gunds before them, provided the resources to make the team successful. Greg Jamison was the public spokesman. A man of deep faith who had been with the club since 1993, Jamison brought years of experience with the NBA's Dallas Mavericks and Indiana Pacers to the Sharks, who hired him as the franchise's Executive Vice President. He was named President and CEO in 1996, and made the transition to the new ownership group.

I thought he brought a sense of professionalism to the organization when it was needed. One of his goals was to make the Sharks a great place to work. He went the extra mile to accomplish that. He used to say, "I need to put my arms around this." He really meant it. He was a father figure in a loving way. I think he did wonders for the day-to-day professionalism when we were going through some challenging times.

Greg is a huge part of the history of this team. He brought the Sharks into the next era when it came to working with the public, dealing with people, and ensuring that top people targeted San Jose as the best place to live and work. The franchise has maintained these characteristics ever since.

Jamison is a religious man, and that's a very important part of his life. I remember when he got up to speak he oten paused and thanked God. It didn't come across as grandstanding or anything orchestrated. He really meant it. I think that his forthright nature rubbed off on everyone. He brought a sense of calm when things weren't calm.

Kevin Compton should get a lot of credit for helping to keep the team here. Compton had a relationship with Hasso Plattner because of their work in tech. They knew each other well, and they liked each other. Along with his lifelong love of hockey, Mr. Plattner was motivated to investigate the possibility of eventually purchasing the team.

By late January of 2013 that purchase became a reality as the German high-tech billionaire, who co-founded business software giant SAP, purchased the ownership shares of two investors to make him the majority owner. Plattner stuck to his word that the successful management structure would remain in place, and that the franchise would have all of the tools needed to pursue a Stanley Cup championship.

The amazing, exciting halcyon years of the Sharks franchise helped to fuel Mr. Plattner's interest in owning the team. When so many people were introduced to the sport in San Jose and became rabid Sharks fans, the future Sharks owner was also in the stands, and the action that he was enthusiastically observing proved to be a link to some of his earliest hockey memories.

Back in Europe, Hasso had particularly enjoyed watching the incredible exploits of the K-L-M Line, featuring Igor Larionov, Sergei Makarov, and Vladimir Krutov. This electrifying trio, one of the greatest line combinations in hockey history, provided him with some of his most enjoyable entertainment. So, one can imagine the delight that he must have felt in the stands at San Jose Arena in 1994, as he watched Larionov and Makarov provide a new generation of fans with some of the same spectacular action.

On the ice, the two hockey legends were joined by Johan Garpenlov, Jeff Norton, and Sandis Ozolinsh to form one of the more lethal, creative, entertaining offensive units in the League in that season. They lifted the Sharks to a 58-point improvement over the previous year, and culminated in the dramatic Game 7 win in Detroit, the spectacularly exciting seven-game series in the second round against Toronto, and the "Celebrate San Jose" parade at the end of the year.

Off the ice, the Larionov-Makarov combination was a very important factor in cementing Hasso's love for the Sharks that eventually developed into ownership of the team. Already with a love of Silicon Valley's entrepreneurial atmosphere, he quickly was able to embrace the team, appreciate the building, and grow in his commitment to the quality of life in the Bay Area.

As far as I'm concerned, the Sharks have the most supportive owner in the game. His company, SAP, holds the naming rights to the building, and has a prominent voice in sponsoring NHL events. That's not only good business, but it proves just how much he loves the game and how much he wants the NHL to grow. He gives GM Doug Wilson and co-Presidents John Tortora and Jonathan Becher the tools that they need for the club to excel.

Yes, from George Gund III to Kevin Compton to Hasso Plattner, the people of San Jose have been blessed with incredible ownership.

Chapter 9

The Playoffs

There is no better time of the year for hockey players, fans, and broadcasters than springtime, when the quest for the Stanley Cup takes center stage.

The regular season is a marathon, no doubt about it. Each year, new life is breathed into the community, and a real sense of excitement begins to build at the very sounds of skates, sticks, pucks, and Zambonis fill the air. The pre-season introduces us to new faces, we get our first looks at the new acquisitions, and the general feeling around town is one of exhilaration and a new beginning, where anything is possible.

The early trends are revealed as the autumn leaves unfold into the increasing drama of the winter months. There are surprising teams off to fast stats, and others with high expectations finding themselves in an early hole. Inevitably, the season reaches the dog days, as injuries, travel, and other competitive challenges mount.

The post-holiday stretch starts to separate the pretenders from the contenders, and that feeling is only heightened as the trade deadline hits three-quarters of the way through the 82-game schedule. The drama of the homestretch nearly always features tight races for so many of those 16 precious playoff spots.

Finally, once the long winter thaws into early spring, the regular season concludes, and the real fun begins.

The Sharks have had an interesting postseason history. As is the case with every franchise out of the post-expansion era, they've certainly learned that the pursuit of Lord Stanley's coveted hardware is a long and unpredictable journey.

In their earlier years, the Sharks produced Silicon Valley euphoria with several Cinderella-style postseason runs. Typical of a young franchise, a couple of rebuilding seasons followed, but then, the team became annual postseason participants, qualifying

18 times over a 20-year period through 2018. During stretches, the Sharks racked up playing as many playoff rounds as anyone along with the Detroit Red Wings and Pittsburgh Penguins.

Still, the degree of difficulty in winning it all is underscored by the fact that the Sharks reached the Stanley Cup Final only once in that span of time, and they fell short with that one opportunity against Sidney Crosby's Penguins in 2016.

How hard is it to win the Cup? Just ask fans in Vancouver, St. Louis, Buffalo, or Washington. How much patience do you need to win the Cup? Just ask fans in Los Angeles. They had to wait more than 40 years before the Kings won their first Cup. How about Original Six cities—fans of the New York Rangers, Boston Bruins, and Chicago Blackhawks lived through long Cup droughts before winning in recent times. Maple Leafs fans were still waiting through 2018 for the magic that hadn't struck since 1967.

It is, however, easy to lose sight of the fact that the pursuit of the Stanley Cup is as much about the journey as it is about reaching the destination. While the Sharks never completely ascended to the peak of the mountain, they developed some hearty rivalries along the way. That's the way it is in the playoffs. Rivalries can't be forced. They occur when two good teams meet with one prize at stake. And that rivalry grows as those same two teams meet repeatedly in a similar circumstance.

When the Sharks entered the league in 1991, most expected they'd develop a rivalry with the Los Angeles Kings, and that happened pretty quickly even though the two teams didn't meet in a playoff series until 2011. The Sharks and Kings met in so many important regular-season games that the two cities didn't need a playoff series to dislike each other.

I believe that certain cities transcend all sports to a degree. Los Angeles is a natural because of its regional proximity in the Golden State. It's Northern California versus Southern California. It's the Giants versus the Dodgers. The 49ers versus the Rams. The Lakers versus the Warriors. And it's the Raiders moving to Los Angeles and coming back to Oakland again. So it's natural to hear "Beat L.A." chants in the arena.

The Sharks developed rivalries, too, with teams and cities that were less predictable at the outset. Why? Because they were all borne out of the playoffs. I believe the Sharks have great rivals in the Anaheim Ducks, the Detroit Red Wings, the St. Louis Blues, the Chicago Blackhawks, the Dallas Stars, the Calgary Flames, and the Edmonton Oilers.

Do you want to rile up fans in San Jose? Just let them catch a glimpse of Theoren Fleury, Ed Belfour, or Chris Pronger. They're all villains in the eyes of Sharks fans. They've all taken something the home team wanted. They've all conspired to break the hearts of San Jose's most loyal supporters. That's why Arturs Irbe was booed in Detroit. That's why Owen Nolan and Bryan Marchment were jeered in Dallas. That's why Joe Thornton and Patrick Marleau heard raspberries in Southern California.

If you were to ask me what my fantasy playoff sequence is— the Sharks getting all the way to the Final and winning their first Stanley Cup—it would go something like the following, although not necessarily in this order: the Sharks would beat Los Angeles, Anaheim, Chicago, and either the N.Y. Rangers or Montreal in the Final.

They're great cities, amazing places and great rivals, and it came oh, so close to actually happening once. In 2014, the Sharks had a 3–0 series lead and lost to L.A. in Game 7. Beyond the general pain that enveloped the Bay Area after that disappointing playoff defeat, note what happened next: the Kings played and defeated Anaheim, Chicago, and the Rangers. Forgive me for being a little upset while contemplating what might have been that year!

Of course, there's nothing that could be done about that. Besides, when the Sharks went to Pittsburgh for the 2016 Stanley Cup Final, it was one of the greatest things that ever happened to me in my hockey broadcasting career, a truly incredible experience, regardless of which captain carried the trophy at the end. It's a real privilege to be able to call a Stanley Cup Final, and when you get to do it once, you want to return again!

If there is any regret that I have with the current system, it's that some of the greatest playoff rivalries have an extremely limited chance of ever happening, let alone on hockey's greatest stage. For instance, the fabulous rivalry that the Sharks and Red Wings built before Detroit was relocated to the Eastern Conference, can only happen if both teams happen to advance to the Stanley Cup Final. As great as such an occurrence would be, it's unfortunate that there weren't other possibilities for it to be scheduled.

My suggested solution for this dilemma would be to take into account that the Clarence Campbell Bowl and Prince of Wales Trophy aren't exactly the most popular pieces of hardware, as significant as they are. How many times have you seen a subdued "celebration" when these trophies are awarded?

The Clarence Campbell Bowl that the Sharks won in 2016 is a beautiful trophy, to be honest. Everyone in San Jose cherished it off the ice, and, much to the note of its Hall of Fame caretakers, made a lot of use of the silverware. It was taken to radio and television stations, client events, and hospitals. I got some really great photos when I took it to San Francisco and got the Golden Gate Bridge in the background.

But when the trophy was awarded after the Sharks beat the Blues to capture the Western Conference, there was no thought about a major celebration on the ice, because captain Joe Pavelski and his teammates had the Stanley Cup on their minds. Similarly, in the East, when Penguins captain Sidney Crosby handled the Prince of Wales Trophy for the Eastern Conference playoff title, there was respect, but no joy, because of the big prize that lay ahead.

If you think about the heritage of the game, there were no conference final trophies. What mattered then, and what matters now, is the Stanley Cup. With four teams to play, there was only the Semifinal and Stanley Cup Final for the teams that earned their way to that point.

With that in mind, I've always said that when you get down to four teams, what about considering the idea of re-seeding? At present, it is impossible for a Canadiens–Maple Leafs, Rangers-Bruins, or Capitals-Penguins Final series. Imagine the excitement if it were possible for it to happen. It would be a paean to the history of the game.

It's the same for the Sharks and Kings or Sharks and Ducks. Great growth is often built on the strength of compelling rivalries, so can you picture how incredible an all-California Final, or a Rangers-Bruins Final series would help grow the game?

In a way, this one change to the current playoff system would be a paean to the history of the game, when six teams fought through to a point where four teams remained, the first seed played the fourth, and the second seed faced the third for the right to advance to the Stanley Cup Final. Some traditional rivals (Bruins-Canadiens, for example) would have incredible attention in a Final series, if it were possible. It would make it possible for anyone to play anyone, with everything at stake.

As for whether a prospective all-California Final would result in compelling growth for the game, consider the fact that there are more people in California then there are in Canada.

What to do with the two other trophies? Well, they could be either retired to the Hall of Fame, or they could be presented to the regular season champions of their respective conferences, thereby putting the Campbell Bowl and Prince of Wales Trophy into a similar category as the President's Trophy, which is also a regular season award.

I think that would be better. That's my suggestion for improving the game.

The 1990s

One thing I wouldn't change is San Jose's introduction to the Stanley Cup playoffs. That came in Year 3 of the franchise—the team's first in San Jose's brand new downtown arena—after the Sharks played their first two seasons at the Cow Palace in Daly City, California. The Sharks were hardly a lock, especially after starting the year winless in their first nine games at 0–8–1. I don't think anyone in Teal had playoff expectations even before that third year started, especially considering San Jose was coming off an 11–71–2 second season.

Well, everyone except new head coach Kevin Constantine, that is.

Prepared as always, Constantine introduced himself to the team with a well-worded speech that hit on the high points, including reaching the playoffs and winning the Stanley Cup. And he wasn't kidding. Jamie Baker was a late addition to the third-year team; he signed a free-agent contract a year after playing for an Ottawa expansion team that won only 10 of 84 games—even one less than the Sharks in the same season of 1992–93.

"Back when the Coach told us we were here to make the playoffs and win the Stanley Cup, there was a bunch of us sitting in the back of the room laughing," Baker later recalled. "We were just hoping not to be an embarrassment. That would have been progress."

Progress was slow, but it was sure. As new-addition Russian greats Igor Larionov and Sergei Makarov rediscovered their magic as linemates, and as Swede Johan Garpenlov rounded out the forward line with slick-skating defensemen Sandis Ozolinsh and Jeff Norton added to the mix, the otherwise defensive-minded Sharks rode that group's offensive creativity to a remarkable turnaround.

The Sharks capped a late-season seven-game winning streak with a 2–1 victory in Los Angeles on April 5, 1994. Baker scored both of San Jose's goals, Irbe stopped 22 of 23 shots, and the Sharks clinched a Western Conference playoff berth with four games still remaining on their regular-season schedule. San Jose finished with a 33–35–16 record. And despite the sub.–500 mark, San Jose's 58-point bump set an NHL record at the time for the greatest single-season improvement in points from one season to the next.

And who should be waiting as a first-round playoff matchup? None other than the Detroit Red Wings, champions of the Central Division and the only team in the conference to crest 100 points. The experienced Wings didn't lack in star power either. The roster was littered with names such as Steve Yzerman, Sergei

Fedorov, Dino Ciccarelli, Paul Coffey, Nicklas Lidstrom, Vladimir Konstantinov, Mark Howe, and Keith Primeau. Oh, and they were coached by Scotty Bowman.

It was like the 1960 World Series—Yankees versus Pirates. The Yankees won three games by scores of 16–3, 10–0, and 12–0. The Pirates won the close ones—6–4, 3–2, and 5–2. That led to a seventh and deciding game won by the Buccos, 10–9, when Bill Mazeroski hit a walk-off home run in the last inning.

Jamie Baker turned out to be the Sharks' Bill Mazeroski.

The Sharks made a statement by stealing Game 1, 5–4. Joe Louis Arena can be an intimidating place to play. But defenseman Jayson More seemed to say "We know we belong here" when he took his hockey stick and stabbed a dead octopus thrown by a fan that landed near his skates just before the opening faceoff.

If that didn't get the Detroit faithful's attention, then the first period sure did. Shawn Cronin was a 30-year-old journeyman defenseman, known more for his fighting skills than anything else. He didn't have a goal in 34 regular-season appearances for the Sharks. His total offensive output as a part-time player was two points.

Well, he scored the very first goal of the series. Larionov and Makarov followed with goals, and the visitors led 3–0 after 20 minutes. By early in the third, the game was tied 3–3 until Baker put the Sharks back up by one. The Wings answered less than two minutes later. No matter. Vlastimil Kroupa, an 18-year-old rookie with one goal in 27 games during the regular season scored the game-winner with less than five minutes remaining.

Detroit restored order—at least to what the Wings were expecting out of the series—by winning Games 2 and 3 by scores of 4–0 and 3–2. But instead of caving in to the expectations of

Jamie Baker fights Steve Yzerman for a loose puck during the epic Sharks–Red Wings series. *(AP Photo/Timothy Fitzgerald)*

the outside world, the Sharks rallied to take a 3–2 series lead. San Jose scored three unanswered goals after falling behind 2–0 at the outset of Game 4 and rode Makarov's third-period tie-breaking tally to a 4–3 win. Three nights later Makarov struck twice more and Irbe made 31 saves during a 6–4 victory in as incredible Game 5.

The Sharks did what they needed to do. They won two of three on home ice to give themselves a chance as the 2–3–2 series format shifted back to Motown for the dramatic conclusion. With the Wings' backs to the wall, they blew out the Sharks in Game 6, 7–1. That was the kind of Detroit domination people expected to see. Maybe the Wings had woken up just in time to save themselves from a gigantic upset. That's, at least, what Detroit fans were hoping.

"Every game we went into saying, 'Let's keep it close,'" Baker recalled later. "They were blowing teams out all year. We had been in playoff mode since Game 10. If it was tied or a one-goal game entering the third period, we were in our comfort zone."

The Sharks got their wish as Game 7 was tied 2–2 after 40 minutes. Garpenlov and Makarov scored goals for San Jose, who watched as Detroit got one each from Kris Draper and Vyacheslav Kozlov to knot it back up. Tensions were running high. One mistake could end it.

"Everybody kept waiting for the wheels to fall off," rugged winger Jeff Odgers said. "We had a couple of bad games in that series like, 'Ah, well, here it is. They're done. Finished.' But it was a resilient group."

That's when Baker did his Mazeroski impression.

Detroit goalie Chris Osgood came out of his crease and played a puck up the boards in front of San Jose's bench. At the same time, Baker jumped on during a line change as teammate Todd Elik came off. Baker's linemates—Ray Whitney and Bob Errey—were already on the ice. Whitney had dumped the puck into a corner and jumped around Lidstrom in hot pursuit while Errey skated hard to the opposite goal post.

"This is like the hockey gods were with us," Baker later said as he described Osgood's clear striking the glass and landing at his feet flat and not spinning or rolling. "I didn't take a full swing because I didn't want (a back-checking Kozlov) to hook my stick. It's a bang-bang play.... I used the heel of my stick, and the rest is history, right?"

Baker's half shot into the vacated net at 13:25 served as the game and series winner.

"What a great feeling for the organization," Whitney said later. "And just a great goal by Jamie."

Look at that series closely and a few things stand out. Larionov led the Sharks in scoring with 10 points on the strength of eight assists. Makarov led the team in goals with six. And Garpenlov was third in scoring with five points. Yet the top-liners were minus–5, minus–3, and minus–5, respectively. Irbe had a .876 save percentage in the series, and his goals against were barely under 4 (3.91). The Red Wings outshot the Sharks 218–153. How the heck did the Sharks win this series?

No matter. They did. And now it was time to get out of Dodge.

Everyone got on the bus and drove out to the airport, and it was fogged in. The team had already checked out of the team hotel. As happens in scenarios like that, no one knew who would win the series, because another Game 7 in Calgary was being played between the Flames and the Vancouver Canucks.

Because the Sharks were the eighth seed, they would face the team with the best remaining record. That meant that if the Flames won Game 7, the group would be traveling to Calgary. If the Canucks won the game, we would head to Toronto.

With the foggy conditions getting worse, the bus pulled into a motel parking lot, and the team walked into the lounge, where the Flames-Canucks game was on TV. There was a pool table in the bar, and a few guys decided to rack up, but most were transfixed on the television screen.

What else could possibly happen? Of course, Calgary-Vancouver went into overtime, and it was quite a show between goaltenders Mike Vernon and Kirk McLean.

By then, the fog was so bad that it became apparent that the team would have to stay over until morning, regardless of the result. But by then, Game 7 in Calgary was going into double overtime.

The weary Sharks were hoping to get some sleep, but it would have to wait for a few more minutes before they learned if the plane needed to turn left to Calgary, or right to Toronto. At 2:20 of the second overtime period, Pavel Bure's incredible goal, off a brilliant pass from Jeff Brown, gave the Canucks the series win, and guaranteed a Sharks' trip to Ontario.

Traveling to Toronto for a playoff series is nothing short of surreal. There is so much interest and attention on the Maple Leafs, and their 13 Stanley Cup championships, and the fans were excited to know that they wouldn't have to deal with the Red Wings in their hopes for a first title since 1967.

Media coverage in Toronto, which seems to rival the Super Bowl on a daily basis, provided all of the fundamentally sound reasons why the Maple Leafs would be a formidable opponent. Pat Burns was the head coach, Felix Potvin was having a strong year in goal, Wendel Clark was a ferocious captain, and Doug Gilmour was one of the more creative players in hockey. The Sharks would be playing Game 1 in Toronto just two days after an emotional Detroit series against a Leafs squad that had two additional days of rest.

But, first things first: Just 48 hours after eliminating the Red Wings, San Jose marched right into Maple Leaf Gardens and took Game 1 by the score of 3–2. Johan Garpenlov broke a 2–2 tie with the only goal of the third period, Arturs Irbe made 29 saves, and everyone in San Jose started saying, "Here we go again!"

Toronto won Game 2, and then it was time for the Sharks to return home to the Bay Area for their first home game of the series. Because of a 2-3-2 series format, Sharks fans had seen and heard the incredible atmosphere beaming into their televisions and radios, and they were determined to give their team the home ice advantage that they deserved.

When it came time for Game 3 against the Maple Leafs, it marked the first time that the fans had been able to get together to enjoy the way that their team had shocked the hockey world. As the Sharks hit the ice for warmups and then again for the game, the absolutely packed arena hit decibel levels that have only been approached on a few occasions in franchise history. It was really something special to see–and hear–for the remainder of the playoff run.

The series went back and forth, with the Sharks taking every odd numbered game and the Maple Leafs responded on even-game nights. In Game 5, the top group put on an incredible show: Makarov (2-2-4), Larionov (0-3-3), and Garpenlov (1-0-1) combined for eight points, and the Sharks took a 5–2 win and a 3–2 series lead back to Toronto.

Who can ever forget Game 6, played on a Thursday night, May 12, 1994? Clark gave Toronto the 1–0 lead in the opening period, but Larionov's fourgh goal of the series tied it 1–1 through 40 minutes. Clark would score again to give the Maple Leafs the lead in the third, but Jeff Norton's first goal of the playoffs brought the Sharks even again, and it was on to a memorable overtime, and a "next goal wins" excitement that was felt everywhere.

Not quite midway through the first period of sudden death, Makarov forced a turnover along the boards in the Toronto end. He used his body to protect the puck and centered it to Garpenlov, whose hard shot from the high slot beat Potvin, but struck the crossbar with a loud clang.

Not long after, the top group again rushed into the offensive zone. Larionov fed the puck to Sandis Ozolinsh, who rushed into the slot. For whatever reason, Sandis elected to return the puck to an unsuspecting Larionov, who didn't seem to have as great an angle to finish the play. It bounced off his stick, and an opportunity for glory was lost.

Finally, a small turnover behind the Sharks net was fed by Gilmour in front to veteran Mike Gartner. As Irbe scrambled to go from one side of the net to the other to meet the play, the sniper slipped the puck past, and this time, it didn't hit the crossbar. At 8:53 of overtime, The Maple Leafs forced a Game 7 in the series. It was *that* close for the Sharks.

I can still hear that crossbar ping in my mind. And I recall the groan from the crowd, who knew that if Garpenlov scored, the

Sharks would have gone to the third round. Had the Sharks won, they would have played Vancouver in the conference final, and the Sharks had played well against the Canucks that year. The Sharks were 3–2–1 against them. It would have been an amazing thing to play them in that conference final.

Instead it was the Leafs who moved on. A fan favorite in Toronto, Clark scored the first two goals of Game 7, and when Mark Osborne tallied early in the third, the Sharks faced a three-goal deficit with less than 17 minutes to play. Gilmour put it out of reach and the Leafs won 4–2. Toronto ended up losing to Vancouver, who met the Rangers in the Final.

Of all of the heroics performed by the Sharks in the losing effort, I need to tip my hat to Doug Gilmour, the never-say-die star of the Maple Leafs that year. Gilmour did everything in his power to push Toronto forward by scoring an amazing three goals, 13 assists, and 16 points, one of the most productive best-of-seven series ever played.

One other memory of that series came outside of Maple Leaf Gardens after the game. A crush of jubilant Maple Leafs fans actually pressed up against two team shuttles that were preparing to take the Sharks back to the airport to head home. These fans actually shook the bus back and forth, prompting one of us to say, "Can't you leave us alone? Your team won the series!" It was just another example of the passion surrounding Toronto hockey fans.

It would have been a dream come true to go to the Final at all, but that was the year the Rangers won the Cup for the first time in 54 years. No more derisive chants of "NINE-teen FOR-ty! NINE-teen FOR-ty!"

In looking back, I have to be objective and admit the Sharks weren't ready for that. Sometimes things happen for a reason. And the reason why the Sharks lost to Toronto was they weren't quite ready yet, and they might have been better off in the long run.

A bizarre result of the series loss was the parade the city of San Jose threw upon the team's return. Hockey parades are always reserved for the ultimate champions, but fans were proud of these Cinderella Sharks, who gave San Jose a new identity in their first season playing downtown. It turns out the fans didn't have to wait long to get excited again.

The following regular season got off to a late start due to a work stoppage that lasted 103 days before labor accord was reached. The schedule was reduced from 84 to 48 games for each team and featured all intraconference play. Another casualty of the lockout was the NHL All-Star Game, which was to be played in San Jose. Fortunately, the Sharks were awarded the 47th NHL All-Star Game two years later.

I'll always remember that first game of the regular season in late January, when St. Louis was the opponent in San Jose. It was Mike Keenan's first game behind the Blues' bench as head coach, months after winning the Stanley Cup with the Rangers and after scores of rumors concerning whether he had negotiated with another team during that Final round.

I remember that Mike didn't want to talk about those rumors when the media asked him about them on the morning of that game. He referred the media to Gary Bettman and stuck to talking about his new team.

Unlike the previous season, when they went on a roll late in the year and catapulted into the playoffs, the Sharks struggled to find their groove this time around. The regular-season scoring list gives some insight into those shortcomings. Ulf Dahlen led the team with 34 points, 18-year-old Jeff Friesen was tops in goals with 15, and Makarov and Larionov, while still very effective, slipped to 24 points each.

In goal, Irbe's save percentage dipped below 90 percent (.895) while his goals-against average rose to 3.26. Wade Flaherty, who would be a postseason hero, was barely better in a backup role—3.10 goals against and .903 save percentage.

But, with Constantine pushing enough of the right buttons, the Sharks squeaked in again despite another sub-.500 finish at 19–25–4. And, because Dallas had an even worse record (17–23–8) with the same number of points (42), San Jose grabbed the seventh seed in the West to avoid a first-round rematch against Central champ Detroit. Instead, the Sharks drew the Pacific titlists, Calgary.

The Flames proved to be another tough opponent. The Stanley Cup champions in 1989, Calgary boasted a roster of stars that included Theoren Fleury, Joe Nieuwendyk, Phil Housley, Robert Reichel, and Joel Otto. There was pressure on this team, too, because they had been eliminated in the first round in every playoff year since capturing the Stanley Cup. Thus, even with a previous track record, the Sharks went in as heavy opening-round underdogs, which is exactly the way they liked it.

Baker scored two second-period goals, the second of which stood as a game-winner, and the Sharks stole Game 1 at the Saddledome by the exact same 5–4 score with which they beat Detroit in their playoff opener a year before. The Flames peppered Irbe with 39 shots, but he turned away 35 to earn the win in goal.

Then, two nights later, when Dahlen scored 12:21 into overtime, the Sharks not only had another 5–4 win, but an attention-grabbing 2–0 lead with the series shifting to San Jose. The Flames came to life on the road, winning 9–2 and 6–4 in convincing fashion. Ex-

Shark Mike Sullivan, who later coached Pittsburgh over San Jose in the 2016 Cup Final, collected a hat trick in Game 3. Fleury went one better in Game 4, as his four-goal, five-point game led the Flames.

Back in Calgary for a pivotal Game 5, the Flames kept it rolling as Fleury scored two more goals and goalie Trevor Kidd pitched a 25-save shutout. Fleury was a thorn in San Jose's side in those early years. It seemed like every time the two teams played he was in the middle of something. And, because of his hearty offensive output, he became the first targeted villain in San Jose. No opposing player got booed more than Fleury early on.

Fortunately for the Sharks, Fleury's goal output in the series would stop at seven. And he managed only one more point that made it an impressive 14 for the seven games. But it was the Sharks' turn to grab the momentum. Back in San Jose for Game 6, Craig Janney scored two goals and Flaherty made 30 stops in a series-extending 5–3 win. Flaherty had earned more of the coach's trust in goal as both he and Irbe fought the puck in the middle of this series.

That set the stage for another dramatic Game 7. The Sharks were playing another powerful team, and could it possibly happen again?

The Flames were questioning what was going on in their goal, too. Even though backup Rick Tabaracci hadn't appeared since the final 19 minutes of Game 1, some started to doubt whether Trevor Kidd could finish off San Jose. It turns out he couldn't.

This was a weird, wild, and unpredictable series. And that theme started even before the Sharks left their team hotel just before Game 7. Standing with teammates awaiting their departure from the lobby, Janney spied a celebrity at the front desk and announced to anyone in earshot, "Friggin' Dudley Moore! What's Dudley Moore doing here?"

Maybe he was inspired by the sight of the English actor and comedian, but Janney led the way in regulation of Game 7. He set up Pat Falloon for his two goals and scored San Jose's all-important fourth tally midway through the third period. The Flames stormed back to score twice within 42 seconds later in the period to force sudden death.

The Sharks were flirting with disaster for sure. The Flames were en route to putting 60 shots on goal on the night they would outshoot San Jose 2-to-1. But, sure enough, the Sharks had a last shred of magic left in this series, and it struck early in the second overtime after the first 20 minutes of sudden death didn't decide anything.

Larionov drove the slot and circled to his left before directing a low shot that was blocked into the corner. Makarov swooped in from below the goal line to pick up the loose puck and survey what was developing as he skated toward the boards. After a deke, Mak wristed a low pass toward the near post that an unmarked Ray Whitney slightly redirected past an upright Kidd and into the net 1:54 into double OT.

Whitney's goal in Game 7 was one of the most electrifying moments in Sharks history. Beating Detroit was special because it was the first time. Going to Game 7 against Toronto and hitting a crossbar in Game 6 were amazing moments. But beating Calgary was an electrifying experience.

"I tipped it just enough that it kind of froze Trevor Kidd into thinking, *Did it really move that much?*" Whitney said later. "When it slid by him, I thought, *Holy shit, we did it again.*" People forget Makarov made the play. They initially announced him as the goal scorer. And, if that had been the case, it would have been like rubbing salt in the wound for Flames fans. Makarov spent the first four years of an NHL career that didn't start for him until age 31 as a Calgary Flame. He scored 24 goals and 62 points in 1989–90 to win the Calder Trophy. Rules for annually awarding the league's top rookie were amended after the season so only players under the age of 26 by September 15 of their rookie year were eligible.

They announced Makarov had scored the goal over the public-address system, and they had to correct it. I was fortunate in that I called the goal properly—I saw that Ray Whitney had barely touched the puck. Of course, it was pretty appropriate that Whitney, an Edmontonian, would get a series-winning goal in overtime at the Saddledome against Calgary!

The Flames got a measure of revenge nine years later, when they beat the Sharks in the 2004 Western Conference Final and went all the way to Game 7 of the Stanley Cup Final.

It was an amazing moment for this team because they weren't as good as the year before. They really weren't. And it was the lockout year, too, so they missed half of the year and the schedule was different.

Round 2 put the Sharks against a highly motivated Red Wings team that still felt the painful sting of the previous year's playoff defeat. Somehow, I just knew that the Men in Teal were going to have Detroit's full attention this time around.

Getting ready for what would definitely be a Detroit onslaught, it was impossible not to reflect for a moment on the amazing series the year before. I'll never forget the late Bryan Murray, GM of the

Red Wings, who had to be bitterly disappointed as Game 7 ended. Leaving the cramped press box at the Joe after that contest, he had to walk by our radio booth. With his assistant Doug MacLean right there with him, Murray graciously stopped to offer a handshake of congratulations. The ashen face that greeted me told me that Murray knew he would not be back following the series loss.

Well, in 1995, Jimmy Devellano and Scotty Bowman were running the show, with Bowman stepping behind the Wings' bench for his second season in Detroit. While the Red Wings featured greater depth and more grit to go along with their fabulous high-end talent, the biggest change was in goal. Future Shark Mike Vernon was now backstopping the Wings, and he was doing his usual fine job of it.

Going back to San Jose's upset in Game 7 the year before, I'll never forget seeing the late Bryan Murray leaving the cramped press quarters atop Joe Louis Arena, yet taking the time to graciously congratulate anyone associated with the Sharks he encountered on his way out. We knew he wouldn't be coming back following the huge Red Wings disappointment.

Scotty Bowman was in his second year behind the Wings' bench, and he had more of his kind of players on the roster now as he shared the GM post with Jimmy Devellano. While Detroit featured more depth and more grit to go along with their fabulous top-end talent, the biggest change was in goal. Future Shark Mike Vernon was backstopping the Wings and doing his usual fine job of it.

The rematch was more of a mismatch, and we called it the "Tennis Series." The scores of the games sounded as if it had come from Wimbledon: 6-Love, 6–2, 6–2, and 6–2. It was like the

190th ranked tennis player going up against John McEnroe. We knew that the Sharks were probably not going to catch lightning in a bottle again, but Detroit manhandled San Jose in every way imaginable.

"We obviously paid the price beating Detroit the year before," Sharks coach Kevin Constantine said later. "They paid us back quite nicely with those big tennis scores."

Detroit's big guns came to play. Sergei Fedorov led the Wings in scoring with four goals and 11 points. Slava Kozlov was next with four goals and nine points. The Wings got a multi-number of goals from seven skaters in all in just four games. Vernon was unflappable. He flashed a 1.50 goals-against average and .902 save percentage while playing every minute of all four contests.

The Sharks' stats were predictably lacking. Larionov was the modest leader in points with three—all on assists. The only multigoal scorer in the series besides Ray Whitney with two was defensive-minded blue-liner Mike Rathje, also scored two. Irbe and Flaherty were equally shelled. Both had 6.00 goals-against averages and dreadful save percentages (.870 and .822, respectively).

There was no way in hell Scotty Bowman, or anybody in Detroit, was not going to take this San Jose team seriously after what happened the year before. They said, "No, this is not going to happen." They were right. It didn't.

Under Bowman's experienced and excellent direction, the Wings were entering a new era of success. They reached the Final that year only to lose four straight to goalie Martin Brodeur and the New Jersey Devils. Their appearance in the '95 Final was Detroit's first of four visits by 2002. The Red Wings won three Cups in that time, including going back-to-back in 1997 and '98, as well as one more Cup in 2002.

Not only did the Sharks fail to win a Cup, but their playoff cupboard went bare, too, for consecutive springs. The new franchise's early-round playoff success was a nice reward for the supportive and enthusiastic fans, but the Sharks still had to do the work of drafting, developing, and focusing on not rushing the process even during tough times.

The 1995–96 season was one of transition as a slow start triggered a domino effect of change. Head coach Kevin Constantine was fired after the team won only three of its first 25 games. A front-office shakeup soon thereafter resulted in Dean Lombardi assuming the role as sole general manager, a position he shared for a couple years with personnel expert Chuck Grillo.

San Jose didn't fare any better in 1996–97, finishing last in the seven-team Pacific Division. Al Sims lasted only one year as coach as Lombardi got a second chance to get it right. He traveled to the Sutter family ranch in Viking, Alberta, and successfully convinced Darryl Sutter it was time to get off the tractor and climb back behind an NHL bench.

The Sharks might have started to wonder when they were going to see results when, at the quarter mark of the 1997–98 campaign, they stood only 6–14–1. The improvement was slow, but steady. San Jose went 28–24–9 the rest of the way—picking up points in all but 24 of 61 contests—to finish fourth in the Pacific and grab the eighth and final playoff spot despite an overall sub-.500 record at 34–38–10.

San Jose drew the Central Division champion, the Dallas Stars, in the first round. It was the third straight playoff year that the Sharks had drawn a first-place opponent. The Stars were a team on the rise, and had won the President's Trophy with 109 points in 1997–98. With a roster stacked with big-name stars, including Mike Modano, Sergei Zubov, Joe Nieuwendyk Derian Hatcher, Jere Lehtinen, and Pat Verbeek, they also had goalie Ed Belfour, who was well on his way to joining Theoren Fleury as a player that Sharks' fans loved to boo.

Belfour was a Shark the previous spring. He came to San Jose from Chicago in late January of 1997 during a four-player trade. Rebuilding San Jose shipped vets Ulf Dahlen, Chris Terreri, and Michal Sykora to the Blackhawks in exchange for Belfour, who after eight seasons and two Vezina Trophies fell out of favor in the Windy City.

The Sharks got an accomplished goalie who could become an unrestricted free agent at season's end, and Belfour made it sound like he could make San Jose a place to call home when he said, "I like [Dean] Lombardi's attitude. He wants to win a Stanley Cup in San Jose. I want to help him do that."

Belfour, however, battled injury during the three months remaining in the regular season. He played 13 games and went 3–9 with a 3.41 goals-against average and .884 save percentage. Despite the subpar results and questions about his health, the Sharks offered a three-year, $10.5 million extension. Instead, Belfour bolted to Dallas on the second day free agents could sign with a new team.

"My main goal is to win the Stanley Cup and be part of a team that is headed in that direction," Belfour told Dallas media after signing for slightly less than the Sharks offered. "That's why I chose to make myself available to Dallas."

And, just like that, the Sharks had another villain.

It didn't take long for the Sharks-Stars series to heat up, and it had nothing to do with Belfour quite yet. Just 16 minutes into Game 1, San Jose defenseman Bryan Marchment rode Joe Nieuwendyk into the end boards as he finished a check, and Dallas's leading scorer in the regular season suffered a torn ACL to his right knee in addition to sustaining cartilage damage. He was done for the series.

The Stars won the opener at home 4–1, which set the stage for more physical drama in Game 2. The Sharks trailed 4–0 four minutes into the third period when San Jose captain Owen Nolan saw an opportunity to possibly knock Belfour off his game and send a message before the series moved to San Jose for the next two games. With the puck dumped into the corner, and just after Belfour stopped it to play it up the boards, Nolan never broke stride and plowed over the unsuspecting netminder.

"He was on top of his game, and I was just trying to think of a way to rattle him," Nolan would say later. "The opportunity presented itself. Still, going in there, I wasn't sure if I was going to do it. It just got to the point where I said to myself, 'I'm just going to ram this guy.'"

The game ended with San Jose piling up a playoff record 72 minutes in penalties. The Stars enjoyed 15 power plays and converted four times during the 5–2 win. The die was cast. Nieuwendyk was out in Game 1. Modano suffered a concussion in Game 2 courtesy of a Marcus Ragnarsson high stick, and now Nolan purposely ran into Belfour.

It was going to be an ugly series.

Dallas played an undisciplined Game 3, putting the Sharks on the power play 14 times, and San Jose responded with a 4–1 victory. Then one of the coolest home playoff memories in team history happened in Game 4. When rookie defenseman Andrei Zyuzin settled a Bernie Nicholls pass and wristed a low shot past Belfour 6:31 into sudden death, the Sharks tied the series at two wins apiece on the only goal of Game 4. It nearly blew the roof off the arena.

I remember thinking it would be great if they could pull it off, but how hard it would be because Dallas was a great team even without Nieuwendyk.

The hometown *San Jose Mercury News* copy editor gets an A+ for the "Suddenly Zyuzin" headline, which made me laugh.

The Stars took a 3–2 series lead in Game 5 when Modano snapped a 2–2 tie midway through the third period with the game-winner. Two nights later Dallas closed out San Jose with an identical 3–2 score in Game 6. The Sharks scored the first two goals, but the Stars stormed back with Mike Keane notching the winner early in the third period.

Belfour definitely got the better of San Jose in the series. He finished with a sparkling 1.95 goals-against average and .908 save percentage. The Stars' run ended with a six-game loss in the West Finals against Detroit a year before they'd go all the way and beat Buffalo for the Cup.

The Sharks, however, were back in the playoffs to stay, and that was a relief around these parts.

Sutter continued to prove that the Sharks were a tough team to play. While they struggled to score goals, they were keenly committed to keeping the puck out of the net. And in 1998–99,

San Jose allowed only 191 goals to go into the playoffs as the second stingiest defense in the West. Again, the Sharks qualified for their fourth straight postseason without a winning record (31–33–18).

The opponent was Colorado, three years removed from their first Cup, and two years away from another. The Avalanche were champs of the Northwest Division with a 44–28–10 record, and the team featured a lineup of stars including Peter Forsberg, Joe Sakic, Claude Lemieux, Adam Deadmarsh, Chris Drury, Shark killer and nemesis Theoren Fleury, and goalie Patrick Roy. Three ex-Sharks dotted the roster, too, including Sandis Ozolinsh, Jeff Odgers, and Shean Donovan. Mike Ricci, a former Av, was on the Sharks' side.

Colorado was set to host Game 1 of the best-of-seven West quarterfinal series. At midday on April 20, 1999, the team was using the Avalanche-provided practice rink in the Denver suburb of Littleton, Colorado.

There was a lot of media watching the practice, getting tape for their telecasts and waiting to interview the Sharks to preview the series. This was before cell phones were everywhere. If the office wanted to get a hold of a writer, sportscaster, or camera operator, they sent an electronic message to a beeper or pager. At mid-day, all the pagers went off at once. That was strange.

That's when we learned that two heavily armed students killed 12 classmates and one teacher at Columbine High School before turning the weapons on themselves. Columbine was not far from the practice rink.

The team went to bed that night not knowing if the series would start the following night, but I knew it wouldn't. Even the morning skates were held, though, before the league announced the start of the series was going to be delayed, and the first two games moved to San Jose.

"If this series goes seven [games], you know there will be four games in five days," Commissioner Gary Bettman announced at the time. "But it was more important, we thought, to slow down the schedule and to move it out to San Jose."

The opener was played on April 24, and the Avs managed a 3–1 victory. They would win two nights later, too, 2–1, before the scene shifted back to their somber home one week after the tragedy. After a day of travel, the Sharks got two goals from Marco Sturm and one apiece from ex-Avs Owen Nolan and Mike Ricci to win Game 3, 4–2.

The off day before Game 4 turned out to be a most poignant moment in Sharks playoff history. And it happened nowhere near a hockey rink. Veteran forward Joe Murphy and seven Sharks teammates took a 20-minute drive into the heart of the Littleton community's devastation to pay respects.

The players placed a 50-foot banner on a chain-link fence surrounding the tennis courts adjacent to Columbine High School. It read, "Our hearts and our prayers are with you." The sign had thousands of signatures of well-wishing fans who attended the first two games in San Jose. And the Sharks Foundation added $10,000 to the $6,000 in donations collected by fans in San Jose.

"Sports are a very minute part of our society," Sharks goalie Mike Vernon said at the time. "This hits too close to home for me. I can't imagine what it's like for the people involved. It's going to affect this community for a long, long time."

The upstart Sharks made a series of it by winning Game 4, 7–3, as Vincent Damphousse scored a Sharks playoff record two short-handed goals and five other skaters added one tally apiece. The Sharks, who chased Roy, knotted the series, 2–2, but remained in Denver with a quick turnaround for Game 5 in Denver the next night.

The Avalanche turned the tables on San Jose by scoring the first five goals to take an insurmountable lead into the third. All of their big stars did the damage as Colorado had goals from Forsberg, Sakic, Lemieux, Deadmarsh, and Fleury (again), who added a second marker in the third as the hosts ran away, 6–2.

The sixth game was back in San Jose, and this one was much tighter. Bill Houlder and Jeff Friesen answered Fleury's game-opening goal, but Ozolinsh got his ex-mates with a tying tally late in the second period. After a scoreless third, Milan Hejduk ended it with his second OT goal of the emotional series at 13:12 of sudden death.

"We feel good about the way we played," Damphousse said at the time. "If we didn't give it our best, then I would be ticked off. We gave it everything we had. Overtime can go either way."

What became abundantly clear as the Sharks approached the end of their first decade in the NHL was that nothing came easy in this league. San Jose GM Dean Lombardi was sticking to a plan that centered around placing character veterans, who had a winning pedigree, around a young core of drafted prospects that would eventually accept the mantle of winning.

The Sharks learned there are no shortcuts to success. Yes, the early franchise playoff upsets definitely provided a spark, but it would continue to be a slow and steady climb. Every spring it seemed the Sharks were always lining up against a first-round opponent that appeared to be a prohibitive favorite, at least on paper.

There was no better example of this than when the eighth-place Sharks went up against the West's top seeds—and Presidents' Trophy winners with 114 points—the St. Louis Blues in the spring of 2000. Coach Joel Quenneville, who not much later would win three Cups in Chicago, led the Blues to a 51–19–11–1 record (the fourth number represents points earned during an overtime loss).

St. Louis was extremely stingy on defense. The Blues allowed a league-low 165 goals. Only four other teams permitted fewer than 200 goals that season. Dallas was the only other one in the West, and the Stars allowed 19 more than the Blues. At the head of that defense was a 25-year-old cornerstone on the St. Louis blue line by the name of Chris Pronger.

Pronger and the Sharks already had a history going back to Pronger's draft year of 1993. San Jose was in possession of the No. 2 overall pick. Forward Alexandre Daigle went No. 1, as expected, to the Ottawa Senators. Speculation was the Sharks would select Pronger, a 6-foot-6 native of Dryden, Ontario, who starred in junior hockey for Peterborough of the Ontario Hockey League.

Instead, San Jose surprised the draft pundits by dealing the second pick to Hartford in exchange for the Whalers' sixth overall pick, their third-round selection, a second-rounder previously acquired from Toronto, and veteran Sergei Makarov. The Sharks used the three draft picks to take, in order, center Viktor Kozlov, defenseman Vlastimil Kroupa, and winger Ville Peltonen. Pronger played two seasons in Hartford before getting traded to the Blues in exchange for Brendan Shanahan.

Established as one of the most dominant prime-age rear guards in the game, Pronger won the Hart Trophy during a season in which Pittsburgh's Jaromir Jagr took the Art Ross with 96 points and Florida's Pavel Bure captured the Rocket Richard with 58 goals. Pronger had a modest 62 points but boasted a plus-52 defensive rating in addition to leading the league in average ice time with 30:14. He was also the Norris Trophy winner that season.

The Sharks, who managed their first winning record (35–30–10–7) in a ninth year of existence, had their hands full. The Blues were not led only by Pronger, but standout players including Pierre Turgeon, Pavol Demitra, Scott Young, Al MacInnis, and Michal Handzus dotted the roster as well.

The Blues were a confident bunch. Marc Bergevin, Craig Conroy, Jamal Mayers, Marty Reasoner, Jamie McLennan, and Handzus all bleached or streaked their hair or eyebrows blond before the start of the series. In the press box before the first puck was dropped, a beat writer for the Blues was asked why he was working alone. He answered, "I'll get more help by the third round."

The Blues' prowess was convincing after a 5–3 victory in Game 1. But funny things happen in the playoffs. Bergevin was struck in the stomach by an intended shot by Sharks defenseman Gary Suter early in Game 2. The Blues defenseman gloved the puck and tried to throw it into the corner. Instead, he accidentally deflected the puck right into the Blues' net for an own goal. And San Jose went on to win Game 2, 4–2.

The fans in San Jose were ready to jeer the confident Blues, and Pronger became their new target. First there was Theoren Fleury, then Ed Belfour. Sharks supporters were clearly now focused on Chris Pronger as the new villain.

San Jose captain Owen Nolan, who had a big moment coming later in the series, scored twice, and the Sharks won Game 3, 2–1. Pronger went to the penalty box three times with minors. When

Gary Suter scored a tie-breaking goal in the third period of Game 4 for a 3–2 win, the Sharks were on the verge of upset and were now up 3–1 in the series.

The Blues returned home to win Game 5, 5–3, and came back to San Jose to spoil the Sharks fans' party with a 6–2 win in Game 6 thanks to Scott Young's hat trick. Pronger enjoyed his most productive game of the series with a goal and an assist and finishing with a plus-3. It was back to the Gateway City for a winner-take-all Game 7.

The Sharks broke on top when grinding winger Ronnie Stern put a backhand shot past struggling Blues goalie Roman Turek just 2:51 after the opening faceoff. The real backbreaker came, however, in the closing seconds of the period. That's when Nolan simply threw a puck from center ice toward the net as he was on his way for a change.

The rising slap shot caught Turek off guard, and when it deflected off his right catching glove to hit the back of the net, the Sharks had a 2–0 lead. The building fell silent. And seconds later the Blues were booed off the ice at the first intermission.

"I didn't even see what happened," Nolan confessed later. "I just shot it and turned to the bench."

Jeff Friesen scored and it was 3–0. Young trimmed the deficit back to two with a series co-leading sixth goal (with Nolan). And Owen would have one last defining moment in the series. Defending a two-man Blues advantage on a late-game power play, Nolan laid out to block a rocket shot by MacInnis, reputed to have the hardest slap shot in the league.

"Those types of plays are bigger than people think," Nolan's teammate Mike Ricci said later. "Owen showed a lot of courage."

Not to be lost in the incredible upset was the steady work of goalie Steve Shields, who faced media scrutiny before Game 7 after his subpar outing in Game 6. Darryl Sutter didn't hesitate to go right back to Shields, who rewarded his coach's choice with 21 stops. Shields played as close to a perfect game as a goaltender could. Some of it was predicated on how the defense was designed, and he didn't steal the game by himself, but he was a huge contributor in that series.

"I'm pretty damn proud of these guys," Lombardi said at the time. "In the three stages of development, there's hope, think, and know. This team knew they could win. That's a big difference from hoping or thinking."

Besides Nolan and Shields, the Sharks got contributions from unsung heroes such as Dave Lowry, Stephane Matteau, Mike Rathje, and Ron Stern throughout. And Pronger's numbers in the Blues' four losses were no goals, three assists, a minus-4, and 22 minutes in penalties.

"They withstood all the Chicken Littles who said they couldn't," Sutter said at the time. "It should have been a seven-game series, and the right team won."

Unfortunately the Sharks didn't have a lot left—emotionally or physically—for Round 2. It started three days later in Dallas against a Stars team that won the Pacific Division with 102 points and steamrolled Edmonton in five games of the first round.

Defending Cup champs en route to another trip to the Final where they would lose in six games to New Jersey, the Stars outclassed San Jose. Dallas won the first two games, each in shutout fashion as Belfour was asked to make only a combined 37 saves. The Sharks gutted out a 2–1 win in Game 3 when Nolan's tie-breaking seventh goal of the postseason stood as the winner.

But Dallas's big guns carried the Stars during a 5–4 Game 4 win on the road—Joe Nieuwendyk scored two goals along with Mike Modano, Sergei Zubov, and Guy Carbonneau adding one apiece. And the favorites returned home to close out the Sharks with a 4–1 win in Game 5.

The 2000s

In 2000–01, their 10th year in the league, the Sharks were moving up in the standings. The upward ascent began with a hot start, something San Jose had never experienced before. After dropping the home and season opener to St. Louis, 4–1, the Sharks rebounded to earn points in all but five of their next 30 games to stand 21–6–4 just days before Christmas.

In the 1999–00 season, Owen Nolan led the Sharks with 44 goals and 84 points. One year later, San Jose featured a more balanced attack. Nolan, who was beset with an abdominal injury and short suspension that limited him to 57 games, finished along with Niklas Sundstrom as the team's second-leading scorer. Their 49 points apiece trailed Patrick Marleau, who was tops on the team with 25 goals and 52 points.

Forwards Vincent Damphousse, Mike Ricci, Scott Thornton, Jeff Friesen, Stephane Matteau, Marco Sturm, and Alexander Korolyuk all contributed while Gary Suter led the way from the blue line. The Sharks were a nice mix of young and mid-age regulars who were playing Darryl Sutter's system to perfection.

Damphousse scored his 1,000th point, Suter played in his 1,000th game, and the Sharks struck a significant deal to land Teemu Selanne from Anaheim in exchange for Friesen and backup goalie Steve Shields. That was a late-season deal that happened at the deadline. Starting goalie Evgeni Nabokov was well on his way to winning the Calder Trophy as the league's top rookie.

San Jose eventually surrendered its hold on first place in the Pacific to a strong Dallas team when the Sharks suffered two late-season, five-game losing streaks. Still, San Jose's 40–27–12–3 record for 95 points was a franchise best, and the Sharks finished second to the Stars to earn the No. 5 seed in the West. Division winners Detroit, Colorado, and Central runner-up St. Louis all placed ahead of San Jose by earning more than 100 points each.

The first round was set, and for the Sharks and Blues it meant a rematch of the first-round series the spring before. That was fresh in the minds of everyone in St. Louis, much the same as Detroit in 1995 had not forgotten what San Jose did to them in '94.

Not only did the Blues have revenge on their mind, they were also embarking on their 22nd straight spring of qualifying for the Stanley Cup playoffs—a streak that would extend to 25 years in a row before getting snapped in 2006. And St. Louis was still longing to return to the Final it not had been a part of since 1970, when Bobby Orr's famous goal that he scored before he took flight in front of the Blues' net enabled the Boston Bruins to win the Cup.

While the 2000–01 Blues weren't quite the Presidents' Trophy team of the year before, they felt the shock of losing would lead to a better focus coming into a new playoff season. St. Louis coach Joel Quenneville noted the most obvious difference right off the bat by saying, "That was nice to see, no more blond hair."

Yes, these Blues were taking the Sharks much more seriously this time around.

The series started just like it had the year before. St. Louis grabbed Game 1 by two goals in a home game, and the Sharks responded with a victory in Game 2. Pierre Turgeon, Scott Young, and Al MacInnis staked the hosts to a 3–0 lead by the midway point of the third period in the opener before Patrick Marleau was the lone Shark to slip a puck past Roman Turek.

Two nights later, San Jose responded to the 3–1 loss to win Game 2, a tight-checking affair, by the slimmest of margins and the smallest of scores. Scott Thornton broke through at 13:52 of the middle period against Turek, who faced only 19 shots in the game. Nabokov was stellar, turning away all 28 shots by the Blues, who went 0-for-4 on the power play.

The scene shifted to San Jose, and St. Louis grabbed the upper hand again with a six-goal explosion in Game 3. Dallas Drake scored a pair while four other Blues added one each in the 6–3 win. Nabokov was replaced at the start of the third period by backup Miikka Kiprusoff after stopping only 16 of 21 shots.

And Kipper's strong third period convinced Sutter he should try to keep it rolling in Game 4, and the Finnish netminder did exactly that. Kiprusoff was outstanding in stopping 39 of 41 shots while Damphousse, Thornton, and Nolan scored goals in a nail-biting 3–2 win for the Sharks to even the series at two wins apiece.

With only five games of regular-season experience with the Sharks that season, the 24-year-old Kiprusoff was called upon again to play the all-pivotal Game 5 on enemy ice. Scott Young, a real pain in the Sharks' side in those years, gave the Blues a 1–0 lead early. But Stephane Matteau answered within two minutes. And, on the strength of a Marleau goal 11:56 into the second, the Sharks led 2–1 after 40 minutes.

San Jose nursed the one-goal edge for most of the final period until Dallas Drake beat Kiprusoff at 17:12 for the final goal of regulation. And the only game that required sudden death in the series wouldn't go San Jose's way, thanks to a fluke ending.

With the teams lined up for a draw in the circle to the right of Kiprusoff, and faceoff ace Mike Ricci going against Turgeon, something odd happened. The linesman dropped the puck right on the shaft of Ricci's stick. Usually, once that happens, although it's rare, the play is blown dead and there's a re-drop. This time, however, that was not the case.

Turgeon took advantage of the fortuitous bounce to win the draw back to the left point where defensive-minded rookie rear guard Bryce Salvador stepped into a slap shot that just eluded the left catching glove of Kiprusoff, who was down low on the ice having done the splits at 9:54 of overtime. How much of an offensive threat was Bryce Salvador? He scored all of two goals in 75 games during the regular season, and that was his first of the playoffs.

Feeling a bit snakebit, the Sharks hoped to regroup in Game 6 at home to try and force another Game 7 in St. Louis. With Nabokov back in goal, the Blues broke open a scoreless game with strikes from Cory Stillman and Pavol Demitra within 52 seconds of the late second period. San Jose could muster only a Brad Stuart goal at 12:31 of the third and saw its season end with a 2–1 loss.

Despite the first-round ouster the previous spring, the Sharks felt like they were a team on the rise. They went into 2001–02 with a healthy Owen Nolan, with late-season acquisition Teemu Selanne in the fold for an entire year, and with the addition of gritty vet Adam Graves and the excellent goaltending combo of Nabokov and Kiprusoff. Vesa Toskala was waiting in the wings should either falter.

San Jose got off to a strong start for the second straight season as they were 18–7–5–3 a week before Christmas. Unlike the year before when the Sharks stumbled in the second half, they were consistent to the finish and were rewarded with their franchise-first Pacific Division crown. San Jose went 44–27–8–3, good for 99 points, to outdistance the Phoenix Coyotes and Los Angeles Kings, who finished with 95 points apiece.

Holding the No. 3 seed in the West also meant the Sharks were going to have home-ice advantage in the postseason for the first time in 10 playoff series. And they took full advantage of that.

The Coyotes were six years removed following relocation from Winnipeg, and they were still more than a year away from moving out of downtown Phoenix into a new arena being constructed in the western suburb of Glendale. And much like when the Avalanche moved from Quebec to Denver, the 'Yotes had a pretty darn good team early on in the Valley of the Sun with Keith Tkachuk, Jeremy Roenick, Mike Gartner, Oleg Tverdovsky, Craig Janney, Cliff Ronning, and Nikolai Khabibulin on the roster.

But this Phoenix team was in transition. There were recognizable veterans such as defenseman Teppo Numminen, agitator Claude Lemieux, rugged Brad May, and top goalie Sean Burke. The Coyotes were also looking for 25-and-under star forwards Shane Doan, Daniel Briere, Michal Handzus, Ladislav Nagy, and defenseman Danny Markov to take the reins.

The Sharks did what hosts are expected to do—they won Game 1. Damphousse opened the scoring with a power play goal in the first, and Marleau broke a 1–1 tie early in the second for a 2–1 victory. Nabokov made 21 saves, and San Jose felt pretty good about its start.

After two idle nights, the Coyotes gave a much better effort in Game 2. Daymond Langkow and Briere scored, and the visitors led 2–0 until Marco Sturm tallied at 14:19 of the third. But when Doan answered just 40 seconds later, the Sharks' doom was sealed in a 3–1 loss as suddenly the series was headed for the desert where the Coyotes would have the home-ice edge.

And when Doan opened the scoring at 1:06 of the first and the hosts had a 1–0 lead after 20 minutes, the Sharks faced their first taste of adversity in the series. Marleau and Graves scored in the second. Scott Thornton and Ricci scored in the third—with each providing a primary assist on the other's goal—as San Jose took home ice right back with a 4–1 win.

A pair of Mikes—first Rathje followed by Ricci—scored in the first period and Nabokov stopped 29 of 30 shots as the Sharks seized command of the series with a 2–1 win in Game 4. San Jose didn't fool around in Game 5, scoring twice in the first and twice in the third after Phoenix cut the margin to a goal. The 4–1 victory matched the series' tally, too. The Sharks were moving on to face a solid Colorado team that needed seven games to eliminate the Los Angeles Kings in Round 1.

The Avalanche were winners of the Northwest Division with the same number of points (99) as the Sharks had to win the Pacific. And while San Jose was more potent with a 248–212 edge in regular-season goals, Colorado was stingier on defense, having allowed 30 fewer goals (169 versus 199). The Avs' goals-against total was best in the league by far, which would come into play in this series.

It took a while for the series to take on a defensive posture, however. The Sharks jumped out with a 6–3 win in Game 1 on the road. Selanne potted a pair and enjoyed a three-point night against Patrick Roy & Co. But the Avs came back to blitz the Sharks 8–2 in Game 2. Nabokov surrendered eight goals on 28 shots. Defenseman Rob Blake, a future Sharks captain, scored the first two for Colorado, which ran its lead to 5–0 by late in the second period.

The teams combined for 10 goals again in Game 3, but two from Nolan led the Sharks to a 6–4 win and 2–1 series lead. Just when everyone wondered when Roy or Nabokov might get hot, the Avs knotted the series with a 4–1 road win in Game 4.

The back-and-forth theme of the series continued in pivotal Game 5 as the Sharks went on the road and surprised the Avalanche, 5–3. Colorado led 2–1 and 3–2, but goals from Ricci, Selanne, and Nolan in the third period sent San Jose home with a golden opportunity to win and advance.

That's when the series finally took a turn for the defensive. A scoreless first period preceded the teams trading their only goals in regulation scored just 24 seconds apart in the middle period— Marcus Ragnarsson for the Sharks followed by Steve Reinprecht for the Avs. Then Peter Forsberg struck with an OT winner 2:47 into sudden death with assists to Joe Sakic and Milan Hejduk.

The fact that a world-class player like Forsberg came through to knot the series and force a Game 7 might not have surprised a lot of people. But few might remember what Forsberg went through that season. He didn't appear at all for the Avs as he took the entire regular season off under doctor's advice after having his spleen removed halfway through the previous postseason when the Avs went on to win a Stanley Cup without him. Amazingly, Forsberg would lead all playoff scorers in 2002 with 27 points.

The Sharks have played in a number of Game 7s, and they're always special. This one, however, ranks right on top as the biggest disappointment for the San Jose faithful. The focal point involved Selanne missing a gaping, wide-open net.

Nabokov and Roy matched each other save for save until Forsberg scored his sixth goal of the series and seventh of the playoffs at 17:50 of the second period. It was an even-strength goal with assists going to Alex Tanguay and Greg de Vries. The Sharks pushed and pushed throughout the third period, and even earned a late power play when Blake went off for a trip with 56 seconds left. Try as they might, the Sharks could not score a tying goal. Roy finished with 27 saves, a shutout, and a hard-earned series win.

Now back to that Selanne miss. Racing in to the goalie's right less than five minutes into the first period, Selanne picked up a loose puck a prone Roy couldn't freeze because he had slid well out of his net. Selanne continued behind the goal in a (Finnish) flash and, with the puck on his backhand, came out front only to send his attempt all the way across the goal line instead of a sure-fire slam dunk goal and an early 1–0 Sharks lead. Instead, the puck rolled right to Roy, who, from his knees and just outside the opposite post, froze the puck.

Selanne stopped in bewilderment. He looked at the open net, looked at Roy, and then glanced at referee Kerry Fraser, who had both hands in the air to signal the stoppage in play. Both Selanne and Fraser seemed to share a smile of disbelief. Selanne had a great series up to that point with five goals and six points. But Sharks fans will always remember the series for Selanne missing an incredible opportunity.

That was a very good San Jose team, and while the mighty Detroit Red Wings lurked in the next round, I thought the Sharks had a good chance to reach their first Stanley Cup Final with that group. Right up until the final horn I felt like they were going to tie Colorado and find a way to win. It was a disappointing finish.

And, as it turned out, that's where Darryl Sutter's team peaked.

The Sharks got off to a slow start the following season of 2002–03. And, a bit surprising, Darryl was let go at the start of December as the team sat 8–12–2–2. The Sharks had new ownership, and the feeling was more change could be coming.

Change *was* coming. After Ron Wilson was hired to replace Sutter, the next big move came at the trade deadline when, with San Jose out of playoff contention, captain Owen Nolan was moved to Toronto. A couple days later Dean Lombardi was dismissed.

The team of Lombardi and Sutter did a tremendous job pointing the Sharks in the right direction. It was now time for Doug Wilson to step in, pick up the momentum, and accelerate the overall level. That's exactly what happened, and the Sharks have not looked back since.

It took until the holiday season for the Sharks to climb over .500 and find their way. They were getting used to Ron Wilson, and the coach who got a four-month head start with his hiring in midseason the year before was getting used to his roster. San Jose just kept getting better and better as the season progressed until they finished with a 43–21–12–6 mark, good for a second Pacific Division title and a franchise-record 104 points.

That good feeling followed the Sharks right into the opening round of the playoffs when they hosted their longtime nemesis, the St. Louis Blues. San Jose had its way with St. Louis, winning the series in five games. The Sharks jumped out with a 2–0 lead on home ice after 1–0 and 3–1 victories in the first two games, respectively.

St. Louis rallied for a 4–1 home-ice win in Game 3, but San Jose took command of the series when Alexander Korolyuk scored two goals including the game-winner in the third period for a 4–3 triumph. The series was clinched two nights later in San Jose when Mike Ricci, Mark Smith, and Brad Stuart scored while Nabokov made 21 saves in a 3–1 win.

The series may have been over, but the drama was just starting for the eliminated Blues. While the losing team boarded a charter the next day to return to St. Louis, fourth-line center Mike Danton attempted to make other arrangements. However, he never made it out of the Bay Area. Police arrested Danton and charged the 23-year-old with conspiracy to commit murder.

In the days and weeks that followed, details emerged of Danton's plan to hire a hitman to murder his agent. Danton's agent had a controlling relationship over him and had coached him in junior hockey. Danton, whose birth name was Jefferson, was estranged from his family. Danton pled guilty to the charge and later claimed his original target was not the agent, but rather his estranged father. Danton spent five years in prison. It was a bizarre story to say the least.

For the advancing Sharks, the second-round series was set against Colorado, a team that also eliminated its first-round foe (Dallas) in five games. Memories of the heartbreaking seven-game loss to the Avalanche in 2001–02 were still fresh in the minds of many Sharks who were part of that playoff run as well. The Avs were stinging from a playoff disappointment since they lost a seven-game first-round series the previous spring against Minnesota while the Sharks were sitting that one out.

With the experience of winning two Cups since 1996, the Avs may have been more familiar with what it takes to reach the third round. But the Sharks were the team who executed, at least at the outset of the second-round series.

Just like the previous series against St. Louis, the Sharks held firm on home ice by winning each of the first two games, 5–2 and 4–1. Patrick Marleau notched his first career playoff hat trick in the opener. And he scored again along with Vincent Damphousse, Jonathan Cheechoo, and Wayne Primeau in Game 2. The pressure was on host Colorado in Game 3, but when Damphousse broke through with the game's only goal 8:59 into the third period, it was the Sharks who held a 3–0 lead in a playoff series for the first time.

Colorado stayed alive—just barely—when Joe Sakic scored 5:15 into sudden death of what was a scoreless Game 4 through regulation. San Jose's Nabokov and David Aebischer of the Avs were hooked into a great goaltender's duel that saw Colorado get the better of the shots, 36–27.

San Jose's hopes of ending a second straight series in five games were dashed at home when Joe Sakic—again—tied Game 5, 1–1, with a goal 9:50 into the third period, and he struck again just 1:54 into sudden death to send the series back to Denver. That was consecutive overtime goals for Sakic against Nabokov, who faced only 18 shots in Game 5. The Sharks needed to regroup or face the prospect of hosting a Game 7 after surrendering a 3–0 series lead.

As it turned out, they didn't have to worry about a winner-take-all deciding game. Instead, the Sharks quieted the ravenous Avalanche crowd at the outset of Game 6 by holding the puck in the hosts' zone the entire opening two minutes. San Jose didn't finally break through until early in the second period, when its territorial dominance led to rediscovering what worked earlier in the series. Damphousse, Marcel Goc, and Cheechoo all scored within less than 11 minutes of the middle period, and the Sharks cruised to a 3–1 series-ending triumph.

This meant a first-ever trip to the West Finals. It was history in the making for the city of San Jose.

The opponent was the Calgary Flames, who'd had a pretty taxing first two rounds. They beat Vancouver in a series that went seven games at the outset, and they were coming off a six-game set against the Presidents' Trophy–winning Detroit Red Wings in the second round. But that's not what made this Flames-Sharks matchup intriguing.

Behind the Calgary bench stood Darryl Sutter, the recent ex-Sharks coach who the Flames hired four weeks after he was let go in San Jose in 2002. Sutter added the title as the team's general manager, too, in 2003. Wearing both hats, Sutter guided the Flames back into the playoffs for the first time in eight seasons.

And that's not all. Calgary rested its goaltending hopes on Miikka Kiprusoff, who the Flames acquired from San Jose earlier in the same season. Kiprusoff was off to a bad start in San Jose when given a chance to win the job early on. The Sharks had three goalies on the roster—Kiprusoff, along with Evgeni Nabokov and Vesa Toskala. One would have to go. When Doug Wilson dealt Kiprusoff to Calgary in mid-November of 2003 for a second-round draft choice, it represented the first deal the new GM swung that included a player on the roster.

Wilson had no idea what might happen by year's end. Then again, that second-round pick turned into San Jose drafting future defensive star Marc-Edouard Vlasic, so that's a deal the Sharks would make over and again.

The Sharks had home ice at the outset for a third straight series, but they couldn't get out front on the Flames like they had against the Blues and Avalanche. The Flames got goals from unlikely sources—a pair from Craig Conroy and one from Krzysztof Oliwa in regulation—and an OT winner from defensive-minded Steve Montador to win Game 1, 4–3. They won Game 2, 4–1, as Kiprusoff got the leg up on Nabokov in a goaltending duel between good friends.

The Sharks needed to rebound quickly, and they'd have to do it inside Calgary's red-splashed Saddledome, where the home crowd was in full-throat support of their focused Flames. Nabokov was stellar in Game 3 in turning away all 34 shots, while Korolyuk scored two goals and assisted another for a 3–0 win. It was more of the same in Game 4 as goals by Rathje, Cheechoo, Damphousse, and Marleau eventually chased Kiprusoff and allowed the Sharks to even the series with a 4–2 win.

The scene was set for a pivotal Game 5 in San Jose. The Sharks knew the importance of using home ice to their advantage. A victory would bring San Jose to within one more win of their first Stanley Cup Final and put reeling Calgary on its heels.

And then the Sharks laid an egg.

I would put that Game 5 right up there with the worst playoff games the Sharks ever played. I believe, if I had to pick one, that *was* the worst playoff game they ever played. San Jose was lethargic. The Sharks had nothing left, and it was obvious. All the odd-numbered games in a series are important. And Calgary won every Game 5 on the road of all four series they played that postseason. Amazing.

Flames leader Jarome Iginla and Marcus Nilson scored in the first period. Conroy added a third tally past the midway point of the second. Playing from behind, the Sharks could muster only a game-total of 19 shots on Kiprusoff. The fans, who were so excited at the outset, had to leave feeling so disappointed.

Two nights later, and back in Calgary, the Flames finally won on home ice. They jumped out 2–0. The Sharks got a goal from Alyn McCauley late in the second. San Jose pressed for a tying goal in the third that never came. Finally, Robyn Regehr clinched it with an empty-netter. The 3–1 win sent Calgary on to a Stanley Cup Final it would lose in seven games against Tampa Bay. The Lightning rallied from a 3–2 series deficit to capture their first Cup, with future Shark Dan Boyle playing a significant role for the winning side.

Looking back at that series, the Flames simply shut the Sharks down. It was a six-game series—with one overtime game that was essentially four periods of hockey—but San Jose generated very little in terms of offense.

The team's leading scorers in the series, Alexander Korolyuk and Mike Rathje, had only four points apiece. Marleau was held to one goal and two points. Jonathan Cheechoo and Mike Ricci scored one goal apiece. Scott Thornton did not score a goal. His only point in the six games was an assist.

Unfortunately, the Sharks had to sit on that tough playoff exit for a lot longer than they expected. The 2004–05 campaign was a wash when owners and players couldn't land a new collective-bargaining agreement in time to save even half a season. The owners eventually convinced the players to accept a new salary-cap system in time for a full 2005–06 season that also featured a serious crackdown on hooking and holding as a way to defend.

When San Jose's modest 8–5–1 start took a disastrous turn with a 10-game losing streak (three by shootouts), Doug Wilson pulled off the biggest trade of his GM tenure to acquire Joe Thornton from the Boston Bruins. Jumbo stepped in to not only feed Jonathan Cheechoo all the way to a 56-goal, Rocket Richard–winning season, but Thornton himself became the first player in league history to win an Art Ross scoring title (125 points on the strength of 96 assists) while splitting his season between two teams.

The individual honors were nice, and the Sharks were excited to jell, as they finished 44–27–11 with 99 points to wind up in second place behind the Pacific Division's runaway winner, the Dallas Stars (112 points). San Jose would start on the road at Nashville as the upstart Predators earned a franchise-best 106 points in their seventh season of existence. Nashville had been to the playoffs once, but lost a six-game set against Detroit in 2003–04.

Nashville made San Jose pay for its trips to the penalty box in Game 1 by converting on the power play four times. Adam Hall had the Preds' last man–advantage strike at 12:06 of the third period to snap a 3–3 tie and send the hosts on to a 4–3 victory. If the Sharks had stopped parading to the box, they could have given themselves a much better chance.

The tables turned even if San Jose still struggled to avoid handing the Predators power play after power play. Jonathan Cheechoo, Patrick Marleau, and Mark Smith all scored with the man-advantage while goalie Vesa Toskala made 25 saves during a 3–0 win in Game 2. While San Jose was 3-for-10 on the power play, the Sharks had to be stout on the penalty kill to help Toskala.

And they were as Nashville failed on all nine of its power-play chances.

As the series shifted to San Jose, the Predators learned they had no answer for Patrick Marleau. San Jose's swift center scored his second and third goals of the series during a 4–1 win in Game 3. Then he notched a second career playoff hat trick with three more, including the game-winner, in Game 4. Back in Nashville, Marleau scored a second straight winner as the Sharks closed out the Preds by winning the last four games of the series.

Marleau finished with a team-leading seven goals and eight points. Defensemen Tom Preissing (6) and Christian Ehrhoff (5) combined for 11 assists from the blue line while Toskala posted a .927 save percentage and solid 2.01 goals-against average. The Preds got five goals and seven points from Paul Kariya, but the skilled winger didn't get enough help to make it a longer series.

San Jose was moving on to face an Edmonton team that disposed of Detroit in six games in the opening round. The Oilers were the eighth seeds in the West, so the Sharks were hoping that they could play the game their way on home ice and land a second straight appearance in the West Finals.

The Sharks got off to a great start in that pursuit as they won Games 1 and 2 on consecutive nights by identical scores of 2–1. Marleau continued his hot hand to score San Jose's first goal in the opener, and he provided the primary assist on Ehrhoff's eventual game-winner scored at 3:14 of the middle period in Game 1. Joe Thornton's power-play goal late in the second period of Game 2 broke a 1–1 tie.

Even though the Sharks got the sweep they wanted at home, Edmonton planted a seed when series villain Raffi Torres delivered a tough hit to Milan Michalek in the neutral zone late in the second period, knocking the rookie winger out of the game and eliciting absolutely no response from the hosts. That was a bit puzzling.

Seemingly undeterred, San Jose went into Game 3 at Edmonton riding a six-game playoff winning streak. And, after getting goals from Marleau and Patrick Rissmiller, the visitors had visions of going up 3–0. Even when Torres tied the game 2–2 late in the third, San Jose was still just one goal away in sudden death from taking complete command.

Overtime period one passed. Overtime period two passed. Oilers goalie Dwayne Roloson made a couple acrobatic stops, one in particular against Cheechoo, to keep the game going.

Finally, at 2:24 of a third sudden death period, Edmonton's Shawn Horcoff punched home a short rebound in front of Toskala following an Oilers cycle off a Sharks turnover, and the hosts had life. That's the game where the momentum shifted. That was a devastating loss for the Sharks, who still were in no mood to seek retribution on Torres taking liberties in Game 2.

The feisty Oilers would knot the series by scoring three unanswered goals in the third period of Game 4 for a 6–3 win. The Sharks appeared as if they'd lost some life. They were getting physically outplayed. They did not look like the same team at the outset of the series. Was it Raffi's hit? Was it their lack of a response?

The scene shifted back to San Jose, but the results were the same. Edmonton steamrolled in a pivotal Game 5 by a 6–3 score again. And, yet again, it was three unanswered goals in the final 16 minutes of regulation that did in the Sharks. After that, the team had a hard time feeling positive they could win a Game 6 on the road to force the series back to San Jose.

Even with two idle nights before Game 6, the Sharks had nothing left. Michael Peca scored in the first, and Horcoff struck midway through the second. That was more offense than Edmonton's Roloson would need. He stopped all 24 of San Jose's shots, and the Oilers marched on with a 2–0 victory. Their impressive run continued all the way to Game 7 of the Stanley Cup Final in Carolina where the Hurricanes won the Cup.

Along with reaching the postseason in seven of the previous eight seasons, the Sharks had clearly entered a new era for the franchise. No longer did the "expansion" label apply. It no longer felt as if San Jose were an underdog. Expectations had risen to the level where the playoff ousters started to sting a bit more.

San Jose approached the 2006–07 campaign knowing they had Joe Thornton for a full season, and the roster was stocked with a nice blend of prime-age, skill players and veterans with something still to give.

The Sharks waged a season-long divisional battle with both Anaheim and Dallas. The Ducks finished first with 110 points to edge the Sharks and Stars, who piled up 107 points apiece. San Jose was second by virtue of winning one more game than Dallas (51–50). It marked the first time three teams eclipsed the 100-point mark since the formation of the Pacific Division in 1993–94. Even two teams cresting 100 points in the Pacific had not happened previously.

The Sharks were now facing former teammate Teemu Selanne as a familiar opponent. He departed from San Jose via free agency in the summer of 2003 to join Colorado. After undergoing surgery and rehabbing during the season lost to the work stoppage, Selanne resurfaced almost as good as new with the Ducks. He had a great year in 2006–07 with Anaheim, leading the Ducks with 48 goals and 94 points.

Dallas had transitioned from the team that played in back-to-back Cup Finals in 1999 (won) and 2000 (lost). Mike Modano was 36 years old now, and holding his own along with other over-32 vets Sergei Zubov, Jere Lehtinen, Eric Lindros, Stu Barnes, Darryl Sydor, and Philippe Boucher. The Stars were stingy on defense with Marty Turco minding the net.

The Sharks figured they'd run into one of those Pacific Division foes in the postseason, and were looking forward to that, but they initially drew the Nashville Predators in the first round for the second straight spring. The Preds enjoyed a fine regular season as well, topping their previous franchise high in points of 106 in 2005–06 with 110 in 2006–07. San Jose and Nashville were two of seven teams in the West that earned more than 100 points. Only eighth-seed Calgary (with 96) fell short.

The Sharks-Predators series started off with a bang. Four different goal scorers staked the visitors to a 4–2 lead after 40 minutes, but the hosts struck back with a pair in the first to send Game 1 into sudden death. There, a tall winger by the name of Patrick Rissmiller beat Preds goalie Tomas Vokoun at 8:14 of the second overtime to give the Sharks a 5–4 win. Typical of the kind of player who is a hero in the postseason, Rissmiller scored 18 goals in 180 regular-season games over his four years in San Jose. It was a great moment.

Determined to not fall into an 0–2 hole, Nashville received two goals each from Peter Forsberg and J.P. Dumont and rallied from an early 1–0 deficit to win Game 2 going away, 5–2.

Home ice proved the perfect tonic for the Sharks to take command over the Preds for a second straight postseason. Milan Michalek and Ryane Clowe scored their second goals of the series in the second period of Game 3 to erase an early 1–0 deficit. Patrick Marleau got on the board for the first time in the third, and San Jose had a 3–1 victory. Two nights later Michalek scored twice, and Joe Pavelski collected his first career postseason goal as San Jose took a 3–1 series lead with a 3–2 win in Game 4.

Hoping to make it a five-game series win over Nashville for a second straight year, the Sharks did just that in Game 5. Clowe scored the only goal of the opening period. Marleau scored late in the second on the power play after Nashville tallied twice earlier in the period, and Marleau added his second of the game at 15:39, a third goal in the series that proved to be the winner.

Marleau was outstanding for a second straight year against Nashville. He led the team with three goals and six points. Joe Thornton provided six points, all on assists. In addition, Evgeni Nabokov was also very consistent in goal throughout the series. He boasted a 2.39 goals-against average and .902 save percentage.

Setting their sights on Round 2, the Sharks knew that they had beaten a very good team without having to extend to six or seven games. Having dispatched the Predators, they moved on to take on Detroit, the winner of the Central Division with 113 points in the midst of making 25 straight postseason appearances.

This would be the first time the Red Wings and Sharks met in the postseason since San Jose's early foray into the Stanley Cup playoffs. Both teams had completely different personnel. However, Detroit carried quite the playoff mystique considering it had won three Cups between 1997 and 2002, and was considered a threat to win one virtually every spring.

The Sharks marched into Joe Louis Arena, a house of horrors for the franchise during regular-season meetings over the first two decades, and stole Game 1. Matt Carle scored a power-play goal 9:45 into the first period, and Mike Grier added one at even strength 24 seconds later against Dominik Hasek. That 2–0 score held up as the final as Evgeni Nabokov turned away all 34 Detroit shots.

San Jose nursed a 2–1 lead through 40 minutes of Game 2 on the strength of first-period goals from Jonathan Cheechoo and Joe Thornton, but Detroit had just enough firepower to fight back. Daniel Cleary and Pavel Datsyuk scored early and late, respectively, in the third period, and Hasek was asked to make only 17 saves as the Wings earned a split of the first two games at home.

The tight-checking, defensive nature of the series continued in San Jose. There just wasn't much difference between these two talented, playoff-tested teams. A Cheechoo power-play goal 13:19 into the final period snapped a 1–1 tie and sent the Sharks on to a 2–1 win in Game 3.

I'll never forget the feeling I had during the morning skate of Game 4. The mood in the Red Wings' room was surprisingly somber. The team seemed lifeless, the room was quiet, the players were moving slowly. Detroit appeared ripe to be beaten. The Wings looked like their spirits had been broken, and it was up to the Sharks to take advantage.

When Cheechoo scored in the first and Marcel Goc followed with one in the second, the hosts were cruising. Only Tomas

Holmstrom's batted-in power-play goal in the final five seconds of the middle period stood as a blemish on San Jose's effort in Game 4. That is until disaster struck in the final 35 seconds of regulation that gave the Dead Wings renewed life.

When the Sharks surrendered the late game-tying goal to Robert Lang it was a mistake shared by all six Sharks on the ice. Everyone had a hand in letting the late-game lead slip away. San Jose had played nearly the perfect game up to that point. The Sharks knew how much it would mean to put Detroit in a 3–1 hole. No one wanted this to happen, but it did.

First, San Jose's three forwards—Marleau, Rissmiller, and late-season addition Bill Guerin—got caught on the wrong side of the puck in the neutral zone. Rissmiller circled away from Marleau and Guerin, who both unsuccessfully tried to win a battle for the puck on the boards against Valtteri Filppula. And all three forwards were slow in their pursuit of Filppula, who had free entry across the San Jose blue line.

Sharks defenseman Kyle McLaren lunged toward Filppula with his stick, but that only opened an easy passing lane to Lang, who was skating free at the top of the left circle. McLaren's partner Craig Rivet couldn't get in any position for an attempted block as he had drifted too far toward the other side of the slot as Lang had a clear look at the net.

He drew back and let go with a low wrist shot that caught Nabokov a bit deep in the net, and he was fooled by the drive that managed to sneak over his left leg pad and under his catching glove. Nabokov rocked straight back and fell to the ice knowing it was one he'd want back.

Jeremy Roenick celebrates after scoring against the Flames in the second period in Game 7. *(AP Photo/Marcio Jose Sanchez)*

The comeback was completed at 16:04 of overtime when Mathieu Schneider intercepted an attempted clear and beat a screened Nabokov with a high slap shot as the Wings tied the series 2–2.

I remember how disappointed coach Ron Wilson was even the next morning as the team gathered to travel to Detroit. He had pretty much ripped them to the media the night before after the Game 4 meltdown, but he still wasn't done when it came time to board the plane. He was still seething.

Detroit was going to be tough after that. The Wings scored the final four goals of Game 5 after Goc gave the visitors an early 1–0 lead. The 4–1 win put Detroit on the verge of a series win. And that came two nights later back in San Jose when Hasek made 28 saves as the Wings rode ex-Shark Mikael Samuelsson's two first-period goals for a 2–0 clinching win in Game 6.

The playoff loss sat like a sour pill in the pit of the Sharks' stomachs all offseason. And it didn't help that division-rival Anaheim not only knocked off Detroit in the conference final but became the first California-based team to win a Stanley Cup when the Ducks beat the Ottawa Senators in five games.

Instead of feeling sorry for themselves, the Sharks came back in 2007–08 with a vengeance. Their season series against Anaheim was extremely competitive. San Jose won twice in regulation and once in a shootout. The Sharks lost once to the Ducks in regulation, once in overtime, and twice in a shootout. Discounting shootout goals, five of the eight games featured the teams combining for four or fewer goals.

In the end, the Sharks outlasted the Ducks for division supremacy. San Jose finished with a 49–23–10 record and 108 points to Anaheim's 47–27–8 mark good for 102 points. They were joined by Dallas (97 points) again as the three teams from the Pacific to advance to the postseason. And, as No. 2 seeds behind the Presidents' Trophy–winning Detroit Red Wings (115 points), the Sharks drew No. 7 Calgary (94 points) as their first-round opponent.

The Flames could be a pesky bunch. Coached by Mike Keenan, Calgary had a number of familiar faces on its roster. Ex-Shark Miikka Kiprusoff had appeared in a whopping 76 games during the regular season. Ex-San Jose captain Owen Nolan managed 16 goals and 32 points as a 35-year-old vet. In addition, Wayne Primeau, one of three players sent to Boston in exchange for Thornton, was also a Flame.

Calgary got San Jose's attention, too, when Stephane Yelle scored twice and Kiprusoff turned aside 37 of 39 Sharks shots to steal the opener in San Jose, 3–2, despite two goals from Ryane Clowe. The hosts tightened up considerably in Game 2. The Sharks permitted only 21 shots, and Nabokov stopped all of them. Joe Pavelski and Torrey Mitchell scored second-period goals, and San Jose tied the series with a 2–0 win.

The Sharks blitzed the Flames at the outset of Game 3. Clowe, Marleau, and Douglas Murray all scored during the opening 3:33 to chase Kiprusoff from the crease in favor of 40-year-old backup Curtis Joseph. And while maybe one ex-teammate came up short, another didn't.

The Flames rallied for three unanswered goals by early in the third to tie it, and then Nolan put it to his former team by scoring his first of the series for the game-winner at 16:15. Owen had provided assists on Calgary's second and third goals of the game, too, as the Flames took a 2–1 series lead with the 4–3 victory.

The Sharks had to grind in Game 4 to even it back up. Down 1–0 and 2–1, San Jose rallied in the third as the first goals of the playoff season from Cheechoo and Thornton slipped past Kiprusoff during the 3–2 win. Nabokov benefited from an unbelievable defensive effort by the Sharks, who allowed the Flames to put only 10 shots total on net.

The competitive and intriguing series continued to unfold in San Jose, where in Game 5 all appeared safe for the Sharks when the second of Cheechoo's two third-period goals gave the hosts a 4–1 lead. But San Jose had to hold on for dear life as Calgary put two on the board, including one late, before succumbing 4–3.

Some behind-the-scenes drama played out before the puck was dropped for Game 6 back in Calgary. Upset at criticism and frustrated that he was scoreless through five games with only two shots on goal and a minus-2, Jeremy Roenick engaged in a heated exchange with Ron Wilson during the second intermission of Game 5. Roenick put an exclamation point on his tirade by flinging a souvenir hockey stick given to Wilson by Martin Brodeur across the coach's office before storming out.

Wilson had no choice but to discipline Roenick with a scratch from Game 6.

"I totally got it, and totally expected it. We've chuckled about it many times since," Roenick said years later. "Ronnie did what he had to do, which I didn't like. I had a little spur up my, um, back. I wanted to show him I could come back, and I was going to make amends."

Roenick got that chance because the Flames evened the series with a 2–0 win in Game 6 as Kiprusoff stopped 21 shots and Calgary got goals from Nolan and Daymond Langkow. It was back to San Jose for a winner-take-all Game 7. A history buff, Wilson delved into Roenick's past and discovered he typically brought his A game when it mattered most. He made a point of mentioning that during the morning skate of the seventh game.

"Ronnie brought everybody to center ice and explained these were the kind of games that make reputations," Roenick later recalled. "And, he said, 'But don't worry about that because J.R. has four goals in game sevens, and he's going to carry us. Right, J.R.?'"

Signed the previous offseason by GM Doug Wilson, who was Roenick's first roommate as an 18-year-old rookie with the Blackhawks in 1988, J.R. was brought on board to give what he had left as a 38-year-old with 18 years of NHL experience and to help mentor San Jose's young talent. His signing came with conditions. He did away with the No. 97 he'd worn in recent years to wear No. 27 with the Sharks. That was his original number with Chicago.

"He put the pressure on me really big," Roenick recalled of Wilson's speech to the team. "And I liked that he kind of called me out for some of the good things I'd done."

Roenick assisted a Thornton goal to give the hosts a 1–0 lead. But Calgary answered back with two of their own, the second of which was scored by Nolan early in the middle period for a 2–1 lead. That's when Roenick left his indelible mark by scoring consecutive goals exactly three minutes apart for a lead the Sharks would not surrender. He assisted a Devin Setoguchi insurance tally to cap a four-point game late in the second during San Jose's eventual series-clinching 5–3 victory.

How sweet it must have felt, too, for Roenick to have that kind of game at the end of his career with Mike Keenan on the opposition's bench. Keenan was Roenick's first coach in Chicago, and the two didn't always see eye to eye early on, though Roenick does credit Keenan for providing a huge boost for him.

"It was just one of those games where I felt great. I felt motivated and I was really fortunate to have that opportunity to play and play well," Roenick said.

Division- and playoff-rival Dallas was up next as the Stars upset Anaheim in six games of the opening round. Not too far in San Jose's rearview mirror were memories of Dallas eliminating the Sharks in 1998 and 2000, both in convincing fashion. This time San Jose would open with the home-ice edge; however, that didn't last long.

Brenden Morrow scored 4:39 into sudden death in Game 1 for a 3–2 win, and the Stars blitzed the Sharks 5–2 two nights later for a two-game sweep on enemy ice. It didn't get any better for San Jose in Game 3 as Mattias Norstrom tallied at 4:37 of sudden death for a 2–1 win and a commanding 3–0 series lead for Dallas.

Determined not to go down without a fight, the Sharks got an early third-period tie-breaking goal from Milan Michalek and 17 saves from Evgeni Nabokov for a 2–1 win in Game 4. Joe Pavelski kept the series—and San Jose's season—alive with his fifth goal of the playoffs 65 seconds into sudden death for a 3–2 win.

It was back to Dallas for what would be one of San Jose's most remarkable playoff games in team history. It was, for one thing, the longest game played in Sharks annals.

Antti Miettinen gave Dallas a 1–0 lead early in the first. Ryane Clowe tied it early in the second. And that's how the score would remain—1–1—through regulation and three full 20-minute overtime sessions. Dallas needed one more goal to advance. San Jose needed the next one to win a third straight and force a Game 7 in San Jose.

On and on, deep into the night and early morning they played.

It reminded me of growing up and watching the playoffs when they were telecast on ESPN. While working in the American Hockey League, I recall watching a playoff game between the Islanders and Washington before I fell asleep. I woke up later with the TV still on. Remember in those days how ESPN used to replay the same game in the middle of the night? I thought, "Oh, they're replaying the game," before I realized the same game was still on!

That game—with Kelly Hrudey in goal for the Islanders and Bob Mason for the Capitals—was the seventh game of the 1987 East semis that started on a Saturday night in Landover, Maryland, and ended in the early hours of Easter morning when Pat LaFontaine scored for New York.

Finally at 9:03 of the fourth OT—16 seconds longer than it took LaFontaine to score his—Morrow converted a Dallas power play, and the Stars had their series-clinching win at 1:21 AM Central time.

Lost in the disappointment of falling short was maybe the greatest save by a Sharks goalie in team history. Nabokov got a strong push to slide all the way from his right to the left side where he threw out his glove and caught Mike Richards' sure-fire one-time attempt from 10 feet away that had series winner all over it 1:30 into the first overtime.

Players on both teams logged incredible ice times during that game: Brian Campbell, 56:23; Marc-Edouard Vlasic, 51:01; Joe Thornton, 47:14; Patrick Marleau, 42:53, and Douglas Murray, 32:10. For Dallas: Sergei Zubov, 53:50; Brenden Morrow, 51 minutes; and Mattias Norstrom, 48:59. Those numbers still boggle my mind.

And shots—the Sharks had 62 shots and the Stars had 55. Not a lot for a four-OT game, but both teams were tired. Kudos to Marty Turco for hanging in there. And, as it turned out, that was Ron Wilson's last game coaching San Jose.

Behind the bench for 385 regular-season games from 2002–08, Wilson advanced San Jose's string of success. His 206–122–19 record and .609 percentage of points earned per outing ranked No. 1 among Sharks bench bosses up to that point in club history. General manager Doug Wilson termed the change as, "a time when the classroom needed a new teacher."

He turned to Todd McLellan, who had served the three most recent seasons as an assistant to Mike Babcock in Detroit where the Red Wings were fresh off winning the Stanley Cup. McLellan not only brought a new voice, but looked to complement San Jose's solid defensive style of play by adding a dash more offense with an emphasis on shot volume.

The Sharks responded with not only the most goals (257) and fewest allowed (204) in the Pacific Division, but they went wire-to-wire to post their best regular-season record in franchise history. San Jose won the Presidents' Trophy for the first time with a 117-point season, thanks to its 53–18–11 record.

San Jose featured a balanced and potent attack. Joe Thornton led the team with 86 points on the strength of his team-high 61 assists. Patrick Marleau led with 38 goals and finished runner-up to Jumbo Joe with 71 points. Twenty-two-year-old Devin Setoguchi burst on the scene in his second season to score 31 goals and add 65 points.

The Sharks featured 10 skaters who finished in double figures for goals. The blue line, anchored by the offensively gifted Dan Boyle, included Rob Blake, Christian Ehrhoff and a young Marc-Edouard Vlasic. Goalie Evgeni Nabokov was still shining in his ninth season between the pipes in San Jose.

While the Sharks were secure down the stretch knowing they were going to face the No. 8 seed in the first round, their opponents weren't as obvious. In the end, Columbus and St. Louis finished with 92 points apiece to relegate Anaheim—one point back with 91—as the final playoff qualifier in the West.

And while the Sharks were looking forward to not having to cross time zones to play either the Blue Jackets or the Blues, they also knew the shorter trek to Southern California wasn't going to be a picnic. One look at the season series between the Ducks and Sharks suggested this could be a low-scoring series. San Jose won four of the six regular season games, but all but one 5–2 loss to Anaheim were games that featured a combined five goals or less.

While the Ducks managed to sneak in by two points over Minnesota and three over Nashville, they were only two springs removed from winning the Stanley Cup. Young stars Ryan Getzlaf and Corey Perry, both only 23, had established themselves as team leaders. Getzlaf was tops on the Ducks' scoring list with 91 points while runner-up Perry, with 72, led in goals with 32. A 21-year-old Bobby Ryan exploded on the scene with 31 goals, too.

They still had Teemu Selanne, who at 38 contributed 27 goals and 54 points. The veteran defense was stout with Scott

Niedermayer and Sharks playoff nemesis Chris Pronger patrolling the blue line. And Anaheim featured a formidable goaltending tandem in Jonas Hiller and J.S. Giguere. The Sharks knew they'd be in for a battle.

The anticipated low-scoring series played out in Game 1, as a scoreless game through 40 minutes was broken up by goals from Niedermayer and Getzlaf in the third period and the Ducks stole the opener behind 35 saves from Hiller, 2–0. Anaheim made another statement in Game 2, scoring twice in the third period to break a 1–1 tie after 40 minutes to jump out to a 2–0 series lead with a 3–2 victory.

The Sharks knew they had to have Game 3, and their big guns came through. San Jose's first three goals came from defensemen—two by Boyle and one by Blake, but for a third straight game it was tied after 40 minutes. That was before Marleau converted on the power play at 10:33 of the third, and Nabokov shut the door for a 4–3 victory.

Anaheim was more ready for Game 4. Ryan scored a pair at even strength in the opening period while Perry and Drew Miller tacked on insurance in the third. Hiller made 31 saves for his second shutout of the series, and the Ducks took command at 3–1 with a 4–0 triumph. The Sharks were starting to feel the heat for sure.

The fifth game back in San Jose was a tight affair. Thornton and Setoguchi scored in each of the first two periods, and the hosts led 2–0. But Ryan Carter and Perry tied it for Anaheim with goals less than four minutes apart early in the third. And it remained tied 2–2 through regulation.

With their season on the line, the Sharks got a clutch goal from Marleau 6:02 into sudden death to extend the series. It felt too close for comfort, but in the playoffs you'll do anything and accept the torture if it means finding a way to live another day.

In Anaheim for Game 6, Thornton skated into the center-ice faceoff circle with one thing on his mind. He wanted to fire up his team and get under the skin of Anaheim's Ryan Getzlaf. The two chirped back and forth waiting for the first puck to drop, and as soon as it did the gloves came off, too. The two alternate captains traded blows until Thornton ended up taking Getzlaf down. Each had to serve five minutes in the box.

The tone Thornton hoped to set didn't faze Anaheim, which scored four unanswered goals after Milan Michalek briefly gave the Sharks a 1–0 lead. It was all over then. Presidents' Trophy winners with high playoff expectations two weeks prior were now making unexpected offseason plans. This one stung.

When I think back to this series one name stands out amongst the role players—Andrew Ebbett. He was a 26-year-old forward on Anaheim's roster. A University of Michigan product, Ebbett typified the kind of unheralded depth the Ducks boasted that season. Before promotion to the bigs, Ebbett logged 74 games in the minors the previous year and spent another 28 for a tune-up in that particular season. Ebbett didn't have a huge series, but his goal did break a tie in Game 2. He was an important piece that helped Anaheim stay a step ahead.

The one difference I kept noticing was that the Calder Cup experience of all those young role players on Anaheim's winning playoff roster gave them an edge over the Sharks. For example, young Sharks forward Marcel Goc had already won an NHL playoff series before he played a full season as a pro, but he didn't have any Calder Cup experience. He didn't have that foundation of experience, and I thought that showed in this series.

Sure, the Sharks won the Presidents' Trophy, but they were beaten by a good team that was better prepared to be in that situation and they used their experience to garner success when they needed to. The Ducks were a great team, but I still maintain that if the Sharks were a little further along in their development, they might have been able to squeak by.

While the series loss to Anaheim was disappointing, it didn't signal wholesale changes. Instead, the Sharks hoped the moves that they made would have an impact moving forward. First off, the captaincy switched from Patrick Marleau to Rob Blake, who at age 40—and with one Stanley Cup title under his belt—was embarking on the last of his 20 years in the league.

Reputed goal-scorer Dany Heatley came via trade from Ottawa ostensibly for Milan Michalek and a declining Jonathan Cheechoo. Grit and veteran depth was added to the lineup in the form of forwards Manny Malhotra, Jed Ortmeyer, Scott Nichol, and defenseman Kent Huskins.

Marleau responded positively to what could have been considered a slight with removal of his five-year captaincy. He scored a career-high 44 goals and tallied 83 points to finish runner-up to Thornton's team-high 89 points. Heatley produced to the tune of 39 goals and 82 points. And the aforementioned depth role players who were added all appeared in between 71 and 82 games.

Another tweak McLellan & Co. made was to get the team in the best health and frame of mind during the regular season instead of chasing every single point possible. They hoped this would give the team a boost heading into the postseason. The previous season's first Presidents' Trophy campaign was a wonderful experience, and the team took a lot of pride in that accomplishment. But understanding the rigors of extra travel as a West Coast team, and the grind of the long season, the Sharks were going to try to position themselves for the best possible playoff outcome by having as much in the tank as possible come mid-April.

And, as it turned out, San Jose didn't slip much in the overall standings—exactly one spot is all. The Sharks won the Pacific Division for the third of an eventual four straight years. They did it with a West-best 113 points and finished behind only Washington (121 points) for the No. 1 overall spot.

This time there was no first-round meltdown. In fact, the Sharks dispatched a couple difficult rivals in Colorado and Detroit over the first two rounds to advance to the West Finals. This would be a long and impressive run by San Jose.

Of course the playoffs are never easy, and nothing proved that more than the first four games of the Western Conference quarterfinal against the Avalanche. San Jose sacrificed home ice with a 2–1 loss in Game 1, and then the two teams battled past regulation in each of the next three games—two of which were won by San Jose.

Devin Setoguchi was the overtime hero in Game 2 with a power-play strike at 5:22 for a 6–5 win to knot the series. A completely different kind of contest unfolded in Game 3 at Denver when the Avs' Ryan O'Reilly snapped a scoreless tie after 60 minutes with an unassisted goal just 51 seconds into OT. Then it was Joe Pavelski with a winner at 10:24 for a 2–1 Sharks victory in Game 4 that tied the series again heading back to San Jose.

Finally the Sharks established their game, and just in the nick of time. Three goals after a scoreless first and two more in the third—with Logan Couture leading the way with a pair—supported Evgeni Nabokov's 28-save effort for a 5–0 win and 3–2 series lead.

Facing the possibility of Game 7, the Sharks rallied from a 2–1 deficit in Game 6 to score four times in the final 12:27 to win 5–2 and advance. Established now as a big-time performer, Pavelski led the Sharks with five goals and eight points in the series. Ryane Clowe, too, showed the determination he brought to the rink every day by matching Pavelski's eight points on the strength of seven assists. Nabby was outstanding with a 1.76 goals-against average and .926 save percentage.

Next up was nemesis Detroit, a 102-point team that earned seven more points than Colorado while finishing second to Chicago in the Central Division. The Sharks knew not to take the Wings lightly, especially after they ground out a 6–1 Game 7 win on the road over the Pacific's runner-up Phoenix Coyotes, who were coming off a fine 107-point campaign.

The Sharks won each of the first three games by identical 4–3 scores. The last goal scored in that sequence stands out most favorably in my mind. It was a pivotal goal because if it went Detroit's way, the Wings were back in the series. But because the Sharks scored, they took command with a 3–0 lead.

Desperate Detroit had the upper hand through 40 minutes. The Wings extended a 2–1 lead at the first intermission to 3–1 through two periods after Henrik Zetterberg struck at 1:42 of the middle session. But goals from Thornton and Couture early and late in the third period sent the game into extra time tied 3–3.

What started as a bad line change, and allowed Detroit a scoring chance on an odd-man break, worked in San Jose's favor in the end. A slap shot by Jason Williams from the right circle caromed hard off Nabokov all the way out of the zone with four Wings caught deep.

Thornton picked the puck up at center, drove the right boards across the Detroit line with Marleau on his left and only 36-year-old Detroit rear guard Brian Rafalski back to defend the 2-on-1 break. Thornton slipped a forehand pass to Marleau just as Rafalski angled himself toward Jumbo Joe, and Patty just one-touched his 39th career playoff goal past a sprawling Jimmy Howard at 7:07 of sudden death.

That was one of those moments when I got the call just the way I would have liked, and it was a great emotional moment to bring to the audience.

Two nights after Detroit avoided getting swept with a 7–1 win in Game 4, the Sharks wrapped up the series and saved themselves another cross-country trip as Marleau scored 6:59 into the third period for a 2–1 victory. It was a great five-game series for the Sharks. Thornton led with eight points while Pavelski and Heatley followed with seven each. Game-winners came off Marleau's stick in each of San Jose's last two victories. The right guys were coming up big.

Chicago needed six games to eliminate Vancouver, and the West Finals were set—the Sharks versus the Blackhawks. It pitted two U.S.-based teams in the conference final, and one from the Original Six to boot. Unfortunately for the Sharks, the series didn't last long despite all the games being closely contested.

The Hawks won the first two games in San Jose by scores of 2–1 and 4–2. When big Dustin Byfuglien scored 12:24 into overtime for a 3–2 win in Game 3, Chicago was one win from its first Stanley Cup Final appearance since 1992. And that became reality two nights later when Byfuglien and Kris Versteeg scored in the third to break a 2–2 tie en route to a 4–2 win.

Future Shark goalie Antti Niemi was a rookie in net for the Blackhawks that season, and he helped Chicago snap a 49-year Cup drought as it went on to beat Philadelphia in six games. And it marked the first time that the Sharks were a victim of an eventual Stanley Cup champ in the same playoff season.

The 2010s

Despite the short summer, the Sharks got right back to the grind of winning the Pacific Division for a franchise-best fourth straight time in 2010–11. And, for the third time in as many seasons, the Sharks had a new captain. Joe Thornton took the C as Rob Blake retired a year after the future Hall of Fame defenseman replaced Marleau. And just before training camp the Sharks signed free agent Antti Niemi, the same goalie who beat them the previous spring and led Chicago to the Cup.

Both Marleau and Thornton continued to lead the way regardless of letter designations. Marleau scored 37 goals—giving him 81 over two seasons—and also led in points with 73. Thornton was next with 70 points on the strength of 49 assists. A breakthrough season came from 21-year-old Logan Couture, however. He scored 32 goals.

Heatley (26), Clowe (24), and Setoguchi (22) all contributed significantly, too, as the Sharks scored the most goals and allowed the second fewest in the Pacific Division en route to going 48–25–9 to finish with 105 points—six more than Anaheim and Phoenix with 99 apiece. The division was strong, however, as it sent four teams—fourth-place Los Angeles included—on to the postseason while only first-place Vancouver represented the Northwest. Detroit, Nashville, and Chicago qualified from the Central.

The California rivals San Jose and Los Angeles finally met in the playoffs for the first time. And the matchup pitted the two most stingy defensive teams in the division, so you had to figure goals would come at a premium. And that's how the series started, too.

Tied 2–2 after regulation, Joe Pavelski scored at even strength at 14:44 of overtime to enable the Sharks to hold home ice with a 3–2 win in Game 1. But the Kings displayed their defensive posture two nights later to take Game 2, 4–0, behind 34 saves from busy Kings goalie Jonathan Quick. Los Angeles received its first three goals from the blue line—Drew Doughty with a pair and Jack Johnson with one—before depth forward Kyle Clifford added one late.

That set the stage for an early-series pivotal Game 3 at Staples Center in downtown Los Angeles, a playoff game that would go down as one of the most memorable in both teams' annals. The Kings flew out to a 4–0 lead in the opening 20:44. Niemi was out after stopping only six shots. He was replaced by Antero Niittymaki, who appeared in 24 regular-season games in his one and only season as a Shark.

Goals from Marleau, Clowe, and Couture by the 13:32 mark of the second period changed the momentum of the game and gave the Sharks renewed hope. But when Ryan Smyth struck 15 seconds after San Jose had drawn within 4–3, it appeared the Kings may have righted their ship.

Time for a history lesson here.

Many hockey fans, and certainly most LA Kings fans, fondly recall the playoff game between the Kings and Edmonton Oilers inside the Fabulous Forum on April 10, 1982. Trailing 5–0, the Kings capped the largest comeback in NHL history by winning 6–5 in overtime. The game was nicknamed the "Miracle on

Manchester" because the Forum—the Kings' original home rink—was located on Manchester Boulevard.

Back inside Staples Center, Clowe and Pavelski scored before the second intermission—capping a five-goal middle-session explosion—to tie the game, 5–5. It stayed that way until Setoguchi scored 3:09 into overtime to complete the coincidental comeback. Sharks win, 6–5, in Game 3—the same game that in the Oilers-Kings series 29 years earlier ended 6–5.

"It's crazy, but before the game I was watching TV," Setoguchi said after the game. "It was about the Kings coming back from 5–0, so it was kind of ironic that we came back from 4–0."

We labeled this one the "Fiasco on Figueroa," (referencing where Staples Center is located). Or from a Sharks perspective: "Fabulous on Figueroa."

The Sharks had shaken the Kings for sure, and when they broke a scoreless tie in Game 4 with three goals during the first half of the second period, the visitors were on their way to a 6–3 win and a 3–1 lead in the series. The Kings picked themselves up again, however, to beat the host and clinch-hopeful Sharks in Game 5, 3–1. So it was back to LA for more drama.

The Sharks struck first in Game 6, but the teams traded the next five goals to finish 3–3 after 60 minutes. Overtime did not last long, however. A Setoguchi drive caromed off Marleau into the slot where Thornton corralled the puck, spun to his left, and swept a low shot past an out-of-position Quick at 2:22 to end it.

Thornton took a few strides, flopped on his back, and slid all the way to center ice with his hands in the air—think a poor man's Theoren Fleury playoff celebration—before teammates mobbed him as San Jose won the series in six games.

If the Sharks thought they were in for less drama in Round 2 against Detroit, think again. When I think about all the Sharks playoff series I've seen—and I haven't missed a single game in person—this series was probably the best, most competitive, cleanest set of seven games I've ever witnessed. It was beautiful hockey. Every game was great and could have gone either way.

It was all the things you want in a playoff series. There weren't a lot of shenanigans. It was intense. It was a rivalry. Certainly there was a hate on for each other, but it wasn't chippy. It was great hockey. And it was exceedingly tense. The margin was razor thin. The teams were equal. Six of the seven playoff games were decided by one goal. The other was decided by two which, of course, included an empty-netter.

Young forward Benn Ferriero scored 7:03 into overtime, and the Sharks won the opener 2–1. How big was this for Ferriero? He would play less than 100 NHL games with three different teams before his five-year career concluded.

The Sharks won Game 2 by the same 2–1 score and went up 3–0 when Setoguchi scored 9:21 in overtime of Game 3 for a 4–3 win. But hold on. The Wings won the next three to knot the series—4–3, 4–3, and 3–1. Unbelievable. In Game 7, Setoguchi and Couture staked the hosts to a 2–0 lead after one period. Henrik Zetterberg drew the Wings within one with the only goal of the second. Marleau scored 12:13 into the third, and Detroit got a goal from Pavel Datsyuk less than two minutes later. The Sharks survived, 3–2.

Miraculously, it was on to Round 3.

The Vancouver Canucks stood in the Sharks' way of a first-ever Stanley Cup Final appearance. But the Canucks were formidable. They had a West-best 117-point regular season, but they also played in a division that produced only the one playoff entry. Vancouver was pushed to seven games by Chicago in the first round, and slipped by Nashville in six during the second round.

The Sharks didn't get off to the start they had hoped for as they dropped each of the first two games, 3–2 and 7–3, respectively. San Jose cut the series deficit to one by holding on for a 4–3 win in Game 3 after it was riding a seemingly comfortable three-goal edge in the latter stages of the third period.

The Sharks failed to convert any of the first five power plays awarded in Game 4, but the Canucks had no trouble once they went on the man-advantage. Vancouver scored three straight power-play goals during a 1:56 span of the second period to seize control. The Canucks skated out of San Jose with a 4–2 win and headed home one win away from closing out the Sharks.

San Jose battled in the do-or-die Game 5, leading 2–1 all the way inside the final 15 seconds before Ryan Kesler tied it at 19:46. The most bizarre playoff goal I've witnessed in person decided the series at 10:18 of the second overtime period. Alexander Edler rimmed a puck on the right boards that went airborne, struck a stanchion holding the glass above the dasher board, and bounced back to the middle of the ice where Kevin Bieksa let go with a low one-timer that Niemi never saw go past and into the goal.

I remember calling it, and I remember the puck getting bounced around the boards. I remember seeing it go up off the stanchion, and then I lost sight of the puck. So I said to myself, "Focus on the front of the net."

When I looked there, I saw the puck as it slipped past Niemi and go in. I knew we had lost, but I still didn't know how the hell the puck got there. I got the call right, but it took me a second to get the name of the player. That was one of the weirdest goals. It was like when Patrick Kane scored the winner against Philly for Chicago to win the Cup in 2010.

Any way you look at it, that was a strange, awful, and disappointing way for a season to end.

After back-to-back visits to the conference finals, the Sharks had a lot of preseason prognosticators on their side. San Jose was viewed as the team ready to break through because they had come so close and because of their balanced attack and commitment to defense.

At the same time, the West and teams in the Pacific were really starting to bunch. Only 17 points separated first from last in the division, and for the first time in 10 seasons no team earned as many as 100 points. It was so close at the top that three teams were within two points of each other. Phoenix snapped San Jose's four-year hold on the division by edging the Sharks 97–96. The Sharks finished just one point ahead of third-place Los Angeles, which grabbed the eighth and last seed in the West.

The usual suspects provided the offense. Joe Thornton led the team with 77 points—59 coming on assists. And the Sharks boasted three 30-goal scorers—Logan Couture and Joe Pavelski with 31 apiece and Patrick Marleau with 30. There was, however, a drop-off thereafter, and inconsistency in line depth cost the team late in the season.

San Jose's first-round opponent was a familiar one in St. Louis. Champions of the Central with a West-leading 109 points, the Blues were joined by Nashville (104), Detroit (102), and Chicago (101) as four of the five teams to crest the 100-point barrier from the same division. That pushed the Sharks all the way down to the seventh seed in what would be a fourth all-time playoff series against the Blues.

St. Louis was stingy on defense during the regular season. The Blues allowed a league-low 165 goals, which was 38 fewer than the next closest team in their division. Jaroslav Halak and Brian Elliott split the goaltending duties for coach Ken Hitchcock.

The Blues didn't possess big offensive threats—David Backes and T.J. Oshie shared the team lead with a modest total of 54 points apiece—but they were a sum of their parts with players willing to play their roles. No question this was going to be a challenging first round for the Sharks and the start of another long postseason run.

The series couldn't have started any better for the Sharks. Dealt from Minnesota in the offseason in exchange for Dany Heatley, forward Martin Havlat had a difficult, injury-interrupted first season in San Jose with seven goals in only 39 games. But, with the reputation as a playoff performer, Havlat scored the first goal of Game 1, and he struck again 3:34 into a second overtime period for a 3–2 win.

Antti Niemi stood tall in the San Jose net with 40 saves while the Sharks found a way to break through the Blues' wall of defense and beat Halak three times. It wasn't a big surprise, however, that the hosts would tighten the screws in Game 2 when Elliott and Halak shared a 29-save shutout with the Blues winning 3–0.

The two teams were assessed a combined 46 minutes in penalties. The emotional outpouring came from San Jose's frustration and St. Louis not being willing to back down. The chippy end to Game 2 marked the last time in the series that the Sharks appeared completely engaged.

In San Jose for Game 3, the Blues converted three of four power plays into goals and led 4–1 until the Sharks scored twice late to make the 4–3 final appear closer than the game felt. And, after two days off, the Blues capped the two-game sweep on the road with a 2–1 victory in Game 4. The only Sharks tally came 67 seconds from the end of the third period. The team just didn't have near the jump it needed or displayed at the outset of the series.

Thornton scored the first goal of Game 5 in St. Louis, but the Blues struck three times in the third period to win going away, 3–1. Just like that, the series and playoff run was over. San Jose only managed eight goals in the five games. Neither Marleau, Ryane Clowe, nor Dan Boyle scored a goal in the series. Havlat's two were contained to Game 1, and that total led the team along with Thornton's pair.

Then, as if to add insult to injury, the Blues were swept in the next round by the Kings. Los Angeles was the eighth seed, yet the Kings waltzed all the way to the Stanley Cup Final. They lost only two playoff games in the West, then dispatched the New Jersey Devils in six games to win their first Stanley Cup under the direction of ex-Sharks coach Darryl Sutter and former San Jose GM Dean Lombardi.

I had a soft spot for Dean and Darryl, and it was nice to see the two get rewarded after all their hard work both in San Jose and Los Angeles.

But back to the Sharks and the Blues series: it was one of the low points in the team's playoff history, because everyone expected so much more. The Sharks didn't seem to have it together, and they didn't seem all that perturbed about it, either. I thought that there would be a few changes after that one.

Once the Kings raised their first Cup, an offseason of uncertainty commenced as the specter of another work stoppage loomed. Sure enough, for the third time in 19 seasons, the league paused while owners and players feuded over rules of free agency and how much hockey-related revenues to divvy between the two.

An accord was reached in early January, and the season's schedule was reduced from 82 to 48 games.

Changes in the locker room were minimal as the Sharks geared up for not so much a marathon but a sprint to the end. The three California teams were the class of the Pacific, but it was Anaheim that went from worst one season to first the next to claim the top spot with 66 points. Defending Cup champ L.A. was next with 59, and the Sharks finished in third place only two points behind the Kings. The shortened season proved how much visiting teams hated that three-game road trip to the Golden State.

The usual suspects led the Sharks during the lockout campaign. Thornton once again was the pace-setter in points. His seven goals were down a bit, but the 33-year-old had 33 assists for 40 points. Couture continued to come through in the goal-scoring department. His 21 goals as a 23-year-old led the team. Marleau and Pavelski added 31 points apiece while Brent Burns started to emerge as a scoring force from the blue line with his nine goals and 20 points.

The Sharks avoided a division rival in the first round by squaring off against Vancouver, the first-place finishers of the Northwest Division with a modest 59 points. San Jose swept the three-game season series against the Canucks, winning 4–1 and 3–2 on home ice and 3–2 in a shootout in Canada.

Because they finished with two more regular-season points, the Canucks were hosts at the outset, but the Sharks quickly grabbed home ice by winning each of the first two games. Couture, Boyle, and Marleau scored after 2011 nemesis Kevin Bieksa opened the scoring in Game 1, and the Sharks had a 3–1 win. The second game was tight, tied 2–2 after regulation, but former Canuck Raffi

Torres enjoyed one of his brief highlights as a member of the Sharks by scoring 5:31 into overtime for a 3–2 victory.

Torres had quite the checkered playoff career against San Jose. As a member of the Oilers in 2006, he turned that series in favor of Edmonton with a huge open-ice hit on Milan Michalek that drew no response from the Sharks. And the Oilers rallied from a 2–0 series deficit to win four straight. In 2011, he hit Thornton so hard Jumbo suffered a separated shoulder that he kept quiet and played through.

Late in the 2012–13 season, Torres was dealt from Phoenix to San Jose, where he played 11 times before the start of the playoffs. That would be the most games in any stretch that Torres appeared in a Sharks uniform over the next two seasons as suspensions and injuries put a halt to his numerous comeback attempts.

San Jose took command with a 5–2 win in Game 3 as Pavelski and Couture scored two goals each and Marleau added one. Then the Sharks earned a measure of revenge for their overtime loss in Game 5 that ended the 2011 playoff series against the Canucks when Marleau snuffed the life out of Vancouver 13:18 into sudden death of Game 4. The 4–3 victory meant San Jose had swept an opponent for the first time in 29 all-time playoff series.

All the big guns came through as Pavelski and Couture led the way in the series with eight points apiece. Thornton had six, Marleau five, and Boyle four. Niemi held up his end of the bargain, flashing an outstanding .937 save percentage with a 2.00 goals-against average. The Sedin twins—Daniel and Henrik—were held to three points apiece as no Canuck scored more than two goals in the series.

It was on to Round 2 and a date with the rival Los Angeles Kings, who booted St. Louis in six games of the opening round.

The Sharks and Kings had finally met for the first time in the postseason two springs prior—with the Sharks winning in six games—and this NorCal versus SoCal playoff rivalry was just about to heat up.

The trend of home-ice dominance in the regular season doesn't always translate for the same matchup in the postseason, but this time around it sure did. The Sharks won both meetings against the Kings in San Jose—4–3 and 3–2 in a shootout—while the Kings triumphed twice in two tries at Staples—5–2 and 3–2.

Amazingly enough, the trend would continue through all seven close-checking, low-scoring, and hard-fought playoff games, too.

San Jose outshot Los Angeles 35–20 in the opener, but Jonathan Quick slammed the door on the Sharks while Slava Voynov and Mike Richards supplied goals in a 2–0 opener that featured only four minor penalties. The Sharks clung to a score of 3–2 late after Marc-Edouard Vlasic broke a 2–2 tie earlier in the third. But Dustin Brown and Trevor Lewis converted power plays into the tying and winning goals for the Kings 22 seconds apart inside the final two minutes of regulation.

The series shifted to San Jose, which meant the Sharks could take advantage of the home rink to knot the series. They won Game 3, 2–1, 1:29 into overtime when Logan Couture scored, and took Game 4 by the same score as Niemi stopped 22 of 23 shots.

The pivotal Game 5 was scoreless until late in the second when the Kings' Anze Kopitar scored. L.A. got two more in the third, and Quick turned away all 24 shots to post his second shutout of the series. The Sharks extended the series to a deciding seventh game by winning Game 6, 2–1. Thornton and T.J. Galiardi scored the game's first two goals, and Niemi made 24 saves to set up the winner-take-all back at Staples.

Whoever scored first won each game in the series, putting extra pressure on scoring first in Game 7. Being the home team didn't matter as much as scoring first. The teams battled through a scoreless first, but when playoff-hero Justin Williams converted on the power play at 4:11 of the second, the hosts had the coveted first goal. Williams struck again at 7:08, and the Sharks faced an uphill battle entering the third.

Dan Boyle managed to slip an even-strength shot past Quick at 5:26, but that's all the Sharks could muster on offense. They had only two power-play opportunities, and none just after the midpoint of regulation. It was hard to really fault anyone. Both teams had played well. Both teams were disciplined, both teams held their defensive posture, and both teams certainly took advantage of home ice.

The Sharks went home, but so did the Kings a round later. It's possible San Jose took enough out of Los Angeles to pave Chicago's way to a five-game win in the conference final. The Blackhawks completed their amazing run by beating the Boston Bruins in six games to win their second of an eventual three Cups in six seasons.

The Sharks and Kings weren't done with each other in the postseason. It didn't take long for a rematch. And it would go down as not only one of the most memorable in Sharks history, but one for the NHL records books as well.

First things first, however.

The league realigned from six divisions to four, and three teams switched conferences with Detroit and Columbus moving from the West to the East and Winnipeg shifting from the East to the West. Now there were 16 teams in the East and 14 in the West. And while the Pacific Division absorbed three Canadian teams—

Vancouver, Edmonton, and Calgary—it lost Dallas to the Central Division.

The NHL tweaked the playoffs, too, as the division winners would face "wild card" teams from each respective conference while the second- and third-place finishers in each division would square off in the first round. The thinking was this would promote more divisional rivalries.

One thing that didn't change was the three California teams' dominance. Anaheim was best of the trio again, winning a second straight Pacific title, this time with a conference-leading 116 points. With a 51–22–9 record, the Sharks were next with a hefty 111 points, and the Kings, probably built more for the postseason, finished third with 100 points.

Joe Pavelski enjoyed an offensive breakthrough during the regular season. A constant on the right side of Joe Thornton's top line, Pavs scored 41 goals and added 38 assists to lead the team in scoring with 79 points. Thornton was next with 76 points, including 65 assists. Marleau pumped in another 33 goals and 70 points, and Couture lost 17 games to injury but still managed 23 goals and 54 points.

Because of the new playoff format, San Jose and Los Angeles met right off the bat. Had the NHL still employed the system from recent seasons, the Sharks would have matched up against Chicago in the opening round. As this one turned out, San Jose probably wished it had gone up against the Blackhawks.

The regular-season series between the Sharks and Kings was tight. San Jose went 2–2–1 against Los Angeles. Four of the five games were decided by one goal. Two went to overtime, and one extended to the limit in a shootout. Bottom line, there just wasn't much difference between these suddenly familiar playoff combatants.

Despite the close nature of the regular-season meetings, and the memory of how goals came at a premium when the two teams battled through seven games the previous spring, the Sharks got off to a rip-roaring start this time around.

Host San Jose scored the first five goals of Game 1—three in the first and two in the second—and cruised to a 6–3 victory. And after the Sharks spotted the Kings two goals in the first period of Game 2, they came roaring back to score three times in the second and four more in the third for a convincing 7–2 win.

"Success has only been two games. We've got a lot left," Sharks coach Todd McLellan said as if to warn there was still a long way to go.

One had to figure Game 3 in Los Angeles would be a tight one considering what was on the line for the Kings. They were looking to tighten up and not give the Sharks as many good looks at the net as in the first two games. And they desperately needed to win or face the unenviable task of climbing out of an 0–3 hole.

The game went back and forth. Brent Burns scored the only goal of the first period. Jarret Stoll and Marian Gaborik rallied the Kings with a goal apiece early in the second. But Matt Nieto tied it 2–2 before the second intermission. First Jeff Carter put the hosts back on top with a power play strike in the third. Then Tomas Hertl re-tied it at 3–3 for the last time before regulation ended.

The Kings came out firing in overtime, desperate to climb back into the series. But San Jose goalie Antti Niemi stopped five early OT shots. Then, on the Sharks' first shot, Patrick Marleau slipped his third goal of the series behind Jonathan Quick at 6:20

of sudden death, and San Jose celebrated a breakthrough 3–0 lead in the series and the first playoff win at Staples in three years.

"They had the bat in their hands, and they were going to swing it," McLellan said at the time. "They had us back on our heels. But sometimes it goes that way. We will take that break."

A fragile Kings team let a pair of one-goal leads slip away by the middle of the second period in Game 4, but they got their legs under them long enough to score three straight for a comfortable lead before surviving, 6–3.

San Jose had an excellent chance to end the series at home in Game 5, but that didn't happen. Instead, the Sharks lost the services of Marc-Edouard Vlasic in the opening period. Half of the team's top shutdown pairing, Vlasic would not appear again in the series. It was a huge blow to the blue line. Quick came up large for the Kings, stopping all 30 shots while Tyler Toffoli, Anze Kopitar, and Jeff Carter provided three goals in the opening 20:22. The 3–0 victory, which included 41 shots on the San Jose goal, gave the Kings renewed hope and planted a seed of doubt in the minds of the Sharks, who were now down a key player.

"We did a lot of good things for three and a half games. Tonight was red rotten," McLellan said at the time. "When we started the series, we talked about leaving games behind, closing the book on it. There's no doubt we'll look at it. We have to improve. But it's put in the bank, and we'll move on."

McLellan had one surprise up his sleeve for Game 6, although some suggested a goalie change could be in the offing. Niemi's backup who appeared in 22 games during the regular season, Alex Stalock, got the call and was asked to jump in on the road and try to win a clinching playoff game. Well, that just didn't happen. Stalock battled, but the Kings broke a 1–1 tie after 40 minutes

Brent Burns (88), Joe Thornton (19), and Patrick Marleau (12) warm up as they prepare to take on the Pittsburgh Penguins in Game 3 of the 2016 Stanley Cup Final. *(John Hefti / USA TODAY Sports)*

with three unanswered goals during the second half of the final period.

The Sharks were now one loss away from joining the 1942 Detroit Red Wings, the 1975 Pittsburgh Penguins, and the 2010 Boston Bruins as the only teams in NHL history to win the first three games of a playoff series only to lose the last four and suffer elimination.

"In my mind, it if gets to Game 7, it doesn't matter how it gets there," Sharks forward Logan Couture said. "It gets there, and you're going for one game. We played all year for home ice. We've got to turn this thing around and win that game."

Defenseman Matt Irwin got the Sharks off on the right skate. His goal just 28 seconds after the opening faceoff energized the sellout crowd to a fever pitch and gave the hosts a much-needed early lead. Let the good vibes flow.

Then Drew Doughty tied it with a power-play strike at 4:57. And Kopitar scored at even strength at 18:39. The second period was scoreless. Toffoli made it a two-goal edge with his 5-on-5 goal at 4:40 of the third. Then the Sharks pulled their goalie late. First Dustin Brown, then Tanner Pearson filled empty nets. And the Kings completed their historic comeback with a convincing 5–1 win in Game 7.

"I look at it as they fixed their problems [and] we didn't," McLellan said afterward. "Our problems got progressively worse. I'm in charge, I'm responsible for the group that performs on the ice. I have to accept that responsibility."

"Every year you lose is pretty low," Couture added. "But this one is the type of series that will rip your heart out."

The resilient Kings used the series to springboard themselves to a second Stanley Cup in three seasons. Incredibly, the Kings won two more seven-game series against Anaheim and Chicago to win the West. And they beat the Rangers in five games to win the Cup.

Teams who reach the final round can expect to battle a Stanley Cup hangover the following season, at least early on, but that might be a good way to describe, too, what happened to the Sharks in 2015–16 following their historic first-round playoff loss to the Kings. The long summer was filled with soul-searching, a degree of uncertainty, and another change in lettered leadership. Coach Todd McLellan opted to ask four alternates—Joe Pavelski, Marc-Edouard Vlasic, one-time captain Patrick Marleau, and Thornton—to share the lettered captaincy.

San Jose hung on in the playoff race, and held a top-eight spot for most of the season, but slipped out for good right around the time they hosted—and lost—an outdoor game on February 21, 2015, against the Los Angeles Kings in front of 70,000 fans at Levi's Stadium (home of the NFL's San Francisco 49ers).

The Sharks finished fifth in the Pacific Division and 10 points out of the final playoff spot to miss out on the postseason for the first time in 11 seasons. San Jose had never missed the playoffs during Doug Wilson's entire tenure as GM. He announced shortly after the season that McLellan and the organization had mutually agreed to part ways.

Peter DeBoer was hired as San Jose's new bench boss, and he arrived with a new coaching staff just in time to make the Sharks' silver anniversary season something special. DeBoer anointed Pavelski team captain at the outset and provided a fresh voice for a talented roster that included a new man in goal—25-year-old Martin Jones.

If there was a silver lining to San Jose's lost season, it was that Wilson was able to acquire the former Kings' backup netminder from Boston within a week of Los Angeles trading Jones to the Bruins. Jones was everything the Sharks wanted in a starting goalie. He had good size, was athletic, and was still young, yet he had experience in pressure games and was part of a Stanley Cup winner.

What DeBoer and Wilson envisioned in training camp materialized by midseason—the Sharks were well on their way to playing the way their new coach wanted to play, and it would definitely lead them back to the postseason. San Jose battled its two other California combatants again to the bitter end, finishing third with 98 points as the Ducks edged the Kings for division supremacy in points, 103–102.

With the current playoff format, that meant revisiting a Sharks-Kings first-round series. There was no avoiding it. San Jose would have to fend off any dark clouds and the ghosts of 2014 as well as a Los Angeles team with its sights set on another even-year Stanley Cup to go with those won in 2012 and 2014.

San Jose jumped out to a 2–0 series lead as Joe Pavelski and Logan Couture provided game-winning goals in 4–3 and 2–1 wins, respectively, at Staples Center. Tanner Pearson scored 3:47 into sudden death in Game 3, and the road trend continued as the Kings beat the host Sharks 2–1. But San Jose chased away any lingering ghosts by beating Los Angeles 3–2 in Game 4 and—in a break from the one-goal decisions—eliminated the Kings 6–3 in Game 5.

Jones, sporting a .912 save percentage, earned the satisfaction of beating his old teammates. Brent Burns was an offensive force from the blue line with eight points, and the Sharks featured a balanced attack from top to bottom.

San Jose next drew Nashville, a speedy eighth-seeded team that upset Anaheim in a seven-game first-round series. And, not to be overlooked, the Predators had only two fewer points in the regular season than the Sharks. That might help to explain why this series would go to the limit.

The Sharks held on to home ice with a pair of wins in regulation at the outset—5–2 and 3–2. Nashville struck back with a 4–1 win in Game 3. The Sharks thought they went up 3–1 when Pavelski scored early in overtime of Game 4, but the goal was disallowed following a long review. Instead, the Preds tied the series when Mike Fisher scored at 11:12 of a third sudden-death period.

The Sharks and Preds traded home-ice wins—San Jose 5–1 in Game 5 and Nashville 4–3 in overtime again in Game 6. San Jose ended the suspense early in Game 7 as Pavelski and Joel Ward scored in the first period. Couture, Thornton, and Marleau followed with goals as Nashville was clearly out of gas. San Jose moved on with its 5–0 victory.

While the Sharks were certainly pleased to advance, let's revisit that Pavelski no-goal in Game 4. If that play were called correctly—and he was pushed into Nashville goalie Pekka Rinne, which should have negated interference—and maybe the Sharks don't have to play two extra games in the second-round series and they have more left in the tank at the end of their run at the Cup.

The Blues were next, and St. Louis was coming off consecutive seven-game series wins over Chicago and Dallas. Because St. Louis had the third-most points in the regular season, the Sharks would start on the road in the hopes that a fourth time in the third round would finally be the charm.

San Jose brushed off a 2–1 loss in Game 1 when Jones made 26 saves in Game 2 and another 22 in Game 3 to post back-to-back shutouts. St. Louis retied the series with a 6–3 win in Game 4. And the Sharks faced a challenge knowing they'd have to win Game 5 on the road, never an easy assignment deep in the playoffs. But they got the job done when Pavelski scored tying and go-ahead goals within 1:43 before Chris Tierney and Joel Ward added insurance for a 6–3 win.

With a chance to clinch at home, and the specter of winning the West at hand, the Sharks jumped on the Blues. San Jose built a 4–0 lead by the midway point of the third period and cruised to a 5–2 win. How sweet it was. The look of pride on the faces of Joe Thornton and Patrick Marleau at the postgame news conference was a sight to behold.

A franchise-first Stanley Cup Final was an unbelievable experience. To think the hockey world was focused only on the Penguins and Sharks was humbling. I felt good for so many of the people who worked so hard in the organization and had finally reached this milestone.

"The subtext of the 25-year journey, and all the people I've known over those 25 years, we're all very proud," GM Doug Wilson said before the Final series started. "For the fans who come up to us and remember the journey, it just goes back to that emotion of pride."

But that last step proved very difficult. The Sharks did a tremendous job of containing Penguins superstar captain Sidney Crosby. Much of that credit goes to San Jose's shutdown pair of defensemen Marc-Edouard Vlasic and Justin Braun. The games were close—five of the six were nail-biters to the very end (two featured empty-netters and the other had a two-goal margin).

But Pittsburgh possessed excellent speed from top to bottom. Normally, no one made the Sharks look slow, but at times the Pens did. An edge in execution led to more offensive-zone time for the Penguins, which in turn translated into more shots and scoring opportunities.

The host Pens won each of the first two games by a goal apiece as Conor Sheary provided an example of Pittsburgh's potent depth. He scored an OT winner 2:35 into sudden death in Game 2. The Sharks got a sudden-death strike of their own in Game 3—Joonas Donskoi with the winner at 12:18 to send the Finn-attics into a frenzy—but Pittsburgh went up 3–1 in the series by winning Game 4 by the same score.

The Sharks made their cross-country flight worth it by ruining the Pens' plans to celebrate a Cup win for the first time on home ice. Burns and Couture scored in the opening 2:53 to set the tone for an eventual 4–2 win. But it was all over three nights later when Patric Hornqvist filled an empty net for a 3–1 win and Pittsburgh's fourth Cup.

The Sharks had nothing to hang their heads over. Couture had a coming out postseason by leading the league with 30 playoff points. Pavelski's 14 goals led all NHLers. Vlasic was a playoff-leading plus-14. Jones posted a .923 save percentage while starting all 24 playoff games.

"Our players played a lot of hockey this year, and in many cases they were fueled with heart," Doug Wilson said afterward. "The heart and character of this group is as good as I've ever seen."

It was a playoff run to remember.

The Sharks had never experienced an offseason as short as the summer of 2016. In addition to playing all the way until June 12, as many as six San Jose regulars had to crank it up even sooner than most because they were participating in the late-summer World Cup of Hockey that started with pre-tournament games September 8.

San Jose's training camp and preseason felt disjointed because regulars such as Joe Pavelski, Joe Thornton, Marc-Edouard Vlasic, Brent Burns, Joonas Donskoi, and Mikkel Boedker were missing at the outset, then given a short time to rest after either their respective countries were eliminated or the tourney concluded.

The Sharks hovered around .500 for the first quarter of the season before finding their legs and firmly establishing themselves safely in the playoff chase. By year's end San Jose finished third in what proved to be a dogfight for the Pacific Division title. Anaheim won it with 105 points, but upstart Edmonton made a late-season push to claim second by four points over San Jose, 103–99. Even a young Calgary team, which finished fourth in the division, qualified for the postseason.

No. 2 versus No. 3 was now a familiar matchup for San Jose, and the Sharks started the series on the road in Edmonton to defend their Western Conference title. The young Oilers were more than ready to make a mark after Edmonton finally broke a 10-year drought of missing out on the postseason.

The Oilers, coached by ex-Sharks bench boss Todd McLellan, were led by hockey's next great superstar—Connor McDavid. The 20-year-old, playing in just his second season in the NHL, scored 30 goals and led the league both in assists (70) and points (100). As the only NHLer to crack the century mark in points, and as a young captain of his team, McDavid won the Hart Trophy as league MVP.

The Sharks boasted a major award winner themselves. Defenseman Brent Burns improved on career-best numbers from the year before by scoring 29 goals and 76 points while posting a plus-19 plus-minus rating to be named the first Norris Trophy winner in team history. Burns, who also led the league with 320 shots on goal, was the trigger on an offense that otherwise uncharacteristically struggled on the power play. Burns stepped up when some of the other high-scoring vets didn't provide the offense that the Sharks were used to.

The Sharks received a huge scare in the final week of the regular season as Joe Thornton suffered a serious knee injury, details of which were not divulged at the time. But two days after the playoffs he underwent surgery to repair tears to both his anterior cruciate and medial collateral ligaments. This kind of injury typically sidelines hockey players for up to four to six months.

In Thornton's case, he was skating three days later. Thornton missed the last three regular-season contests and the first two games of the team's conference quarterfinal playoff series. Only those in the locker room knew what he was trying to play through.

San Jose got off to a great start on the road when Melker Karlsson scored 3:22 into overtime to allow the visitors to grab Game 1, 3–2. Edmonton answered two nights later with a gutsy defensive effort as the Sharks could muster only 16 shots on goalie Cam Talbot and the Oilers won 2–0.

Thornton's inspirational return to the lineup did nothing to end San Jose's goal-scoring drought as the Sharks were shut out again in Game 3—Talbot had 23 saves—in a 1–0 Oilers win. Then, out of nowhere, the Sharks exploded for a 7–0 win in Game 4 to even the series. Couture and Pavelski scored two goals each and Martin Jones made 23 saves.

San Jose spotted host Edmonton the first goal of Game 5, then rallied for three straight to lead 3–1 late in the second. But the Oilers struck once late in the second and again late in the third to force overtime before David Desharnais was a hero by scoring at 18:15.

Unfortunately, it wasn't meant to be. Edmonton broke open a scoreless Game 6 in San Jose with a pair of goals in the second period before McDavid ended it with only his second goal of the series into an empty net at 19:59. The 3–1 win sent Edmonton on to the second round where it would lose in seven games to Anaheim.

For the Sharks, Patrick Marleau led the team with three goals in the series, and it would memorably be his last of 19 straight seasons in teal. Marleau, who left via free agency for Toronto, departed as the franchise playoff leader in games (177), goals (68), and points (120). For the rest of the Sharks, it was time to heal and rest up after a long, long stretch of hockey.

Maybe it was karma, but when San Jose's other longtime franchise cornerstone, Joe Thornton, went down with a season-ending knee injury in late January, the team's quest for the playoffs were in question.

But with the emergence of a group challenged in training camp to reach another level, which included Chris Tierney, Tomas Hertl, and Joonas Donskoi—plus the integration of youngsters such as Timo Meier, Kevin Labanc, Marcus Sorensen, and Dylan DeMelo—San Jose sure enough was in the hunt late, despite the absence of its superstar center. That motivated GM Doug Wilson to acquire powerful scorer Evander Kane from Buffalo at the trade deadline.

The Sharks responded by going 12–6–1 after Kane's arrival to finish third in the Pacific Division with 100 points for the first time in four seasons, and clinched a 13th playoff appearance in 14 seasons. San Jose boasted 11 players with double-figure totals in goals. And Kane made it 12, combining the nine he scored with the Sharks after the 20 he had with Buffalo. The only time the Sharks had 12 double-figure goal-scorers was in 1993–94, and the NHL was a lot more wide open then than today.

In the first round, San Jose met SoCal rival Anaheim—a point better than the Sharks—for only the second time in the playoffs. And, over the span of seven nights, San Jose dominated Anaheim to record only its second series sweep in club history.

The Sharks outscored the Ducks 16–4 in the four games. Goalie Martin Jones was fantastic. He stopped all but four of 132 shots for a .970 save percentage. San Jose's power play went 6-for-20 (30 percent) to make Anaheim pay for its undisciplined style. And 15 of the team's 18 skaters showed up on the score sheet as the regular-season depth continued right into the playoffs.

That meant a second-round matchup against equally successful Vegas, the surprising expansion division winner. The Golden Knights were coming off a similar four-game sweep that included only three goals allowed against Los Angeles.

Vegas threw a scare into San Jose in Game 1 with a dominating 7–0 victory, but the Sharks rallied behind a Logan Couture power-play goal 5:13 into a second overtime session to even the series with a 4–3 victory in Game 2.

Upstart Vegas answered in San Jose, when William Karlsson scored 8:17 into sudden death for a 4–3 win in Game 3. But the Sharks knotted the series again as Jones made 34 saves for his sixth career playoff shutout in 38 starts during a 4–0 win.

Pivotal Game 5 went to the host Golden Knights, who withstood a late San Jose comeback attempt to hold on for a 5–3 victory. And Vegas' magic ride continued two nights later when

Marc-Andre Fleury stopped all 28 shots during a series-clinching 3–0 victory in Game 6.

Captain Joe Pavelski summed it up best when he said, "We knew we were a good team. There's some good teams that didn't make the playoffs. We'll be just as hungry next year. We'll have to be a good team again, and try to turn into a great team."

Chapter 10

The Tough Guys

Fighting in the NHL has changed so much in the relatively short time the Sharks have been in the league. Take, for example, these penalty-minute leaders and how much time they served in a penalty box during San Jose's inaugural season of 1991–92.

- Mike Peluso (Chicago), 408
- Rob Ray (Buffalo), 354
- Gino Odjick (Vancouver), 348
- Ron Stern (Calgary), 338
- Link Gaetz (San Jose), 326

There're some tough guys on that list for sure. Peluso's pugilistic pile of penalty minutes, accomplished over an 80-game schedule, ranks third all-time for a single season. One-time Sharks assistant coach Paul Baxter compiled 409 penalty minutes while skating with Pittsburgh during the 1981–82 season that was 80 games for each team. And the list is topped by Broad Street Bullies' headliner Dave Schultz of the Philadelphia Flyers. He was booked for 472 minutes in 1974–75 when teams were again playing 80 games each.

Peluso's figure represents the single-season high during San Jose's time in the league. Things started to change in the late 1990s when Ray's accumulation of 261 minutes in 1998–99 marked the first time since Washington's Randy Holt logged 275 in 1982–83 that the league leader dipped under the 300-minute plateau. And only three times since the 1997–98 campaign has the leader crested 300 minutes over a full-season schedule.

A couple factors led to the change in attitude about fighting in the game. While there are and will always be hard-line traditionalists who refuse to allow fighting to be legislated out of the game, staged fights at faceoff and line brawls have largely left the game. A good power play could make undisciplined actions on the ice pay dearly on the scoreboard. And coaches, too, started to demand more from third and fourth lines to push the pace and make opponents' defense feel more pressure.

If all a player could do was fight, he soon found himself out of the league. Policing the ice for transgressions that might be missed by the officials, or simply keeping everyone in line, is still very much part of the game. But players can't just police; they have to bring more to the table in terms of skating and scoring than ever before.

That being said, the Sharks still had their share of tough guys. This was especially evident early on when a young Sharks franchise felt the need to fight back when they were either getting taken advantage of or opponents were taking liberties against the non-glove-dropping skilled skaters.

There's another thing you need to know about the players who were labeled fighters. Nearly across the board, these are the nicest, funniest, most outgoing guys off the ice. They're not only the most popular guys with the fans, but they're the most popular in the dressing room, too.

Teammates really understand what they put on the line every night, and that's a big deal. The best so-called policemen, as I refer to them—I don't call them enforcers—have a sense of right from wrong, and they have a keen sense of justice. They know when it's time to stand up for their team, and they are willing to be there when no one else is there to help. And I think that's why those guys are appreciated and they're liked so much. That's the difference between a guy who polices on the ice and a flat-out goon.

Glance back at the list of the leading penalty minutes from the 1991–92 season and you'll notice a Shark sitting there at No. 5—Link Gaetz. One thing to note about that inaugural season for San Jose. Gaetz rolled up those 326 penalty minutes in 48 games.

The other four ahead of him on the list needed between 63 and 72 games each to achieve their punishment in minutes. Link was clearly the team's first policeman, but I guess you'd run across a number of people who'd more commonly refer to the Linkster as simply a goon.

Link is a unique character. He showed up at his first training camp with a black eye. The story goes he got into a barroom brawl the night before. And two days before that he was arrested for trying to shoot a bell hanging from a tower at a church. His aim for the bell was off and he took out the stained glass window of the church instead.

Here's what else you need to understand about Link. He was a great hockey player. He had the best shot on the team. He was one of the better skaters. And he had the toughness we all knew about. He could pass the puck and do just about everything on the ice when he was in the right frame of mind. But Link had his demons off the ice, and they led to many well-chronicled incidents that helped to greatly shorten what could have been a promising career.

I remember one time at the Cow Palace—the team's home rink for their first two seasons—at a time Link wasn't playing. He was walking around the archaic building, and there was an area that was basically open space between the lower-bowl seats and the upper bowl. It was a big and wide landing that was visible no matter where you were inside.

Link walked around with a crowd of at least 20 kids following him. That had never happened before, and I've never seen it since. He was like the Pied Piper. A crowd of people would just follow him around. That was the mystique of Link. First-year executive Dean Lombardi said Link had a cult following similar to Joe Montana, the star quarterback for the 49ers' Super Bowl teams at that time.

Link could have been elected mayor of San Jose, and he probably would have made $6 million a year. He was a good enough player to do it.

I remember one time Link came on the air with me as a guest. And this is the kind of thing that would happen to him all the time. Wrong place, wrong time. However, this is a lot more innocent than most of his other transgressions, whether they occurred on or off the ice.

We were just coming back from the commercial break. We could hear the commercial winding up in our headsets, and we started to hear the volume of the crowd in the background. I was about to say, "Welcome back," but instead Link belched on the air. Burp! Just like that. And I followed up with, "Well, welcome back to the Cow Palace." We've laughed about that for years up in the broadcast booth.

Any time I happen to hear the theme song from that old television series *The Mod Squad* I think of Link. Actor Clarence Williams III played the character of Linc Hayes, who was an undercover cop on the series. I hear that music, and it reminds me of Link.

A sequence of events that started on the night of March 6, 1992, led to the end of Link's time with the Sharks. The Sharks were hosting Pittsburgh in a late-season game. The Penguins were defending Stanley Cup champs, and they'd shown no mercy during their first two meetings with San Jose.

Pittsburgh won 8–0 at the Cow Palace in early December. Penguins captain Mario Lemieux scored two goals and added four assists for a six-point game where Kevin Stevens also collected a hat trick. Less than two weeks later, the Pens beat the visiting Sharks, 10–2, on a night where 16 different Pittsburgh skaters picked up points. Lemieux, who often tortured San Jose, again led the way with two goals and three points.

Pittsburgh capped a season-series sweep with a 7–3 road win in early March as Lemieux went for four points on a goal and three assists in that game. Link seemed particularly ornery that night. Gaetz skated to the penalty box five times by late in the third period for two cross-checks, a hold, a slash, and an unsportsmanlike conduct minor—the last of which did little to deter Rick Tocchet from eventually collecting a hat trick.

Gaetz was still serving his slashing minor when the final horn sounded, and he burst out of the penalty box when the door swung open, intent on throttling anyone wearing black and gold. Gaetz was assessed 17 more penalty minutes and earned an automatic 10-game suspension for instigating a fight while exiting the box at the end of a game.

A month later, just as his suspension ended, Gaetz was involved in a serious auto accident when he was thrown from a car driven by a friend who was under the influence. Link was in bad shape for more than a week with back and facial injuries. He suffered a bruised brain stem, which left his left side partially paralyzed, and he had no memory of the accident. Link was laid up in the hospital for six weeks.

Once discharged, Gaetz rehabbed over the summer, intending to resume his hockey career. But he saw his playing days end with San Jose when he was traded in the fall to Edmonton. Unfortunately for Link, he never appeared in another NHL regular-season game.

Jeff Odgers logged 217 penalty minutes in Link's shadow that first season, and he assumed the full-time policing duties by Year 2. Now here's a guy who was given nothing in the game. He realized he was not as talented as most, yet he was tougher than everybody.

It reminds me of the stories you hear about the guy who is the worst hockey player on the team—and I'm not suggesting that Jeff was a bad player—and who goes out and beats the crap out of someone in tryouts. The coach sees that and says, "We need him on our team."

Jeff Odgers had a great sense of justice. It's part of who he is. He's a rural farmer. He knows the difference between right from wrong. Any time Odgie fought, it was not considered dirty, and it was not considered out of line. He was a policeman who protected his teammates. He fought for the honor of the jersey when it was being tarnished by an opponent.

He always had that aura—not of a vigilante, but maybe of a frontiersman of the wild, wild west. Whenever I looked at Jeff Odgers, especially when he had that thick mustache, I pictured him fighting in the Civil War. Maybe he fought for General Ulysses S. Grant and then went out to the Badlands with Teddy Roosevelt. Odgie was one of those frontier guys.

Odgers' first NHL game was on Long Island. It was Mike Sullivan's first game that night, too. And Odgers showed a willingness right off the bat to throw his weight around. He got into a fight with Mick Vukota of the Islanders. Vukota was a pretty tough dude. Odgers was giving away two inches, some reach, and 25 pounds. Vukota was also three years older.

From that moment on you knew Odgie was going to be there for his teammates. And to this day he's the club's all-time penalty-minutes leader with 1,001. Never mind he was the slowest skater on the team. He certainly had a choppy stride that might move an NHL scout to ask, "Why are you showing interest in him?" But Jeff had so much heart, and so much character. He was able to dole out justice in a way nobody saw as unfair, and I think he'll always be respected. That's why he became captain of the team by 1995. Usually you don't have a fourth-liner become your captain, but that was the kind of guy he was.

Jeff is one of the great stories of the franchise. He's from a small town—Spy Hill, Saskatchewan—and nobody lives there but the Odgers family, I think. He's on a fifth-generation cattle farm. And as so many small towns in Canada do, this one has erected a sign that says: "Welcome to Spy Hill, home of Jeff Odgers," and it had a picture of him in a Sharks uniform.

Lyndon Byers was at the tail end of a 10-year NHL career when the Sharks signed him early in the 1992–93 season. With 959 penalty minutes in nine seasons, the former Boston Bruin was a piece of work. He appeared in only 18 games for the Sharks. But that was enough to log 122 PIM to shoot his career total over the 1,000 mark.

I remember one time he sat in the booth with me for a game. The Sharks were hosting Calgary in late January of 1993, and another guy who was reasonably rugged at times—Sharks defenseman Jayson More—scored a beauty of a shorthanded goal. More made a brilliant move, skated through a couple defenders, and went top-shelf against Calgary (and future Shark) goalie Mike Vernon. Jayson put it top shelf and it stuck to the top of the net. Like Buffalo Sabres legend Rick Jeanneret used to say, "Where Momma hides the cookies."

Well Lyndon Byers got on the air with me and said, "I just want you to know Jayson More did not score that goal." I thought, *What the hell is he talking about? Oh my God, did I mess up?* And he said, "Jayson ORR scored that goal." Remember that More's number was 4, the same as the great Bobby Orr. That's the kind of personality L.B. had. Of course, he went on to do radio in Boston. He had the media in the palm of his hand, and now he's a part of it.

The Sharks selected a tough character by the name of Darin Michael "Dody" Wood in the third round of the team's initial NHL draft of 1991. Reared in Chetwynd, British Columbia, and of Saulteau First Nations ancestry, Wood only appeared for the Sharks during an NHL career that spanned from 1992 to '98. He logged 471 penalty minutes in 106 NHL games, but he spent most of his time in the IHL or AHL.

Dody was a tough kid. How tough was he? Dody took a short leave from the team when a family relative passed away. He returned to the reservation for the funeral where afterward a will was read. As the story goes, at the reading somebody got into an argument, and Dody came back to the team with a black eye.

One of the funnier moments I recall involving Wood came during a preseason game against Vancouver. Dody was trying to make the team, and he got into a situation where he felt like somebody hit him, he retaliated, maybe another hit came a little from behind. The opponent dropped his gloves and turned to face Dody, who dropped his gloves as well. Dody looked up and saw Mark Messier. Dody got a shit-eating grin on his face, because he was about to fight Mark Messier. The only reason Mess was engaging Dody in preseason was because he'd signed a free-agent contract to move from the Rangers to the Canucks, and he was just trying to set a tone with his new team.

David Maley was another one of those early-franchise glue guys who wasn't afraid to drop the gloves. He'd already spent eight seasons with Montreal, New Jersey, and Edmonton before, at age 29, getting claimed off waivers by San Jose. Maley compiled 156 minutes in 62 games before moving on to the Islanders late in

1993–94. I give Dave credit, though, for returning to the South Bay after his playing career was over. He was one of the first ex-Sharks to invest in the community by becoming a business owner. You have to respect that.

When I hear the name Andrei Nazarov I immediately think of the 1960s television sitcom *The Munsters*. In fact, GM Dean Lombardi described a young Nazarov to us that way one night on the air: "Oh, yeah, he's a real Herman Munster type."

First of all, I could visualize two electrodes coming out of Nazarov's neck. And second, I recall the scene in *The Munsters* where Herman gets hit in the middle of the street by a tractor trailer. The tractor trailer is totaled, and Herman is fine. That's what Nazzi was like on the ice.

Thanks to Dean's comment, the Sharks' original in-house organist, Dieter Ruehle, played *The Munsters* theme song when Nazzy took a seat in the penalty box. Anytime we heard that music, those of us in the broadcast booth were trying not to die of laughter.

I remember a time against Colorado when Nazarov took an innocent, innocuous-looking shot from center ice. The puck rocketed off his stick, rang off the crossbar, and went all the way up about 50 rows in the seats. I couldn't help but start laughing.

The Sharks used a high pick to select the Russian-born Nazarov—10th overall in 1992. He spent a good share of his time in the minors over four different seasons as property of the Sharks. One time early on while Nazarov was in Kansas City, Blades coach Kevin Constantine was mad at him for something, as happened often. Nazzy just looked at Kevin and said, "How much the fine, how much the fine?"

Nazzy tried to use the language barrier to his advantage. He supposedly couldn't speak any English the season of his first training camp. When Nazzy showed up for the first road trip in flip-flops, shorts, and a T-shirt, he was told he had to wear a suit and tie. He acted like he didn't understand. One of the team's public relations guys took him to get a suit. That's when Nazzy looked at him and said, "Hugo Boss." He wanted a designer suit! Nazzy knew what he was doing.

There was the time, too, when Nazzy head-butted Stephane Quintal not once but twice in a fight. Afterward Nazarov said, "In Russia, this is allowed." Well after his career, Nazzy ended up going back to Russia to coach. And every one of those teams he had turned into a goon fest. Every one of them! But he wore a Hugo Boss suit with a nice pocket square to coach. You can find videos online that show him swinging sticks at fans in the stands.

I'd place four tough guys who came to the Sharks at the end of their careers in much the same category—Ronnie Stern, Dave Brown, Tim Hunter, and Marty McSorley. Boy, talk about a group no one would want to mess with. All but McSorley capped long careers with San Jose as their last stop. Marty played one season each for two more teams—a return to Edmonton and a finale in Boston—before retiring.

All four were so well established in terms of toughness by the time they got to the Sharks that not a lot of opponents wanted to issue a challenge. They didn't have to do a whole lot to deter trouble. But if a physical response was necessary, they didn't need to be asked twice.

Dave Brown signed as a free agent just before the start of the 1995–96 Sharks training camp. San Jose was coming off consecutive Cinderella runs in the postseason. They'd upset Detroit in Round 1 in '94 and Calgary in '95, same round. The team wasn't necessarily built to contend for a Cup, but reaching the postseason and knocking off a worthy opponent each of the two previous seasons suggested San Jose was on the right path.

And while the 1995–96 roster was sprinkled with a number of hard-nosed competitors in Jeff Odgers, Owen Nolan, Dody Wood, Andrei Nazarov, and Jimmy Kyte, there were also a number of coveted young draftees that could use some protection. That talented group included Ray Whitney, Jeff Friesen, Viktor Kozlov, and Ville Peltonen. Again, Brownie wasn't asked to fight much—he logged only 46 penalty minutes in 37 games, after compiling 1,743 minutes in 13 previous NHL campaigns. But just the sight of his 6-foot-5, 222-pound frame—and listening to that soft, deep, and authoritative voice—was enough to keep things calm.

Tim Hunter was the perfect replacement for Brown. With 3,011 minutes over 15 NHL seasons before signing a one-year deal as a free agent in the summer of 1996, Hunter had a little more fight left in him when he arrived in San Jose. Hunts logged 135 minutes in penalties on a team that lost a whole lot and had other guys in a cranky mood, too: Nazarov (222 minutes), Wood (193), McSorley (186), Todd Ewen (162), Tony Granato (159), and Nolan (155).

Hunter was truly a student of the game. It's not necessarily a trait you'd expect from someone who was expected to throw his weight around. But a couple months after his only season with the Sharks concluded he was hired in Washington to start a career in coaching.

He was an assistant under Ron Wilson with the Caps through 2002 and followed Wilson to San Jose, where Hunter was an assistant coach again through 2008. Hunter was an astute, well-spoken, and prepared individual. You always learned something

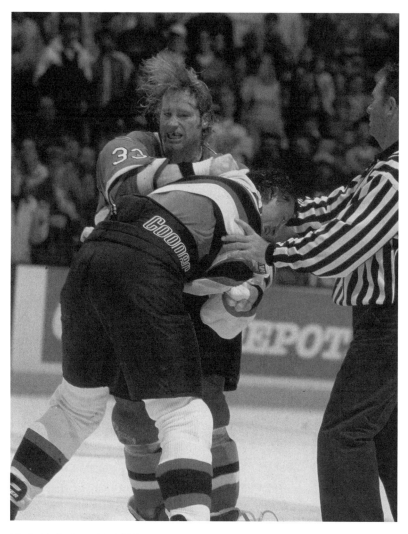

Marty McSorley added 326 penalty minutes during his two years spent in San Jose to a career total of 3,381 over 17 NHL seasons. (Jim McIsaac/Getty Images)

when you talked to Hunts. And if he told a player to do something, odds are they were going to try their best to get it right!

McSorley needed no introduction to Sharks fans. They were plenty familiar with him running alongside Wayne Gretzky and all those other skill guys that had become division rivals as members of the Los Angeles Kings. And the fans knew that McSorley and Gretzky's connection started when both were with the Edmonton Oilers.

Unlike free agents Brown and Hunter, McSorley came in a trade with the Rangers before the ill-fated 1996–97 season, but he was a pretty significant presence in terms of physicality the following season when San Jose rallied to return to the postseason for the first time in three seasons. Marty logged a runner-up 140 penalty minutes in 56 games. Coach Darryl Sutter was strict about not taking unnecessary penalties, so discipline was important. Still, if McSorley felt like he needed to stand up for a teammate, he dropped 'em.

Stern signed as a free agent in the summer of '98, and he played in San Jose for the final two seasons of his 12-year NHL career. Ronnie blended in well with the close-knit group. He played through injury but still had something to give. He took pressure off Nolan to feel like he had to drop the gloves. Stern led the team in penalty minutes his first season with 158 and was tops again in 1999–00, playing in 67 games.

The Sharks went through a period where they continued to search the market high and low for a hired gun. And they always seemed to land a veteran who was well qualified for the job but was at the end of a long career. When San Jose signed free agent Brantt Myhres early in training camp of 1998, the Sharks were going a different route.

An Edmonton native, Myhres was only 24 years old with just 85 games of NHL experience in three seasons with two teams—two with the Tampa Bay Lightning and one with the Philadelphia Flyers. Myhres was a personable and tough winger. He was more than willing, but he had trouble staying healthy and off the NHL's suspended list. Myhres appeared in 30 games one season for the Sharks and only 13 the next—logging a combined 213 penalty minutes.

Brantt fought a lot of demons, as many of the guys who are primarily asked to fight often do. He liked to take his jersey off and have just his shoulder pads on, sort of showing off for the girls. And we liked to tease him by calling him Dirk Diggler. He tried to climb the glass between the team benches in a playoff series against Nashville to get at a Predators player after a game. Thank goodness he was unsuccessful.

Myhres cleaned up his life after his playing career ended, which is nice to see. He had received a lifetime ban from the NHL, the final blow after he previously failed four drug tests that resulted in suspensions. But Brantt became clean and sober and even studied substance abuse behavioral health at a university in Calgary before returning to the NHL to help others with similar problems. I respect him for getting his life together because things weren't going well there for a while.

The next two tough guys who come to mind—Scott Parker and Jody Shelley—are connected because one was brought to San Jose because of the actions of the other. Shelley was a member of the Columbus Blue Jackets in 2002–03 when he took offense to a hit delivered by Sharks defenseman Brad Stuart. The teams met nine nights later in San Jose, and Shelley had revenge on his mind.

He clocked an unsuspecting Stuart, who suffered a concussion and missed the final 21 games of the regular season.

When general manager Doug Wilson traded for Scott Parker during the 2003 draft, he said, "What happened to Brad Stuart will never happen again." And, sure enough, when San Jose and Columbus first met the following season—December 31, 2003—Parker dropped the gloves against Shelley only 2:16 after the opening faceoff.

Parker was a first-round draft pick, and he could play a little. But he was also tough. As it turned out, his body took a pounding, and he's living outside Colorado Springs after having been diagnosed with traumatic brain injury. There are some days he just can't do much. You hate to hear stories like that.

Coincidentally, Jody Shelley was dealt by the Blue Jackets to the Sharks 11 months after Parker was moved to Colorado. Jody, too, was a decent player. He could skate and make plays. Shelley provided muscle for the better part of three seasons in San Jose before he was shipped to the Rangers. He scored some goals in big games for New York and Philadelphia, and nobody would mess with him. And he was one of the nicest guys. They loved him in Columbus. He's an intelligent guy who can describe the game well. That's why he's been a good fit in the broadcasting field since his playing career ended.

Another tough skater who certainly knew his way around the ice was Ryane Clowe, a homegrown Shark. San Jose selected the 6-foot-3, 225-pound rugged winger who hailed from St. John's, Newfoundland, with a sixth-round pick in 2001. Clowe had to bide time in the minors. During his two full seasons with Cleveland of the American League he proved he could score, he could set up goals, and he could fight.

Once he got his promotion, he showed what we had heard. He was as tough as absolutely anybody, and half the time no one would fight him because he was so tough. And he could play. He could make you pay. Look at the numbers he finished with as a Shark: 101 goals, 271 points, and 567 penalty minutes in 423 regular-season games over eight seasons.

Brad Staubitz played the role of policeman for half a season's worth of games in 2008–09 and 2009–10. He was more of a light heavyweight. At 6-foot-1, 215 pounds, Staubitz was like Billy Conn, the light heavyweight who put on a few pounds and fought Joe Louis for the title and almost won. Staubitz was another one who knew right from wrong and tried to do something about it.

Understanding that the police—i.e., the referees—aren't always there to adjudicate problems. So you could call them a second amendment advocate, if you know what I'm saying. I remember one fight Staubitz got into with Jordin Tootoo in March of 2009 when Staubitz basically rearranged his face. It was a pretty devastating bout. Staubitz pumped in one right after another, then switched to the left hand and got a few more uncontested shots in right on the button. That was one of the more one-sided bouts we've ever had in San Jose.

Mike Brown, like Staubitz, was not overly big at 5-foot-11 and 210 pounds, but there wasn't a guy in the league he'd back down from. By the time the Sharks dealt with Edmonton for Brownie, fighting in the NHL was not only on the decline, but the player who filled that role needed to do other things, too. Like play. And Brownie wasn't bad.

The other thing I remember about Brownie was how quickly he could grow a mustache. He'd grow one for Movember real thick and real fast. He had one of those 1890 waxed mustaches with points on the ends early on with the Sharks. I also recall when he broke his leg in a game. He didn't say anything...he just came off the ice—and he'd broken his leg! That's another tough character.

Micheal Haley is one of the true tough guy players on the team, too. The difference is he added a lot more than just having the ability and willingness to drop the gloves. He added a little bit of everything. He could skate and he could pass.

I give Micheal Haley a lot of kudos because if you think about all these policing guys, they had to work their way up. They weren't first-round draft picks most of the time. They were guys who had to fight their way literally and figuratively to get to the NHL and make a living. And they've endured a lot. Look at what some of these guys have had to deal with. We've heard stories about substance abuse and other difficulties. That's why they're so respected.

Big John Scott, too, was quite the deterrent. No one would fight him. I liken him to Nick Fotiu—not a lot of guys wanted to fight him back when he patrolled the ice in the 1980s. John is a smart guy. He got an engineering degree from Michigan Tech, which is not an easy school. It's a pretty difficult program, and as a hockey player, too, it's not easy. But he did it.

I don't think anybody was happier than the people in San Jose when that whole 2016 All-Star Game scenario went down. I think about some of the goals he scored for us more than the fights. "Deterrent" is a good word for him because no one would fight him much, but if anything happened, he would go over and settle things down. He'd say, "You're going to stop this right now," and he did it with a sense of humor, too.

Chapter 11

The Bruce Black Story

Sometimes, something happens that is truly remarkable and makes a difference in someone's life. That's what happened in the 1996–97 season, when a few fortuitous events placed me on the same plane as a Bay Area businessman with a unique connection to hockey.

It was one of those rare occasions where the Sharks made a trip for two on the team plane available to someone who bid on the trip to benefit a selected charity. We have seen these a few times in preseason in recent years, but it's exceedingly unusual to have such an opportunity in a regular-season journey today.

On this particular trip in 1997, the team was introduced to Bruce Black, a successful Bay Area entrepreneur who was an avid follower of Sharks hockey. It was a thrill for Bruce to bring his son with him on an excursion that not only benefitted a charity and allowed him to see Sharks hockey behind the scenes, but it brought him closer to a mystery from his own past.

While the aircraft jetted on its way to the first leg of the journey, Bruce let me in on that mystery. "I was born in Bell, California, in 1947, and was adopted by my parents there," he said softly. "I know a little bit about my birth parents, but I have a bit more information on my birth mother than my birth father. All I know about my birth father is that he played in the National Hockey League."

I was immediately interested. "What's his name?" I asked. "Let's look him up." "His name was Don Gallinger," he said. I immediately recognized the name, but couldn't recall much more.

We had a few books on the plane that could provide some answers: several editions of the *NHL Guide and Record Book*. We looked at the Retired Player section, and saw that Gallinger had played in the NHL from 1942 to 1948, and had scored 65 goals,

88 assists, and 153 points in 222 NHL games, all for the Boston Bruins.

One notation in the Retired Players section is important here: a large dot printed next to the player's name means that he is deceased. I looked at Gallinger's name, hoping that there would be no dot. Of the two editions of the guide that were available, the earlier one had no dot next to his name, but when I turned to the same page in the later edition, I felt a tinge of disappointment when I saw the large dot next to his name.

I shook my head and said to Bruce, "It's too bad that we met one year too late, because maybe we could have located your birth father before he died." I promised to look into details when the trip ended, we exchanged phone numbers, and that was that.

Well, for some reason, that dot kept nagging at me. "What if it was a misprint, and he isn't dead?" I asked myself. "I think I'll do a bit of checking, just to be sure, and maybe I can get a copy of the obituary at least."

I couldn't find an obituary, and a call to the NHL Players' Association produced something else entirely. "We have him listed as still alive," the representative told me. "But we can't provide any details to you as to where he is, due to respect for privacy."

That made sense, but I knew that Bruce still had a chance to meet his birth father in person. We began the process of searching him out.

Meanwhile, a few things continued to nag at me. It seemed unusual that a player with decent NHL production had only played for a few years without talk of a career-ending injury. Gallinger was an exceptional athlete and had been one of the top candidates for the Calder Trophy during his rookie NHL season. He set a record that is still held today: at age 17, he became the youngest player ever to score an overtime goal in a Stanley Cup playoff game for Boston against the Montreal Canadiens. He had served his country in World War II, staying active in the game by playing for an RCAF hockey team composed of pros, and he had taken up with the Bruins again after the war was over.

Gallinger was well thought of as a baseball player, too, so much so that he was offered a contract by the Philadelphia Phillies and Boston Red Sox to abandon hockey and play baseball. But he had no baseball career after 1948, so that wasn't the reason why his career had suddenly ended.

There was something else, too. I knew that I had read about Don Gallinger before. I was familiar with his name, but couldn't recall why.

The reason suddenly appeared, almost as a footnote, in a list of notable dates in NHL history. Given the gravity of it, I was amazed that it wasn't a 100-point headline, and that it was no longer even a topic of conversation.

As it turns out, Bruce Black's birth father was one of only two players in history expelled from the NHL for life by league President Clarence Campbell for gambling on games. Along with Billy Taylor, an established star six years older, Gallinger had been shunned from the game in perhaps the most scandalous moment in NHL history. Due to an earlier gambling incident involving Toronto Maple Leaf star Babe Pratt that resulted in a nine-game suspension, the League was ready to lower the boom on anyone associated with anything approaching the 1919 Black Sox baseball scandal. Campbell lowered that boom in September of 1948 and expelled both Taylor and Gallinger.

This was turning into quite a detective story. A National Hockey League player had fathered a child in 1947 who was given up for adoption over 2,000 miles away from home; the player was expelled from the league a year later for the most notorious of reasons; and no one had talked about either of these events for years! Why not?

We had ourselves quite a mystery, but the bigger question was whether it would be possible to unite Bruce Black with either of his birth parents. We had no idea whether these people were in good health, and had no idea whether they would have any interest in meeting him. The mystery turned into a race against time.

The race began where it had started, in the NHL guides and club yearbooks, where we searched for any information that we could find on Don Gallinger. It seemed that everywhere we turned, we found something fascinating.

For instance, we found that Gallinger was born on April 16, 1925, in Port Colborne, Ontario. Coincidentally, Bruce Black was born on April 16, 1947, on his birth father's 22nd birthday.

It was just days after Gallinger had skated in what would prove to be his final Stanley Cup playoff series, the 1947 NHL semifinal round against the Montreal Canadiens. In that series, won by Montreal in five games, Gallinger dressed for the first four contests, winding up with one fighting major against Canadiens legend Emile "Butch" Bouchard in the game won by Boston.

The search continued. We found the names of several people in the Port Colborne area with the last name Gallinger. Several calls produced people who sounded as if they were in their 20s or 30s, and none recognized the name Don Gallinger. The search had stalled.

A final phone number was on the list. When a woman answered, her voice sounded older. *Maybe she'll know something about Don Gallinger's whereabouts,* I thought. *Maybe she'll remember him.*

I gave her my name and explained that I was the play-by-play radio voice of the San Jose Sharks, looking to track down the former NHL player Don Gallinger. Her voice, while friendly, suddenly sharpened. I realized that I had hit pay dirt.

"Are you a lawyer?" she asked suspiciously. When I replied in the negative, she asked, "Does he owe you any money?"

"No," I replied.

"Well, he is my brother-in-law," she said. "My husband, Keith, who is dead now, was his brother, and he was a wonderful man, nothing like his brother."

I repeated the story that some accounts had him alive, while others listed him as dead. "Oh, he's alive," she said, somewhat sarcastically. "But I don't have anything else to add to that."

Sensing that the phone conversation might end with her hanging up on me, I figured it was time to toss the Hail Mary. I explained that I was trying to track Gallinger down because he had fathered a child who had been given up for adoption and who was looking to meet him.

There was silence at the end of the line. "Well, I'll be damned," the elderly lady blurted out after a while. I had told her something about her brother-in-law that she hadn't known. And then she began to share more information, first in bits and pieces, and then in a steady stream.

Gallinger had married a woman—not Bruce's birth mother, but someone else. The couple became the parents of four children, three boys and a girl. He had used what money he had made in the NHL to invest in a hotel property somewhere near Kitchener, Ontario.

From there, a series of downward spirals placed tremendous stress on this Gallinger family.

First, the business failed, dooming the marriage in the process. There were stories of infidelities on both sides. The daughter lived to be nine years old, dying of leukemia. Then the children's mother was killed in an alcohol-related automobile accident. Struggling to make ends meet, Gallinger held a variety of jobs, eventually becoming a shirt salesman for a clothing company. Because he was always on the road or otherwise AWOL, the children were sent to live with their maternal grandmother, who provided a home for them.

The phone crackled. The elderly lady continued to speak, and I continued to scribble on whatever scraps of paper were nearby. "One of the boys hated his father so much that he changed his last name to his grandmother's," she said. I dutifully wrote all of it down. "What are their names? Where do they live?" I asked.

I learned from her that the oldest son was named Donald Gallinger Jr., and he lived in Collingwood, Ontario.

Suddenly, the information slowed to a crawl. "So, you're not a lawyer, right?" she asked. I once again replied that I was not, sensing that she was suspicious again. "Some lawyers have been calling me about him," she said.

I assured her that I was telling her the truth, and thanked her for the information. She thanked me for the revelation that I had shared with her.

"I don't know why anyone would ever want to find him, and if they do, they'll be happy that they never grew up in that family," she said. It wouldn't be the last time that I heard such a sentiment.

After that conversation, the search continued in Collingwood, Ontario. I found a home number listed for Donald Gallinger Jr.

and a number for a flower shop that he owned. During business hours, I called the flower shop.

It was perplexing. I was calling a business during business hours, and I kept getting an answering machine. *What kind of a business was this?* I wondered. But the answering machine kept picking up, and on it was an important bit of information.

"Hello, you've reached Don and Judy Gallinger," the voicemail said. We now had someone else's name.

After several calls that went to voicemail, I decided that there was a reason why I wasn't getting through: Bruce Black had to make this call. I gave him the information and told him that I hoped that when he called, the wife answered the phone, not the husband. "She has no history with what you have to say, so she won't hang up on you," I added.

Two days later, the phone rang, and Bruce was on the line, sounding excited. "I just had a nice chat with Judy," he said, "and she didn't hang up." The reason why the answering machine had kept picking up was because they had been on vacation and had just returned to work. Don Jr.'s wife told Bruce that she couldn't wait until her husband came home to hear the latest news about his family history.

Shortly afterward, the two half-brothers were on the line with one another. They found that as fellow business owners, they had a lot in common. They liked to play golf. They had families. Two other brothers were still alive, too, although Don Jr. did not have a lot of contact with them. There was also a reason why the elderly lady in Port Colborne had been so suspicious: a lawsuit was pending between father and son.

Don Jr. gave Bruce his father's address and phone number, and the addresses of his newfound brothers. Bruce said he would send a family photo, along with some basic information, to each brother, and to his father. Bruce and his wife made plans to fly to Toronto to meet the brothers separately from the father.

And so the packages were mailed, and all were the same, with one exception. The package that was mailed to Don Gallinger Sr. had an additional note after the introduction. "I have your telephone number. If you would like to speak with me," the note said, "I will call you one week from Wednesday, at 8:00 PM Eastern Time, and we can speak then."

Time passed, and the fateful day came closer. It was the day before the scheduled call. Bruce gave his brother a call to see what he thought of the package. What he heard was a bit disconcerting.

"We haven't received your package yet," Don Jr. said. What if Don Sr. did not receive his package before it was time for the promised telephone call the next night? There was clearly only one way to find out, and because of the letter, Bruce had to call.

Wednesday, the day of reckoning, arrived. Bruce's telephone rang, and Don Jr. was on the line: the package had arrived on that very day, and that meant that there was a good chance that his father had received his, too.

At 5:00 PM Pacific Time, 8:00 Eastern, Bruce picked up the phone and dialed. The phone rang and rang and rang. It rang 11 times, as if someone on the other end of the line was making a decision whether to answer or not. On the 11th ring, Don Gallinger Sr. answered, and when he started to talk, it seemed as if he wouldn't stop.

"I've been looking at the package that you sent all day," he said, and so the conversation began. For the next two hours, Don Gallinger Sr. talked, a flood of emotional memories bubbling to the surface and crackling over the phone line to California.

He had met Bruce's birth mother, Ruth Gordon, somewhat accidentally during the summer. He was a high-flying young star with the Boston Bruins, one of the better young players in the National Hockey League. She was the daughter of a top executive at Inco Limited, the largest nickel miner in the world. They hadn't known each other for a long time, had gotten together, and she had become pregnant.

Don found out about the pregnancy from his father, a welder, in a call he received while at Bruins training camp. "I was willing to marry her," he said. But when the welder met with the executive back in the fall of 1946, the societal gulf, along with the shame that accompanied out-of-wedlock pregnancy, was too great.

Her father told his father that there would be no marriage. The executive's daughter would not be marrying a welder's son who was "only" a ne'er-do-well hockey player. Don't worry, her father said. He would take care of everything.

Ruth's father did take care of everything. It was all arranged. She did what a lot of young women did under such circumstances back in those days. She would leave town immediately, live with a relative, have the baby, give the baby up for adoption, and return home after physical evidence of her pregnancy had subsided. For the rest of the world, she would "go away to school" for a year, and no one would find out. It would be her secret. Her father's career would not be affected by family scandal. Don would have no contact with her again.

Discussion turned to the lifetime ban, and Don began to show his deep-seated bitterness. Babe Pratt, the NHL's Most Valuable Player in 1944, had been suspended for nine games due to gambling on games, and others had been convinced to gamble, in part because their salaries were low.

When caught gambling on games early in 1946, Pratt served his suspension, promised never to gamble on games again, and was allowed to return to the ice. He was traded by Toronto to Boston in June of that year. Pratt's final NHL season was spent as Don Gallinger's teammate with the Bruins in 1946–47, the same year that Bruce Black was born.

The interconnected web continued with Billy Taylor, who was also an established star at the time. He had been in Toronto during the Pratt affair, but was traded to Detroit, where he set a record that has only been equaled by Wayne Gretzky: he recorded seven assists in a game against Chicago on March 16, 1947.

After that one season in the Motor City, Taylor was traded to Boston in the fall of 1947, and it was here that he also came to influence Don Gallinger.

Gallinger had already enjoyed gambling, but it was Taylor who convinced him that he could double his $7,500 annual salary by betting on his team to lose. They did so, but only on games that they believed the team would lose anyway. It happened on eight occasions in that 1947–48 season, and the seeds for scandal followed the tangled web that wove back through the cities where Taylor had played.

James Tamer, a known figure associated with the Motor City underworld, was being monitored by the authorities for illegal gambling activities. On a wiretap just before a game in Chicago in February of 1948, Tamer was recorded talking with a Bruins player. Making a few notes on the physical condition of the Bruins, the voice later identified as Gallinger instructed Tamer to bet $500.00 for him. By this time, Taylor had been traded to the New York Rangers. Tamer would phone New York, where Taylor placed the bet for Boston to lose. Ironically, Boston won the game, but the authorities had enough information to contact NHL President Campbell, and the scandal broke.

Interestingly, Tamer would show up in the public eye two decades later. The man in the middle of hockey's gambling scandal in 1948 eventually became the "entertainment director" at the Aladdin Hotel in Las Vegas. After being indicted by a grand jury for holding a hidden interest in the hotel and for his association with known organized crime figures in the Motor City, he was denied a casino license by the State of Nevada. He was later banned forever from setting foot in any Nevada casino. Tamer died in 2003 at the age of 91.

When confronted with the scandal, Gallinger denied his participation to the public, but privately confessed to Campbell, in the hope that his honesty would result in a suspension and reinstatement similar to that of Pratt. However, the NHL president was not as lenient with Gallinger and Taylor as he had been with Pratt just one year earlier, and the result was a lifetime expulsion from the NHL, with the right to appeal also removed by a change in the league's constitution.

Pratt remained involved in hockey for the remainder of his life. In spite of his nine-game suspension for gambling, he was inducted into the Hockey Hall of Fame in 1966. A legendary figure in Western Canada, he was a popular CBC television commentator, became an ambassador for the Vancouver Canucks, and died of a heart attack in the media lounge of the old Pacific Coliseum on December 16, 1988. Canucks players wore the letters "BABE" on their jerseys for the remainder of that season.

After a series of articles by Hall of Fame writer Scott Young in the 1960s, a case was made for reinstatement. President Campbell continued to resist, but finally, in 1970, both Taylor and Gallinger were reinstated, allowing them to pursue careers in the game.

While they were well beyond their playing years, things went better for Taylor. He became a scout for the Pittsburgh Penguins, and his son, Billy Taylor Jr., had a brief career that included two NHL games played.

Meanwhile, Gallinger never got another job in hockey, and he became bitter whenever he talked about the other players who got back in the game.

The telephone conversation continued that night, and Bruce Black learned more. The photo of the Black family had stirred another memory for Gallinger. "The picture of your daughter in this photo that you sent me really reminds me of Ruth as I remember her," he said.

He also learned of Gallinger's work as a traveling salesman for a men's shirt company. His travels brought him often to Southern California, where, unbeknownst to him, Bruce had been raised by his adopted parents.

Don's other children were eventually raised by their maternal grandmother, and they were estranged from their oft-absent father while they were growing up as well.

Bruce was excited to learn so much about his past. He made plans to travel to Toronto with his family to get together with all of his newfound Gallinger brothers: Don Jr., Michael, and Kim. On the same trip, he would venture to Burlington, Ontario, where he would meet his birth father face-to-face.

Bruce was very enthusiastic about this journey into his past and his added appreciation of what his adopted parents, his true parents, had done for him. As we spoke about his experiences, he showed a renewed interest in learning more about his mother,

Ruth Gordon, so it was time to restart the investigation, this time from the maternal side.

Bruce's parents had diligently saved all the records of their son's adoption, and in that record, there was a bit of paperwork that had his birth mother's signature: her full name was Elma Ruth Gordon, so we knew that she was referred to by her middle name instead of her given name.

Even though we had more information about Bruce's birth mother, there was no guarantee that we could find her. After all, it was likely that she had eventually married, changed her name, and vanished into thin air. There were no guarantees that she was still alive, or that she would want to have any contact with Bruce.

One bit of information proved to be the best clue: a listing in *Canadian Who's Who*, part of the well-known reference publication series. Ruth's parents were listed, along with two brothers and one sister. We had more names to add to the growing compilation.

One of her siblings, her brother David, was also listed as an attorney with a law firm in Toronto. It seemed like a good place to start. "Why not call the law firm, if it is still in existence?" I told Bruce. "David is probably long since retired, but if he's still alive, perhaps they could put you in touch with him, or if he isn't, someone in his family."

Bruce enthusiastically agreed, and called the law firm. Little did he know that the next dramatic turn in the story would take place. As it turned out, this particular brother was 13 years younger than his sister, and he was still working at the same law firm!

In one instant, Bruce was on the phone with the brother of his birth mother. He began to tell the story of his search, but the reaction he got was different than the Gallingers' reaction.

David spoke with the professional voice of an accomplished attorney. "I'm sorry," he said. "You have the wrong person. My sister Ruth never had any children until she married Dr. Fraser Parrott. I know them all. There is no history of this in our family. You must have the wrong person."

Bruce maintained his calm. "Before you hang up," he said, "I'd like to ask you one question. Did your sister ever go to school in California for a year?"

The question was answered by dead silence on the other end of the phone line. About 10 seconds went by before Bruce asked if David was still on the line.

Then David said, "I forgot about that! I was only about five or six years old when it happened, but yes, she went to California to school for a year."

"Well, that's when she had me."

"I think that I'm going to have to have a conversation with her about this."

A few days went by, and then Bruce's phone rang. David Gordon was on the line. He had asked Ruth to meet him to talk about an important family matter, and asked her to come alone. She had complied.

"My sister has confirmed your story. She is very upset," David noted. "She said that it brought back the memory of the most difficult time in her life. She said that she thought she let her family down. They told her that no one would ever find out about this." He continued: "She wants me to let you know that she is very happy that you have made a successful life for yourself. She's grateful for that. But she also wants me to tell you that she just can't see you right now."

313

Perhaps she had never told anyone, not even the man that she married, about the child that she had delivered in Bell, California, on April 16, 1947. Moreover, Ruth's own brother had no knowledge of it until he had received the call from Bruce Black. It had to be a very traumatic event.

Bruce said he understood and respected her decision. He offered to send David the same package that he had sent to the Gallingers, including that photo of his daughter that had reminded Don of Ruth. Ruth could open it if she wished and could respond if she wished. Perhaps, if that family resemblance were close, he reasoned, Ruth might one day be motivated to reach out. David agreed to accept the package.

Several things happened to follow up on this chain of events that began in the fall of 1998, and two decades later, the story is still unfolding.

First, Bruce did make that trip to Toronto with his family. While there, he met his brothers, Don Jr., Michael, and Kim. Each of his brothers would unknowingly echo their aunt's earlier assertion that he was fortunate to be raised by the people who adopted him, his true parents. They agreed to keep in touch.

Bruce then went alone to meet his birth father, Don Gallinger Sr. He came out of that meeting appreciative of his part, and of the couple who had raised him as their own.

Less than a year after meeting his birth father, Bruce received the news that Don Gallinger Sr. had died of a massive heart attack on February 3, 2000. His obituary acknowledged Bruce along with his brothers Don, Michael, and Jim as surviving children.

Not too long after that, David Gordon also died. Ruth had never contacted Bruce, and he had no idea whether she had seen the package that had been mailed to the law firm in 1999.

Years passed without any news, but Don Jr. continued to be on the lookout for any information about Bruce's birth mother. Finally, the news came. Ruth had died on May 12, 2015, in Cambridge, Ontario, a town about 45 minutes from where Don Gallinger Sr. had lived for so many years.

Through her obituary, Bruce learned that Ruth was predeceased not only by her brother David, but by her sister. One brother remained. More important, her marriage produced three children, who were named in the obituary. Bruce found out that he had two additional brothers and a sister, all of whom were still living. He was able to get contact information for them with Don Jr.'s help.

In the fall of 2017, Bruce and his wife made another trip to Toronto to meet his mother's side of the family. It was there that he learned that Ruth had been sent to California to stay with a relative who owned a bar in Bell. The children knew that relative well and were stunned that the secret had been kept from them for 70 years. It was another successful visit, and it provided closure for all concerned.

Ruth's husband had died in 2010, but her health had begun to fail. All her life, Ruth had been heavily involved in charitable organizations, many of which helped children.

Bruce also told his new family members his adoption story. On the day that his parents came to the hospital, there were over 20 baby boys to choose from. Of all the baby boys there, Bruce was the one who looked up and smiled at them. They loved that. They selected him. It was a smile that changed many people's lives.

Bruce Black is now enjoying retirement with his wife and family in the Bay Area. He continues to stay in touch with his birth family, and he's a strong supporter of the San Jose Sharks.

His story is one that continues to amaze us, and it's one of the things that I'm proudest of in my play-by-play tenure with the club.